Refiner's Fire

Refiner's Fire

A Religious Engagement with Violence

Cheryl Kirk-Duggan

FORTRESS PRESS

MINNEAPOLIS

REFINER'S FIRE
A Religious Engagement with Violence

Cover photograph by Don Farrall copyright © 2000 by Photodisc, Inc.
Cover and interior design: Beth Wright

The poem on pages 70–71 from *Images in Black,* copyright © 1969 Jewel C. Larimore, is reprinted by permission of Third World Press, Inc., Chicago, Illinois.
The excerpt on page 166 is reprinted with the permission of Scribner, a division of Simon and Schuster, from *For Colored Girls Who Have Considered Suicide/When the Rainbow Is Enuf,* copyright © 1975, 1976, 1977 by Ntozake Shange.
The excerpt from "Memorial I" on page 162, from *Chosen Poems: Old and New,* copyright © 1982, 1976, 1974, 1973, 1970, 1968 by Audre Lorde, and the excerpt from "Holographs" on page 169, from *Our Dead behind Us,* copyright © 1986 by Audre Lorde, are both used by permission of W. W. Norton and Company, Inc.

Library of Congress Cataloging-in-Publication Data
Kirk-Duggan, Cheryl A.
   Refiner's fire : a religious engagement with violence / Cheryl A. Kirk-Duggan.
     p. cm.
   Includes bibliographical references and index.
   ISBN 0-8006-3253-2 (alk. paper)   94220426
    1. Violence—Religious aspects—Christianity. I. Title.

BT736.15 .K57 2000
241'.697—dc21   00-046267

The paper used in this publication meets the minimum requirements of American National Standard for Information Sciences — Permanence of Paper for Printed Library Materials, ANSI Z329.48-1984.

Manufactured in the U.S.A.   AF1-3253
05   04   03   02   01   1   2   3   4   5   6   7   8   9   10

To the pedagogues and muses
Who nurtured my earliest beginnings, to age 13
As I Refined the Fires of
Divinely-given creativity:

Rose Yvonne Chretien
Dorothy Handy
Mary Lue Chavis Jones
Leroy Gilliam
George Kramer
Tommy Martin
E. H. Walker
Christine Martin
Louella Walker
Marion Mayfield
Geneva B. Jackson
Juanita Mouton
Hazel Bishop
Weldon Knighton
Esther Williams
Melvin Guice
The Rev. Willie Mays
Rebecca Brooks
Rudolph and Naomi Kirk

Contents

Acknowledgments

There are conversations and relationships in works of art, music, science, and literature that are born from experiences of sharing thoughts and ideas. Many encouraging voices have greatly supported this project in varying ways. My deepest gratitude goes to the many colleagues, institutions, and support staff that have made this journey a process of Refining the Fires of prophecy and completion. I offer words of thanks to the research librarians at Meredith College, Raleigh, North Carolina, and at the Graduate Theological Union (GTU), Berkeley, California, for their expertise and support in getting interlibrary loan materials and for having robust collections and phenomenal on-line databases available. My deepest appreciation to my editor, Michael West, who could visualize these Refining Fires and whose editorial acumen enabled me to chart a course to bring these Refining Fires to fruition in this volume.

Thanks to the Presidents, Dean, colleagues, and students at the GTU for being excited with me, for listening for the umpteenth time when I talked about ideas from *Refiner's Fire*. Much appreciation to my colleagues and friends in the Colloquium on Religion and Violence (COV&R) where I found certain concepts and language to talk about my passions: especially Thee Smith, Diana Culbertson, René Girard, James G. Williams, Julie Shinnick, Sandor Goodhart, Gil Bailie, Raymund Schwager, Robert Hammerton-Kelly, and Caesareo Banderas. For conversations that invited me to explore new areas of thought that resulted in new thinking and presentations, I am grateful to Dwight Hopkins, Simon Harak, Sharon Moore, Neil Elgee, M.D., and the Ernest Becker Foundation, and the members of various sections and groups from the American Academy of Religion and the Society of Biblical Literature. Special thanks go to the Womanist Approaches to Religion and Society Group, formerly chaired by Katie G. Cannon, and the African American Biblical Hermeneutics Section, which Hugh Page and I cochair.

To my GTU students and colleagues; the members of the Center for Women and Religion staff and advisory board, who are always encouraging my work; my various prayer groups across the country; my Phillips Temple CME Church family, where I serve as an associate pastor with senior pastor Rev. Anthony Summers; and several Bay Area preacher friends, Faye Morris, Joyce Cooksey, Wayne Mays, who continuously say, "Go ahead!" To my family, the clouds of witnesses—my late parents, Naomi Ruth Mosely Kirk and Rudolph V. Kirk, who always made a way and who so loved me as to let me paint a mural on our living room wall when I was in fourth grade—refining my artistic fires, so young; to my siblings, Rudolph II and Dedurie, whom I love dearly and who love me as I am, I say thank you. To my husband and confidante, who deliberately, delightingly, and mischievously encourages me to light all my fires, the Hon. and CDR, USNR (ret.), Michael A. Kirk-Duggan, my eternal gratitude.

Preface

Handel's setting of Mal. 3:2 in his oratorio, "The Messiah," has a continual, sturdy rhythmic pulse for the bass voice. The aria opens with the questions: "Who shall abide in the day when the Lord comes?" and "Who shall stand when the Lord appears?" The bass answers in a dynamic, virtuoso aria, "Why do the Nations so furiously rage together?" In response, the tempo and rhythmic scene painting change to a vigorous pulse with great agitation in the orchestral and vocal parts, for the subject of inquiry is "like a Refiner's Fire."

The dynamics of a Refiner's Fire were poignantly, passionately revealed to me during a Wabash Teaching and Learning Workshop in January, 1998. When asked to present a symbol or artifact that best described each of us, my dear friend Dr. Marsha Boyd, now with the American Theological Association, said that her metaphor is a welder. Welders artistically use fire to refine metals. On our last day of this workshop, I perused the reference materials on the bookshelf in my room and discovered *The Welder's Bible*. I remembered my years of biblical history and could quickly recall a Geneva Bible, the Bishop's Bible, the Wycliffe Bible, The Woman's Bible, et cetera, et cetera, but no Welder's Bible. My excitement and curiosity got the better of me. I brought the Welder's Bible to Marsha for her to see and then I began to flip through its pages. This was not a Bible that contained Hebrew and New Testament texts. This was a complete encyclopedia of everything one needed to know about welding, from terminology and temperatures at which various metals can be refined, to the different types of joints one welds and the safety precautions one ought to take when welding.

Welding is serious, dangerous business. Using language and exploring religious concepts is also serious, dangerous business, but it is a business that I am called to do: welding and Refining a Fire, molding thoughts across time, emerging out of various temperatures and various contexts to explore the intersection of violence, power, and religion. This volume, itself a process of Refining the Fire of passion amid theological discourse in exposing violence, viewed through the lens of a Womanist approach that welds and explores the fires created at the juxtaposition of creative theory and praxis.

Using *Refiner's Fire* as a metaphor of social change and abusive control, this book explores the intersection of violence and religion, creative/destructive systemic forces, in biblical and contemporary society. Throughout literature and history, personal, communal, and institutional violence has existed intimately with religious practice. The creation of the world out of chaos into order was an evolutionary, violent act. The thrust of a child out from the protective birth canal into a hostile, outside world is violent. The mandate of law enforcement to maintain order often requires violent acts by authority. The "Three Strikes" law and the death penalty are violent acts allegedly designed to quell violence. Statistics show that neither the "Three Strikes" law nor the death penalty has worked as a successful deterrent. Many of those trapped by the three strikes are couriers of dope for dealers and suppliers. Many of those who are employees of the illegal drug industry are there because they are addicts, and some are there because of the equal opportunity employment benefits. The death penalty is a sophisticated, high-priced lynching, given the cost of appeals, housing, and the elaborate system designed to make this state-ordered, state-administrated act of violence a humane "mercy killing." *Refiner's Fire* analyzes the effects of religion as catalysts that help humanity to foment and/or transcend violence.

Using historical and contemporary situations and narratives, *Refiner's Fire* analyzes religions' involvement in violence. Building on a Womanist theology and ethic, *Refiner's Fire* addresses issues concerning women, religion, and violence in language, the Bible, slave spirituality, the 1960s Civil Rights Movement, the protest ministry of Martin Luther King Jr., and female social groups—sororities and gangs. After the section that presents a preliminary or exploratory study for a constructive theology and ethics of violence toward transformation, the book concludes with a liturgical treatment of death that transcends ultimate violence.

Chapter 1, Eyes on the Prize: Womanist Reflections, introduces a hermeneutics, or methodology, focusing on ways of seeing and exorcising that facilitate consciousness-raising, analyze complex realities, and ultimately, help transform injustice. Chapter 2, Take No Prisoners: Biblical Women Engaged in Violence, began as a presentation, "What's Violence Got to Do With It?: Inflamers, and the Lizzie Bordens of Ancient Israel: Women Who Slay and/or Cause Wrongful Deaths" for the 1996 Colloquium on Violence & Religion (COV&R) Symposium. This chapter analyzes pairs of women in the Bible who work together for divine or human purposes and who Refine the Fires of leadership, seduction, and rage to do violence; they instigate and/or commit murder within a framework of mimetic desire, from ethical, Womanist, psychosocial, theological, and legal perspectives, to achieve their goals. These women represent a stunning reality: these stories of prominent women are saturated with violence. Tragically and regrettably, nowhere in the entire Hebrew Bible or New Testament does a positive story of a mother/daughter relationship exist. Chapter 3, Lay My Burden Down: Spirituality Transcends Antebellum Violence, is a discourse on the inherent spirituality that emerges from those powerful psalms of slaves, selected African American spirituals. Those songs, emerging from the African diaspora in the United States during the antebellum period, when the enslavement of African Americans was a legal and accepted practice, and during the 1960s Civil Rights Movement, Refined the Fires of protest, assurance, dignity, justice, and equality. This essay on spirituality signified was prompted by conversations with my friend and associate, Professor Dwight Hopkins, University of Chicago.

Chapter 4, Sojourner's Sisters: 1960s Women Freedom Fighters Right Civil Wrongs, celebrates the outstanding contribution of the women who were rarely feted in the media but who defied violence and kept the 1960s Civil Rights Movement going by working behind the scenes. They Refined the Fires of justice by challenging systemic and personal violence, and their actions helped strengthen the community as they handled communications, brainstormed, marched, were beaten, or died early as a result of the process. Chapter 5, Ballads, Not Bullets: The Nonviolent Protest Ministry of Martin Luther King Jr., was part of a presentation for the 1996 American Academy of Religion session of the Peace and War Group. This chapter explores the powerful function of music in King's nonviolent, direct protest action ministry and the interpersonal dynamics of this Nobel Prize winner's activity as a "Drum Major for Justice." Both the music and King's ministry are Fires Refined to affect social justice in the midst of blatant oppression.

Chapter 6, Soul Sisters: Girls in Gangs and Sororities, was first presented to the 1995 Annual Meeting of COV&R in the session, "Violence, Mimesis, and the Subject of Responsibility." This chapter explores the many interrelated complexities of soror and sistah imitative or mimetic societies and the levels of internal and external apathy and responsibility, fires left unrefined by society or family in loving, meaningful ways. Interest in this material began during my days as a doctoral student at Baylor University, in conversation with fellow student of ethics Sharon Moore. Reading a *Washington Post* Sunday magazine article pressed me to begin researching the topic of girl gangs. Chapter 7, Build Up, Break Down: Language of Empowerment and Annihilation, analyzes the implications of the power of language as a Refining Fire of communication on a continuum from violence to virtue. These interests first came together in a presentation to the Ernest Becker Society in Seattle, Washington. There I used the work of cultural anthropologists, in dialogue, to note how we daily use words either to empower or to denigrate ourselves and others. The impact and power of language to enhance or destroy, in daily parlance, the academy and the pulpit has become a burning passion. I see how we are usually adamant about the mounting violence from guns and drugs but are nonchalant, cavalier, and dismissive when it comes to our careless use of our most accessible tool for creating violence—language.

Chapter 8, Daughters of Zelophehad: A Constructive Analysis of Violence, uses the metaphor of the Daughters of Zelophehad to engage a Womanist constructive theological and ethical analysis of violence, towards Refining the Fires of transformation. This work developed from a conversation with the editor for this project, Michael West. We agreed that in a work delving into the intersection of violence and religion, it is important to engage the analytical, the descriptive, and the prescriptive, since we question the necessity of human violence and work towards a therapeutic answer. We must ask: What are our options? Chapter 9, Death as Worship: Celebrating Dying as Part of Life, explores death as a part of life. Using liturgical expressions, seasons, and the experience of certain liturgical moments during the worship service proper, the chapter illumines these sensory experiences as moments of Refining divine Fires of praise and inspiration, as the locus of death as worship. This chapter was written as a celebration, a response, and reaction to the spring 1991 death of a most brave, courageous woman, Mary Helen Bell. I had the privilege of giving her last rites; I stood and ministered at her bedside, witnessing her final breath; I told her mother, "She's gone."

As we move quickly into the new millennium, into the twenty-first century, we have opportunities to be our neighbor's sister or brother. We have new options for living transformed lives where we acknowledge the *imago dei* within each other and ourselves, where we face new challenges, with enhanced technologies that allow us to annihilate ourselves totally. We have the gift, the challenge, and the opportunity to create and embrace new socio-historical and economic configurations of community, in which we can make a difference and not be self-absorbed. We have an opportunity to live out of a spiritually, socially, physically, and economically salvific model of community in which everyone matters. We have countless decisions to make that can affect this world for millennia to come.

When we take a liberationist stance, in which salvation is holistic, encompassing everything that shapes our lives from the spiritual and economic to the emotional, sexual, and physical, what must we do to be saved? What can we do to move ourselves to a lived ecology of human spirit? Why do we need a crisis to garner our attention? Are we so transparent and fearful that we can only move forward or come to action if our environment is one in which we live in pain, deceit, or fear, when dysfunctionality and lies are our only options for coping? What Fires need to be Refined, and which Fires need to be stifled? Clearly, to live a holistic life as a healthy, balanced global community of mutuality as opposed to one of exploitation, we must address the apparent penchant for human-induced, human-created, human-celebrated, bought-and-paid-for violence (for example, gossiping, libel, boxing, pornography).

Many persons imagine that there are places on the planet where violence does not or cannot exist by definition. Many, in religious institutions, imagine that their sanctuaries, temples, and mosques are immune to societal violence. Unfortunately, the data tell a different story. What is the possibility for a healthy, serene society? Incredible historical evidence for violence of all kinds exists—holy war, domestic, spousal, workplace, child abuse, and ecological violence, as well as libel, theft, racism, sexism, classism, homophobia, and the seemingly aphrodisiacal allure of power, which has brought scandal in many "high places," including the Vatican and the Oval Office. What must we do to be saved? How do religion, spirituality, and faith affect violence? Are human beings capable of living in a context of justice? *Refiner's Fire* explores living, historical, and literary texts to mine the role and impact of violence at the intersection of religion. In this exploration, we look to the altars of faith, hope, and love—courageously exposing and unmasking the violence couched in the narratives of the lives of many. Such a journey of theory and praxis relies on analytical, critical, passionate listening to offer a crucible in which individual and communal Refiners shape their Fires into transformative passion.

A Refining Fire is an impulse, a creative energy given to us by God, in a context of choice: we can choose to do justice out of love, or we can choose to be violent out of pain. Ultimately, the only visceral, underlying choice is for our world to Refine the Fires of peace, justice, and freedom—we must see each individual as holy, as sacred. Without this qualifying certitude, rumors of wars will always result in war. We will forever find newer and more precise technological ways to kill ourselves and others. Our world will be a haze of deferred dreams, dysfunctional, depressed, disembodied people who create dangerous liaisons and deadly dialogues.

The power of God's grace, which gives us the phenomenal gifts to think and speak, reminds us not to give up too easily. At the end of the day, there are but two modes of change: conversations and relationships. We need to learn how to talk and listen as sacred ritual; we must connect with each other as sacred association. Either we live as holy people, or we die. To what music shall we dance? Which Fires shall we Refine?

In each instance, I have been the welder; the text and I have braved a Refining Fire.

1. Eyes on the Prize: Womanist Reflections

She looked in the mirror:
No immediate image did she see;
The vastness of the horizon
Seemed to mock her: she could not see her reflection.
Through the skewed lens of dominant culture:
She saw nothing
A sister came along,
With dignity and joy,
And a different way of seeing.
She was mesmerized.
A thing she could not fathom
Was about to cross her path,
And that incomprehensible other
Opened her mouth;
And spoke;
And lovingly said: "You are somebody."
She looked in her mirror, again.
And this time she saw
Gazing back at her, a beauteous vision:
Nobility and peace.
The empty objectiveness that was but a shadow
Had been replaced
By her mighty image.
And she heard God say:
"That's good!"

To know who and what you are and to whom you belong is to embody the divine good, is to be clear about what is at stake, and is the cost and benefit of the prize of total, salvific grace and freedom. The wounds of oppression were created by slavery, abscessed by Jim Crow, and festered by internalizing the hurt; venting the injury on others oozes the poisons of pain, self-hatred, self-defeatism, insatiable desire, and rage. The wannabe-like-white-folks syndrome and the failed project of integration have exacted a tremendous cost. Although the "For Colored Only" and "For Whites Only" signs have been painted over or dismantled, the poisons and prisons of racism, sexism, classism, ageism, and heterosexism now wear different masks. "Keep Your Eyes on the Prize; Hold On!" affirms and avows the attitude of Womanist scholars as they study, teach, preach, and write about the tridimensional race/sex/class oppressive experience of Black women, tempered with the life-giving power that ruminates in the beingness and doingness of women of the African diaspora. Keep Your Eyes on the Prize is an invitation to confront systemic and personal evil.

This chapter introduces a hermeneutic, a way to see and hear and exorcise the evil and violence that exist in various pockets of society in these United States and the world. This methodology and embodied way of living facilitates consciousness-raising, analyzes complex realities, and ultimately helps transform injustice. Womanist theory, the language of Womanist thought, is itself the anvil and the kiln for Refining the Fires of analysis towards the reformation and transformation of individual, communal, and systemic violence. After indicating the origins of the term and the theoretical basis of exploration, I express my own rubric of doing Womanist analysis.

What is a "Womanist"?

Alice Walker coined the term "Womanist" and claims that a Womanist is courageous and in charge; a Womanist loves and commits to the wholeness and survival of all people.[1] Many strong Black women have not heard the term *Womanist* and have not identified themselves as such. *Womanist* is a confessional term; thus some strong Black women do not make this claim nor support all the components of the Womanist definition. Nevertheless, many strong Black women are Womanist by virtue of the experience of oppression and the desire for liberation, which serves as a catalyst for empowerment, exhaling, and excelling. A Womanist, sometimes denigrated as "domineering castrating matriarch," is a strong Black woman who has developed survival strategies in spite of the oppression of herself in order to save her family and her people. She takes charge; she acts; she is;[2] she Refines the Fire of justice as she keeps her eyes on her prize.

> Paul and Silas, bound in jail,
> Had no money for to go their bail.
> Keep your eyes on the prize,
> Hold on, hold on.
> Hold on, hold on,
> Keep your eyes on the prize,
> Hold on, hold on.
> Freedom's name is mighty sweet,
> One day soon we're gonna meet. . . .
> God, my hand, on the gospel plow,
> I wouldn't take nothing for my journey now. . . .

The only chain that a man can stand,
Is that chain of hand in hand. . . .
The only thing we did wrong,
Stayed in the wilderness a day too long. . . .
But the one thing we did right,
Was the day we started to fight. . . .
We're gonna board that big Greyhound,
Carryin' love from town to town. . . .
We're gonna ride for civil rights,
We're gonna ride both Black and White. . . .
We've met jail and violence too,
But God's love has seen us through. . . .
Haven't been to heaven but I've been told,
Streets up there are paved wit gold. . . .[3]

The term Womanist arises from the use of the term "womanish" in African American communities and refers to a Black feminist who takes seriously the experience and oppression due to gender, race, and class. Walker's definition of Womanist is complex and fertile as a foundational rubric for doing critical analysis. In addition to the components of survival, of loving, of taking charge, the term also conveys a vitality of life, a quest for knowledge, and the paradox of being young and living wise or grown. Womanist sensibilities provide the freedom of being able to love all people, sexually and nonsexually, and give credence to the manifestation of woman's culture and life. To be Womanist invites holistic health and loving the spectrum of colors of Blackness, like the flora and fauna in beautiful gardens. Womanist theory is aesthetic, physical, spiritual, emotional, and creative.[4] Womanist evokes a palette of kaleidoscopic reality, daily Refining the Fires of passion, love, hope, and change.

Womanist Theory's Inclusive Call

Womanist theory, from "a least of these theology,"[5] invites an inclusiveness that is a call to love and care. Such sensibilities provide uplift for Black women and for all people experiencing oppression and marginalization because of labels and categories used to displace and control those who are different. While the "whys" behind the distaste for difference are beyond this chapter, people who are different often prove to be psychologically unsettling and seem to undermine personal confidence in a dominant worldview. This kind of dysfunctionality causes a series of behaviors—from conversion to destruction—that serves to reduce anxiety, perhaps to the point that denies the right of the other to exist. Such behavior may involve (1) conversion—changing ourselves or being changed by circumstances; (2) missionary work—convincing others their view is wrong; (3) accommodation—incorporating some of their belief systems so the minority report is no longer threatening; (4) destruction—annihilating the person who is different.[6] One way to understand war, for example, is not from a perspective of the political, economic, or rational, but to note that all wars are rationalized by ideology and deal with conflict that we have with people who are different from us. Why? We seek to deny the right of the other to exist. The undergirding "least of these theology" includes the disappeared, those who are marginalized and relegated to the realm of the insignificant, and the "other," who is treated as an object and with a "we'll get to them if and when we can, but no rush" mentality.

A "Least of These Theology"

A "least of these theology" embodies a God who cares and who looks with disgust on anyone who dismisses a person made in the divine image with the same disdain as dismissing a speck of dirt. A "least of these theology" is a mode of God talk where all "I's" are important and are relational. These I's have eyes that may reflect light and hope. These eyes may reflect insanity, fear, or absence—the body is present but the essence is so damaged that it appears no one is truly present in that particular human being. These I's/eyes want, need, and desire love and compassion but have been denied such embodied grace from their communities for so long that they have given up hope. These I's/eyes have become objects, things, bits and pieces of trivia. Their eyes no longer have a vitality but have become riddled with spiritual cataracts, thwarted by severe emotional glaucoma.

These I's/eyes often get lost in a schema of bureaucracy, social mobility, gentrification, downsizing, prisons, poverty. These objectified sentient beings have become just another number in an overworked, unpaid caseload: the I's/eyes become weary and disheartened and sometimes engage in self-destructive behavior. The I's/eyes sometimes become a problem to be paid off or settled, without any due process. In these moments, the Refining has stopped. The Fires have died down; only ashes remain. The person is trapped by the greed of a corporation that seeks to downsize domestically and then move the entire facility to Central America or Asia, in search of ever lower wages. Some poor youths, often runners for drugs and firearms, hustling to make ends meet, wind up in the prison systems when they barely can walk. How does one speak to such graphic need? How does one answer, "What must I do to be saved?"—saved from my destructive tendencies, my circumstances, the oppression imposed by systemic, institutional injustice? "What must I do to be saved?" by my own relatives, my own communities, particularly if I know that I do not matter and that you couldn't care less and are careless about my existence?

Womanist theory, midst a faith-based curiosity, seeks to discover, analyze, and honor the lives and gifts of these I's/eyes and souls of the forgotten and dismissed. Womanist theorists want us to focus the eyes of Black women on and toward the transformation of themselves, other African Americans, and of society, of the complex, pathological institutions and communities that are ailing and wounded: empowerment instead of denial and destruction. Cloaked by oppression, my Christian Womanist stance involves theology (dialogue, identity, sacrality, spirituality, and power); Bible and narratives (authority, characters, rituals, language, and history); ethics (value, behavior, visibility, integrity, and praxis); and context (autobiography, culture, aesthetics, ecology, and community).

Womanist Theology Is Conversation

Womanist theology celebrates the identity of individuals and communities where hope remains an option to overcome lived oppression. The awareness of the value and aesthetics of God and human life is the presence of the sacred. Sacrality, a tenet of life, flows through everyone with the beat of the human heart and the pulsating movement of blood coursing the miles of veins and arteries throughout the body and the community. The reality of sacred beings evokes a charisma, an imbedded divine interest within people, which provokes a need for the spiritual for the sake of health. Womanist spirituality is one of the languages for a Refiner's Fire that allows for conversation, conversion, change, and hope, in spite of and for all people. Womanist spirituality yokes an energy, a power that sustains one when it seems all hope is lost and any efforts to make a difference are futile. Womanist theology Refines the Fires of outrageous opportunity and anticipatory accomplishment amid the wrath and scorn of cruelty and hatred.

Regardless of her life context, a Black woman does not avoid oppression. Some people practice a "theology of otherness": since God obviously made them (usually of dominant culture) superior, the other, an African American woman, because she is Black, must be inferior. Society tells the Black woman she cannot really be made in God's image; consequently she is either a servile machine or a sexual, erotic thing. In either case, the fearful or dominant one desires to reduce her to a commodity. Many people choose to see her Blackness, her gender, her age, and her class as categories that legitimate and sanction their right and ability to control her. The daily reality of tridimensional oppression uses violence to subjugate her as the objectified "other."[7] Both interracial and intraracial attitudes create problems for Black women and cause a gross imbalance in families and societies, an otherness, like a cancer that no treatment can cure. Within and outside of African American culture, the issue of skin color is profound.

There are situations in which a dark-skinned person wants to relate only with other dark-skinned African Americans, and some lighter-skinned African Americans may only associate with those of a similar shade. The outsider, the one who is lighter or darker, is other. In the process, societal injustice and prejudice warp the theological health of individuals and whole societies: there is no Fire, but there is a lot of smoke. The smoke perverts one's sensibilities and creates an environment of communal and self-deprecation and hurt. The systemic tyranny of racism has become so internalized, so embodied by some within the race, that any difference in skin hue within the race provokes hatred of self and gives individuals permission to designate as "other" those that do not have the same skin tone.

This otherness, shared by all African Americans, helps to form the African American female experience, which uses domination to make Black women invisible.[8] Notably, Black women were rarely selected to hold national leadership positions in the 1960s liberationist, social, political protest organizations.[9] The Womanist perspective seeks to make the invisible visible as part of the fight for the rights of all people. Theologically, Womanists seek to identify relevant issues and resources, uncover discrepancies, right the wrongs of sexism, classism, racism, ageism, and homophobia in narrative and society, and make Black women visible.

Womanist Theology as Champion for Freedom

Womanist Theology champions Black women's struggle for freedom and deals with social and ecclesial oppression in the mandate for silence and submission[10] by unfolding an African American vision of freedom and justice. Womanist theologians, like other theologians, do not agree on all issues. Cheryl Sanders argues that Christianity forms the center of ethical and theological identity, that the term Womanist overemphasizes secularity and lesbian love over heterosexual love and does not focus on Christianity enough. Not all Womanists are Christian. Most Christian Womanists, however, myself included, affirm a strong biblical and christological heritage in our understanding as we embrace most tenets of Womanist theory. Many of our sister Womanists have other faith traditions that are not steeped in the Christian story, and we celebrate and equally welcome their voices. The impetus for Womanists giving assent to the freedom and survival of all people springs from the feminist aspects of the Black religious folk expression of mothers to their children.

Womanist Vision: Thinking and Seeing

A Womanist vision Refines the Fires of thinking and seeing that are: (1) eschatological or goal-oriented; (2) concerned with physical, mental, emotional, spiritual, and economic health and liberation of individual and communal mind/soul, spirit, and body; (3) about the relational, historical Black experience; (4) based on real feelings, experiences, and actions; and (5) a transformational, life-changing process that enhances everyone. Through a liberating, biblical Womanist vision, identification and healing intensify in communion with a living God. Thus, people know God as a personal, powerful, compassionate liberator who encompasses and transcends masculine and feminine qualities and cares about individuals and communities. A Womanist biblical vision gives one the room to be chary, cautious, and creative in the reading of Scripture—careful to note androcentric and oppressive texts in the Bible while keeping the faith and remaining in the Christian tradition. In concert with the gift of seeing is the gift of naming and expressing one's own voice.

Naming and Expressing

Naming, as a metaphor for both pronouncement and personal identification, makes a political and liturgical statement. In the received biblical texts, God spoke, and the world came in to being. Human beings speak and in the process produce something on a continuum from chaos to comfort. Naming in the biblical sense is attributing a mode of identity to someone, assigning that person's or being's demeanor and character. There are many names for God: Yahweh (I am, that I am becoming), El, Elohim (God or gods), El Elyon (God most High, Exalted One), El Bethel (House of God), El Roi (God of Seeing), El Olam (Everlasting God), El Shaddai (God Almighty, God of the Mountains), El Berith (God of the Covenant), El Elohe (God of Israel), and Adon(ai) (Lord of the Earth). Similarly the names of persons in the biblical text also exemplify either their character or its antithesis: Anna (grace), Esther (star), Leah (wearied), Naomi (my delight, sweetness to bitter), Salome (peace), Adam (of the earth), Amos (to be burdened), David (beloved), Gabriel (God's strength), Jesse (wealthy), Joseph (increase), Michael (who is like God?), and Nathan (gift of God).[11] Names identify and reveal much.

My experience of God is a creative, way-out-of-no-way God. This "making a way out of a no-way God," is a "mother to the motherless and father to the fatherless."[12] Relationship with this God allows one to survive and transcend and to accept and celebrate the gifts of creation. "Making a way out of no way" means that when all seems hopeless, impossible, or irreversible, when despondence, despair, and desperation are one's best friends, God can still bring life, renewal, and light. This God brings new life, nurture, and relationship. A Womanist relational view of God produces intimacy, mercy, love, compassion, and solidarity. This God is real and present. This God creates persons as *imago dei,* persons who embrace diversity, mutuality, and wholeness. Such a theology provides identity and respect for all life. An awareness of the historical and current basis of such a theology calls for a theological, archaeological excavation of past narratives: to learn our origins, see our present reality, and learn how we can hope for the future. This God is a consummate Refiner of fiery lives and shuns the use of human violence.

The Study of God-Talk

Womanist theology is the study or discipline of God-talk that emerges out of the rich yet oppressive experience of African American women. This God-talk analyzes and critiques human individual and social behavior in concert with the Divine toward analyzing the ramifications of injustice and malaise due to gross oppression and the use of power, moving towards change, balance, and promise. A Womanist emancipatory theology embraces a message of hope and transformation toward engendering mutuality and community and honors the *imago dei* in all persons. Womanist theology builds on the essential goodness of humanity and focuses on liberation amid personal and societal fragmentation in general and theological discourse in particular.

Womanist theology intentionally creates arenas where one makes visible African American women's experience. Womanists expose cruelty and all forms of violence—subtle and shameless, are serious, and commit to the survival, wholeness, and health of all people. I am a Womanist storyteller, poet, preacher, professor, and performer; I embrace the Christian story with an appreciation for the richness of God's revelation in the world through many faiths and with a theological bent and ethical sensibility toward creating new avenues of possibility and communal solidarity. Consequently, my use of Womanist theology embodies reformation. Such reformation confronts the many complex issues of individual and communal daily life amid the grace of God, including social justice issues, and promotes a vision of life that champions immediacy and inclusivity. My Womanist vision searches for a way to champion the freedom, dignity, and justice of all people—a prelude to the praxis of morality, a prelude set not to music but to the rhythm of words, of poetics.

Emancipatory Womanist Theology

My vision of emancipatory Womanist theology Refines the Fires of transformation by using many texts: living texts scripted by the lives of persons and set in oral stories, the Bible, and other written and artistic narratives. These texts afford the ability to stipulate authority—that is, who is in charge and who gets to subvert others and exercise dominance to thwart the utterances of new voices. Such authority becomes a vehicle for strengthening one's present communities and reshaping them. Within communities, the reality of human characters engaging and confronting other humans and societal issues through time creates history and herstories that need to be told, studied, and repeated. Part of their stories are the celebratory practices or rituals that mark certain events and the language undergirding the signifying that occurs when people gather together. Within ancient, recent, and ongoing history and language systems in communities, we can also study human behavior and their sense of commitments, values, and the good (or ethics).

Ethics provides a vehicle for educating ourselves to move aside and to partner with others that they might claim their visibility and we might craft a socio-cultural context in the world whereby we can live with integrity. This socio-cultural movement is not about sacrifice but about genuine sharing. The sharing is moments of praxis in which engagement can lead to liberation. That liberation occurs in our context, which unfolds as the place at which culture, aesthetics, and community converge. Personal accountability is substantive to integrity and esteem within our own autobiography. If we are wise and attentive, if we share resources, if we appreciate the beautiful, if we embrace a spirit of thanksgiving, but also an attitude in which we hold ourselves and others accountable and we do not allow our communities as individual and collective spirits as well as the land to be desecrated, then we become good stewards of our resources. We have but to study many his- and herstories to see that this level of sharing and committed stewardship has not been and is not always the case. In the United States, we have not always been good stewards of our resources.

The Suffering of Black Women

The history of Black women in America reveals abuse, exploitation, separation, incompletion, and suffering; yet thousands of African Americans kept their "Eyes on the Prize" and did not despair, give up, or acquiesce. Many slave women had a theology of suspicion, resistance, redemption, remembrance, and retelling that undergirds the Spirituals that Martin Luther King Jr. preached. Stories of slave women note both their belief in a "mighty God" and the savagery, violence, and sexual abuse from their arrogant male slave masters and jealousy, rage, hatred, and harassment from their ambivalent slave mistresses.[13] Nevertheless, many slave women used their resources of Christianity, biblical imagery, the Spirituals, African traditions, "mother wit," and language to survive, to develop self-esteem, to protect themselves, to bolster their spiritual, psychological, and emotional health, and to speak the truth. These women, who used their suspicion to explore situations and to be leery of naive idealism that did not support their realities and values, are the ancestors of Womanist scholars. These bonded women honored themselves and their ancestors through Refining the Fires of remembrance and retelling. They celebrated God's redemptive nature, resisted their incarceration, and developed their own sense of Christianity in defiance of the religious

hypocrisy practiced by their owners. The language of retelling and remem-
bering occurs in slave narratives, the Spirituals, and slave sermons.

Sermon texts deal with reality, God, and the meaningfulness in the lives of
Black folk and are fodder for Womanist analysis. These sermons rely on a
poetic, dramatic delivery and a text of biblical imagery and symbols that
name the oppressions and present hopeful possibilities. When sermons have
negative female images and sexist models,[14] however, Womanists ask, "How
has the rhetoric of the pulpit contributed to the empowerment and abuse of
Black women?" The use of dramatic, biblical language and its transmission
process, so rooted in Black culture, can be liberating or oppressive.

Too often, church leaders use biblical texts to brainwash women into
believing that women ought not to preach, that women have no business in
the pulpit, that women must be subservient to men. Since God has the audacity to call some women, some women have the audacity and joy to step out on
faith and minister. How is it that certain folk think they have the inside scoop
on what God knows, wants, and does? Many Black women experience God in
Jesus as a co-sufferer and an empowerer.[15] One who empowers is a friend.
True friends do not abuse or identify persons with the job they perform and
do not label one who serves as menial, beggarly, low. The tridimensional
experience of Black women pushes society to refrain from: (1) covering up
harsh realities with conciliatory language; (2) categorizing people; and (3)
devaluing people's lives because of who they are. Womanist theology calls for
a reworking of the language of inclusive discipleship:[16] an experience of partnerships, justice, mutuality, and liberation. Liberation is the task of reexam-
ining and refashioning a faith language. Faith language exposes abuse, gives
voice to Black women, and deals with the language of sin and surrogacy.

Womanist Theology: A Prayerful Faith Journey

Womanist theology often grows out of a prayerful faith journey of pedagogical testimony, midst a wilderness/survivalist/re-productive ministerial experience, that teaches the sacred, spiritual, and secular moments of Black
women's everyday lives. Those lives gain strength by reading the Bible
through the lens of a survival/quality-of-life tradition. Biblical and extra-bib-
lical materials reveal the many experiences of women, from survival and rape
to the wilderness experience, surrogacy, and forced motherhood. The forced
motherhood of Black women involves the exploitation of Black women by
White men, White women, and Black men. Motherhood envelops the rise of
stereotypes, authority shifts, and the celebration of Black women's spirituality and their contributions to social change.[17] Acts that assault motherhood
and exploit Black woman personhood devalue God's children, thwart right
relationship, and produce sin.

Some Spirituals view sin as trouble and as a heavy psychological state, with Jesus as the one who conquers sin. Sin also concerns White oppression, stumbling blocks to community development, certain wrongdoing for the sake of survival, and collective social wrongdoing or evil. Sin from a Womanist perspective concerns: (1) physical abuse and the loss of one's sexual being; (2) devaluation of the image of God present in Black women as sexual beings; (3) anything that creates a sense of unworthiness or lack of self-esteem in Black women; and (4) the violation of Black women and of nature.[18] Overcoming sin is a shift toward atonement, being at one with God and with others.

Theologian Delores Williams[19] asserts that the crucible of atonement lies in the ministerial vision of Jesus. Such a vision teaches, loves, and empathizes but does not subjugate, belittle, take advantage of, make one a surrogate, or defile creation. Intraracial oppression, pathological white racial arrogance and narcissism, and stereotypical socio-political symbolism affects Black women's survival and resistance in the wilderness. The "wilderness" experience symbolizes the place where Hagar and Black women and their children Refine the Fires of overcoming as they encounter, name, and are cared for by God. The wilderness is the place of "risk-taking faith," exercised in a crisis when a woman meets and receives individual direction from God.[20] For many Black women, risk-taking faith involves their commitment to and intimacy with the one who is their rock, sword, shield, friend, defender; the Doctor who never lost a case; the one who always answers because "Central is never busy": Dr. Jesus.

Christian Womanists Refine the Fires of salvific health as they call us to embrace a holistic, life-giving, relational God, a caring Jesus, and an empowering Holy Spirit, as we engage and nurture each other through reciprocity, equality, and respect, fostering the survival and wholeness of the extended, communal human family. This life-giving God is incarnated in a Black Christ.[21] A Black Christ calls the community and the church toward a wholeness, allowing Black people to see Christ in themselves and themselves in Christ, in the "lived sermons" of their ancestors.[22] The image of a Black Christ symbolizes a message of empowerment and freedom, moving toward an ethical life, a life of stewardship.

A Life of Stewardship

Stewardship comes from the Greek term *oikonomia,* a compound word meaning to manage a household. The steward is the person who manages the household and is called a steward (*oikonomos,* law of the house) or an overseer (*epitropos*). One classic overseer is Joseph in the house of Potiphar (Gen. 39:4-6). Interestingly, the term *epitropos* arises out of the institution of slavery, in which the master appoints the overseer to be in charge of the household. The

New Testament has many examples of the ordinary concept of stewardship, for example, the unjust steward (Matt. 20:8, Luke 12:42; 16:1-8). Stewards can also be public officials or guardians of minor children.

Other biblical uses of stewardship include one appointed over all things except him or herself, which concerns how one deals with the world and his or her personal life (Gen. 1–3). In the New Testament, an unusual use is one who manages or administers the gifts of God, notably the preaching of the gospel. Stewardship also concerns holding the gospel in trust (1 Cor. 4:1-2; 9:17; Eph. 3:2). Another atypical use of stewardship concerns the training and discipline of Christians regarding their faith. Stewards are required to be faithful; that is, stewards of God or people are to hold the responsibility of management and administration in trust (1 Cor. 4:2). The chief duty of a Christian steward is toward the gospel, which involves the use of one's life and the use of one's money. In sum, from the Hebrew Bible a steward is one who rules, oversees, governs, is worthy, is appointed to the position to be in relationship; the New Testament expresses the role of a steward as one who is involved with religious economy, a domestic manager, guardian, and tutor.

Womanist Ethicists as Good Stewards

Some Womanist ethicists, acting as good stewards, reject suffering as the mode of existence for Black women and seek to develop shared authority as partnership. Womanist ethics studies and applies holistic core values and beliefs that help people develop healthy practices and rules to govern human behavior for the benefit of personal and societal well-being. Suffering for Black women is not God's will. Suffering is sinful for Black women, for it thwarts God's gift of wholeness.[23] Shared authority helps a community cooperate and respect each other in the quest for justice. Rooted in the risen Christ, such justice generates accountability, mutuality, conversation, critical evaluation, healthy relationships, intimacy with God, and a prayerful, active personal and social witness of togetherness out of the faith community into the world. Social witness supports total human liberation: freedom from poverty, wrongdoing, poor self-esteem, narcissism, and brokenness, and freedom to be in healthy, life-giving relationships.

Womanist social witness, grounded in spirituality, requires personal and communal love and justice. Such social witness screams with outrage at the lynching via toxic waste, marginalization, social and political control, self-destructive behavior, elitism, skewed agendas, passivity, and blindness to who we are. Womanist spirituality calls for an ethics of accountability that looks at what destroys Black extended families and the results of Black middle class flight. Womanist spirituality knows that to change the lived experiences of the underclass, we must build new allegiances, and that the Black

Church must do a reality check by asking, Who is God, who is our neighbor, and how do we minister?[24]

Components of Womanist Engagement

For Womanist theologian Delores Williams, Womanist theology has several components of engagement: dialogical, liturgical, confessional, ecumenical, and pedagogical.[25]

The Dialogical—The dialogical engagement Refines the Fires of honest conversation and ethically based research to expose evils and empower conclusions that require an ethics of accountability and sensible praxis toward possible solutions benefiting the "least of these."

The Liturgical—One type of dialogue, the liturgical, concerns worship. The liturgical daily Refines the Fires of celebrating life as gift and being responsible for making a difference and empowering—not fixing—people. Thus, worship services are designed to inspire and not to perpetuate oppression, from an aesthetics in which salvation concerns all basic human needs[26] and practices a divinely inspired sense of gratitude that makes it unacceptable to violate ourselves, other persons, or our universe. The liturgical sets the framework for the confessional.

The Confessional—The confessional Refines the Fires of acceptance and letting go as it invites us not to be ashamed of our bodies, our wants, and our needs. The confessional challenges us to identify and give witness to the *imago dei* within all humanity; to use language carefully; to enjoy an eschatological, holistic life; not to take anything for granted; and not to take more than we give back. Confessionally, one can avoid always measuring progress in dollars and clout, can plant a tree when someone is cruel to us or our loved ones, and can keep from worshipping a God who does not love us.[27] A solid confessional base makes it easy to build bridges across ecumenical lines.

The Ecumenical—The ecumenical invites us to affirm stewardship, Refining the Fires of being responsible and accountable as we hold our lives and blessings in trust as part of our religious life. The ecumenical reminds us of the tensions between religions, the frequent ecclesial control of women, and the divisiveness of denominational religious practices that pollute our spiritual environment. Given that most people understand *ecumenical* to pertain to the variety of Christian denominations, I suggest that Womanist theology is also interfaith—open to the global representations of religious faith. Ecumenical/ interfaith communion and community remind us that change cannot occur without modeling or teaching: the role and function of the pedagogical.

The Pedagogical—The pedagogical Refines the grace-endowed creative Fires that call us to teach, preach, write, and live in an exemplary manner, cognizant of who we are and why we are here, and to see and respect our lives and our universe as gift. The theological Refines the Fire of openness to see and embrace the blueprint for action; that action becomes lived in the realm of ethics. Womanist theology and ethics provide the lens for constructing and reading stories and analysis of violence in living and written texts, as we Refine the Fires of oppression to weld visions of hope and possibility.

bell hooks and Killing Rage

One voice significant in the process of awakening our sensibilities and then choosing liberatory action is bell hooks. Her voice provides a vehicle of cultural critique and analysis that helps disrupt those cultural productions that celebrate White supremacy, White privilege, and all hegemonic, oppressive discourse. She reminds us that oppression is insidious; if we pretend it does not exist, that we do not see it or know how to change it, then the oppression never has to go away. Change requires a major wake-up call. Denial allows us to be complicit in oppression. To transform denial requires "killing rage" as militant resistance. Killing rage, the fury and anger that bubble up amid an experience of violation, is painful; without an outlet the rage can evolve into intense grief and destruction. The locus of this rage is a place of aliveness, of immediate presence, "the assertion of subjectivity colonizers do not want to see."[28]

Killing rage, a source for metamorphosis and empowerment helps one to name, unmask, and engage the self and others in profound politicization and self-recovery. Such rage—a catalyst for courageous action and resistance—helps one grow and change. Pathological, addictive, and dysfunctional behaviors dull the pain and the rage. In those moments, we become complicit with White supremacist patriarchy. Killing rage, a destructive or creative force, gives us the choice to comply or resist, to be pessimistic or hopeful. Because rage can be consuming, it must be tempered by using a full range of emotional replies or responses to employ us in self-determination. Sharing rage spawns communication and facilitates connections. Shutting down rage leads to assimilation or absorption or forgetfulness.[29] The historical Black church was the place where the Refining Fires of one's killing rage fueled opposing ways of thinking and being that enhanced our ability to survive and thrive. The antithesis of engaged rage is victimhood. To offset the rhetoric of victimhood, hooks encourages Black folks to participate in a dialogue of self-determination, as we work to end racist, sexist, classist, heterosexist domination.[30] Killing rage is a Refining Fire, an electrifying tool for change, a catalyst viable for public and private sectors. Killing rage energizes and encourages; titillates but thwarts violence; instigates yet incriminates apathy, dominance, misery and complicit behaviors, thoughts, and processes. Killing rage is a healthy "board of education" that affects teaching, learning, and living. Violence reduction and education as the practice of freedom calls for a distinctive, Refining Fire of rebellious intellectual action and related rigorous praxis.

The absence of the vitality of killing rage fosters complicit behavior. The misinterpretation and fear of killing rage causes us to experience intimidation, and we cannot know pleasure anywhere else. The absence of empowering killing rage means that patriarchy and its related oppressions remain alive and well. Miscommunication and marginalization arises out of domination. Instead of loving the whole people and dealing with the sacrality and preciousness of people's lives, we continue to practice dominance and cruelty, creating bifurcated modes of being that lead to increased hypertension, migraines, depression, cancer, and premature deaths. Killing rage as transgression toward liberatory praxis signals an alternative lifestyle and undergirds my understanding of Womanist theory and theological ethics as praxis in several ways:

1. Radical—the methods, processes, and modes of being are original yet rebellious;
2. Revolutionary—the context is nonconformist, activist, and reforming;
3. Righteousness—the model is sacred, holy, honorable, faithful, grace-filled, healthy;
4. Revelation—the process involves discovery, disclosure, and prophetic intent;
5. Rhetoric—the imagery is eloquent, values orality and stories, is sensuous and expressive.
6. Realization—the creativity presses for awareness, understanding, and actualization;
7. Risky—the work is dangerous, complex, sensitive, and probably offensive to some;
8. Representational—the process is artistic, functional, and organic;
9. Relational—the experience embodies love and builds alliances and connections;
10. Rising—there is intense movement across a continuum;
11. Restorative—the model nurtures corrections, healing, and visibility toward justice;
12. Resilient—the experience is buoyant, flexible, and expansive.

Womanist Theory: A Refiner's Fire

Womanist theory, then, embodies a Refiner's Fire: God's powerful grace lived out in humanity, moving toward transformation. In the crucible of life, this Fire can assist us in addressing issues related to women, religion, and violence. Womanist theory Refines our seeing, thinking, and hearing so that our discernment allows us to see the oppression and the possibilities, the gifts and graces, the complexities and ambiguities, the stereotypes and healthy balanced lifestyles regarding gender. By definition, Womanist thought requires that we both celebrate and honor the holiness and sacrality of all humanity and of creation itself and that we see, name, and help transform the numerous personal and systemic injustices. Womanist thought serves as a corrective for the oppression in religious and secular institutions. Womanist theory seeks to Refine dysfunctional systems by firing up healthy relationships and opportunities for renewal and reconciliation, for admitting the androcentric and patriarchal nature of many of our religious traditions and dogma. The theology and ethics that emerge from a Womanist ethos seek to save the whole person and are diametrically opposed to divisive, fractured ways of being. In seeing and then helping to redeem the violence of our religious traditions and systems, Womanist theory can affect violence in larger society. Separation of church and state, notwithstanding, religious practices, faith, and spirituality have tremendous influence on our daily lives, even when the religious rhetoric is couched in secular terms. In mapping out strategies for wholeness, Womanist thought and praxis can serve as a powerful catalyst to help us embark on Refining the Fire of life in our hearts, the Fire that resurrects love, hope, and faith as a blessing to God and ourselves.

2. Take No Prisoners: Biblical Women Engaged in Violence

Woman, girl child, concubine,
Damsel, daughter, vixen
Women of old,
Women today,
Females signifying themselves
Dancing with God.
Mother, prophet, judge
Midwife, entrepreneur, incubator
Of ideas, of semen, of righteousness
On the wings of another's thoughts
Who controls and dictates and decides
Her beingness in the world.
Instigator, ingenious, intelligent
She who marries and births well
She who inherits
A culture of indifference to her:
She who kills,
From Divine command,
From husband's need,
Out of jealousy,
Out of need;
She destroys
So she can be.

The Bible has few substantive stories about women, and none portray mothers and daughters in meaningful, healthy relationships. Usually the functions of biblical women hinge on the male offspring they produce to secure land, position, or a promise (for example, Sarah, Rebekah, and Jephthah's daughter). Some women in the biblical narratives face humiliation, rape, or death (Genesis 38; 2 Samuel 13; Judges 19), and the erotic love story the Song of Songs, in which two lovers are treated with equality, is the only biblical book in which a woman actually speaks for herself.

A few biblical narratives depict women not as victims but as perpetrators of violence. Asking "what's violence got to do with it?"[1] we examine several texts that Refine the Fire of violence and smelt the passion of love in a mix of power and sex. Focusing on women who instigate or commit murder, this chapter begins to explore the phenomenon of mimetic desire, that is, the violent impulse to seize or destroy another person or a person's goods. That impulse, which becomes transformed into religious sacrificial systems, is evident in many biblical narratives about women. This chapter discusses its meaning and its deep ambiguity. After qualifying several female biblical coconspirators and their socio-historical and theological locations, this chapter explores: (1) their sources of power and the impact of their sexuality and (2) the glorification of sanctioned violence and the cost of idolatrous violence, mimetic activity, and forms of rejection.

Women Warriors and Coconspirators

Deborah and Jael

The biblical figure of Deborah (Judges 4 and 5) is portrayed in narrative and poetry as a courageous leader and judge. Though attempts were made later to domesticate this fiery figure,[2] her saving Israel in a time of crisis shows her as a prophet, judge, military commander, wife, and mother, blurring traditional boundaries with her Refining Fire for God.[3]

The narrative is straightforward: Having again done evil in God's sight and threatened by the Canaanite King Jabin, Israel cries out for help. Deborah enters, and Israel comes to her for judgment (4:1-5). Deborah calls for the Israelite general, Barak, to take position, and she draws out Sisera, Jabin's general, into Barak's hands. Tension mounts with Deborah's boast to Barak that a woman would save the day for Israel and the fulfillment of her prophecy in Jael's murder of Sisera. The story contrasts Deborah's and Jael's prowess with Barak's cowardice. When Sisera abandons his men and then Jael murders Sisera, victory goes to the Israelites, and Deborah and Barak sing poetic praises of the Lord.

The poem recounts the deeds of the tribes, the course of battle, and Sisera's death. Deborah functions as God's spokesperson but not as a true military leader. Ultimately, God subdues King Jabin on behalf of Israel. The victory poem balances Deborah, "mother of Israel," with the image of Sisera's mother awaiting his return. Each mother justifies her children's violence by dehumanizing their victims. Jael, allied with Deborah, a self-motivated Bedouin housewife and friend of King Jabin, "mothers" Sisera and then drives a tent peg through Sisera's head. Jael may also be a survivor who deals with her husband's politics and saves herself and her family.[4] The narrator sees Deborah's and Jael's actions in light of Israel's relationship and dependence on God.

Deborah's song celebrates a salvific, sovereign, covenantal God of history who judges, practices righteousness, blesses, and helps those who yield themselves. Conquest of land theology stands with remnant theology, as God's promises to Abraham continue; God wants relationship with those who love God, as their praise and life reflect God's splendor.[5] Deborah and Jael salvifically Refine the Fires under maternal guise and with military cunning by using strategy, hospitality, and divine sanction to kill in God's name.

Jezebel and Athaliah Do Battle—and Murder

During the monarchy, a mother-daughter duo Refines the Fires of murder in the name of Baal. Jezebel, the Phoenician princess (1 Kings 16:29–22:40; 2 Kings 9:30-37) married to Israelite King Ahab, and Elijah, Yahweh's prophet, mirror each other in behavior and ontology. Both scheme, plot, and murder. She worships Baal; he worships Yahweh. The text honors him and demonizes her. Although they never meet, they are inextricably linked together, from Naboth's vineyard to their final ends,[6] and they remain enemies. The legends of Elijah's opposition to King Ahab, Queen Jezebel, and her Baal entourage, which fueled the factions against the house of Ahab, were woven into a written cycle to authenticate Elisha's revolutionary, prophetic role and the revolution itself.[7]

In the Elijah-Elisha stories, natural disasters, warfare, heavy land taxes, rural land buy-outs, and debt-slavery create peasant dislocation and dissatisfaction. Upper-class displeasure emerges in the Naboth incident and in Elisha's fraternization (2 Kings 6:32). Women outside of Jezebel's entourage remain outsiders. With the tensions over socio-economic and political factors and the syncretism of the worship of Yahweh and Baal, God's apparent disfavor of the house of Ahab ends in bloody revolution.[8] Jezebel's story pits Yahwism against Canaanite-Phoenician religion.

Jezebel's story also depicts marital devotion, religious zeal, and a strong personality as she Refines the Fires of violence amid religion. The text condemns Jezebel for being a Baal worshipper, a persecutor and murderer of Yahweh's prophets, a patron housing Baal and Asherah's prophets, and an instigator of Naboth's murder. Elijah pronounces gruesome, total destruction to the house of the King and to Jezebel. Jehu accuses Jezebel of being a madam, a prostitute, and a sorcerer who thwarts peace (2 Kings 9:22).[9] Thus, Jezebel becomes the scapegoat for the evils of the divided monarchy and a symbol of a monstrous woman. The symbolism persists even into American history, in which the name Jezebel denotes:

> wicked; scheming; whore; cheap harlot; either promiscuous or a complete whore; female form of gigolo; the name has seductive connotations; . . . evil and treacherous; two-faced; . . . not ashamed; bimbo; . . .

a Southern belle with a mind and will and sex drive who is damned for
not fitting the stereotype of a helpless, frigid woman; . . . condescend-
ing term used for African American women in the time of slavery; . . .
sensual; in the Bible [Jezebel] serves as the archetypal bitch-witch-
queen. . . . The contradictory, controlling, carnal foreign woman . . . sexually evil and a demon woman: Ahab's evils are laid at her door.[10]

Only the 1895 Women's Bible views Jezebel as a generous, brave woman who
goes to any length to appease her husband.

A second queen, a descendent of Ahab, married a king of Judah and is also
seen as monstrous.[11] The reign of Athaliah, wife of the eighth king of Judah,
Jehoram, and the only woman to rule Israel or Judah, is problematic (2 Kings
8:25-27). While most scholars agree that Athaliah is the daughter of Ahab
and Jezebel, some question her paternity, because she is listed as daughter of
Omri and daughter of Ahab.[12] Here we suppose her parents are Ahab and
Jezebel. In any case, Athaliah blasphemes because she worships and supports
the Baal gods in the South as Jezebel did in the North. Athaliah marries Jehoram, later king of Judah, strengthening the political bonds between the
Davidic and Omride houses. Ahaziah, their son, becomes king of Judah in
842 BCE and reigns for a year, until Jehu kills him. Hearing of Ahaziah's
death, Athaliah sets about to kill or have killed all the males of the court,
including her own family. Unknown to Athaliah, a grandchild, Jehoash,
Ahaziah's baby son, is hidden and kept alive in the Temple. Athaliah reigns
as queen for six years until her assassination in 836 BCE by priestly order. The
priest crowns Jehoash king under the royal guard's protection.

Judith and Her Maid: Beauty as a Weapon

Unlike these queen mothers of dominance, idolatry, and aggression, Judith, a
female activist from the Apocrypha, stands on the side of Yahweh. While
Judith's story (in the Book of Judith) is Jewish fiction, with many historical
and geographical discrepancies and inaccuracies, it has similarities to that of
Deborah and Jael: in each, female heroines single-handedly kill Israel's
enemy. Each story begins with a political skirmish between a foreign power
and Israel; each includes a private scene with the female heroine and the
enemy; in each the enemy dies at the hand of the female; and each story clos-
es with a victory song.[13] Judith, like Jael and Deborah, seems barren and is
described as a married woman with an absent husband. These women see
themselves as acting under God's will for peace, and God receives credit for
the victory in the woman's "salvation by human initiative."[14]

Judith echoes other biblical female characters and other ancient heroic
women—for example, Clytemnestra, Elektra, Helen of Troy, Miriam, Deborah, Jael, Sarah, Rebekah, Rachel, Tamar, Naomi, Ruth, Abigail, Esther, and
Susanna. Judith's story uses direct speech with irony and has three main char-

acters: the hero, the heroine, and the villain; in a sense, Judith plays the first two.[15] Judith, a good listener and a wealthy widow, is well respected, wise, beautiful, discerning, pious, and God-fearing; she prays as she works toward a community reversal.[16]

Judith Refines a salvific Fire in Yahweh's name when she saves her people from Assyrian pride and their own misery. She helps transform a cowardly and compromising people. Holofernes desecrates Israelite cultic sites, and Israel fears losing its temple. Holofernes discounts Israel's covenantal protection and comes to overtake Judith's town by stopping its water supply.[17] The Book of Judith sets off Israel's fear or its denial of true deity and true sovereignty in times of struggle (1:1—7:32) against Judith's beauty, resolve, and victory (8:1—16:25). When Holofernes's god Nebuchadnezzar challenges Judith's God, Judith's God succeeds.

Judith's late entrance in the work (not until chapter 8) signifies her prima donna status, like one who enters the stage as the orchestra plays the themes or *leit motifs* that symbolize her presence. Aesthetically, Judith's strength illumines the frailty and adversities of Israel; she liberates using seduction. Judith overrides the sexual ideas of Holofernes which commingles penetration of the city and penetration of Judith: she decapitates him.[18] With her maid, Judith returns with the head of Holofernes and leaves a disoriented, defeated Assyrian army behind. After a victory celebration, Judith returns to a sedate life as a widow and dies at the age of 105.

Retold in over 150 literary works of drama, poetry, and fiction and in numerous hymns, oratorios, operas, cantatas, and ballets, Judith's story echoes themes from Deuteronomistic theology and some Wisdom literature. First, God uses the weak to bewilder and overcome the strong; second, observance of the Law accords one victory over one's enemy. This work, written around 150 BCE, was meant to encourage "patriotism of the Judeans against their Seleucid enemies and to encourage fidelity to the Jewish Law."[19]

The text is rife with ambiguity (Judith's morals and motives), double entendres, and irony,[20] as Judith defends God and country. Israel sees their distress as a trial sent by God. Yet since God is with them, they will have victory through Judith. God's ways differ from those of humanity, but if people absolutely trust God, salvation occurs. The conflict between Holofernes and Judith revisits that of Pharaoh and God in Exodus. One can imagine Judith as a messianic figure and her murder of Holofernes as a sacrifice that saves the Bethulians.[21]

Herodias and Salome: Coconspirators in the Death of John the Baptizer

Shifting to the Greco-Roman rule of Palestine, we study Herodias and Salome, coconspirators in the death of John the Baptizer. Herodias was the granddaughter of Herod the Great and daughter of Aristobulus.[22] She married her father's brother, Herod Beothus, according to historian Josephus, though the Gospel of Mark claims she was married to a Philip Antipas, who had divorced his wife to marry her. Popular tradition later saw divine retribution for John's death in the Arabian defeat of Antipas. According to Mark (6:17-29; also see Luke 9:7-9), Herodias was upset with the Baptist for condemning her incestuous marriage to Antipas: she was forbidden to marry her uncle (Leviticus 18). While Antipas seemed to respect and protect John, Herodias exacts revenge during Herod's birthday banquet. Herodias's daughter (Herod's stepdaughter) Salome dances and so delights and/or sexually arouses Herod that he promises to grant her anything. On Herodias's motherly advice, Salome asks for the head of John the Baptist. Antipas grants the request. The guard brings John's head on a platter and gives it to Salome, who gives it to her mother.[23] A dance has set the stage for the beheading of an apocalyptic, eschatological prophet, as lust, seduction, adultery, and incest derive death from a dance.

Why is John such a threat? John, Jesus' cousin, preached a messianic, eschatological Day of the Lord. As prophet and priest, John rejected the corrupt society of his time and strictly adhered to Torah. Herod Antipas and other Judean authorities sensed the danger of John's popularly received preaching. John was probably arrested as an instigator of a rapidly growing messianic movement. Though John's arrest is meant to squelch activity, he becomes a martyr.[24] His imprisonment and execution occurred at Macherus, the Maccabean-Herodian mountain fortress, near the Dead Sea.[25]

Assets of Power and the Place of Sex

The stories of Deborah-Jael, Jezebel-Athaliah, Judith-her maid, and Herodias-Salome all relate violence and religion, Refining the Fires of desire that in each instance devised the death of at least one man. We will now examine the roles of power and sexuality in these biblical women's lives.

Biblical texts define women, named and unnamed, in terms of their relationships with men. Otherwise, the biblical text usually ignores them. These texts often blame men's problems on women and label women foreign, idolatrous, wicked, and only occasionally powerful. But, as we have seen, in the stories of Jezebel, Rebecca, and their husbands, the women are in control.[26]

Women today are often in the same boat. Currently, less than 10 percent of the highest representatives in global governments are women. In international organizations like the United Nations, women hold less than 5 percent of the posts. The Margaret Thatchers, Golda Meirs, Indira Ghandis, and Tintoria Buttis are exceptions. Women's viewpoints, knowledge, sensibilities, feelings, and needs in health care, housing, education, economic and community development, or employment security are often left out of policy making and administration; top female governmental office holders are mostly in education, health, and social welfare. Such policy ghettoizes women and keeps them ineligible for the traditional male occupations.[27] How does the interplay of gender, power, and sexuality figure in the biblical narratives we just examined?

Deborah and Barak

Deborah's vocation may or may not have transcended an ancient glass ceiling. She wields divine authority, yet she needs Barak, a man, to fulfill her prophecies. From one view, a female Deborah cannot carry out God's will herself.[28] In fact, in the text God is the central hero; Deborah mediates between God and Barak. Barak becomes the metaphor for Canaanite oppression. The text differentiates between human and divine characters by using in-motion verbs for human beings, verbs of control for the Lord, and stylistic and situational repetitions.[29] One scholar argues that poetic imagery, evoking notions of Anat (the ancient Canaanite goddess of love and war) occurs in Judges 5 to denote the religious import to Deborah's role in the Canaanite war. Anat is to Yatpan (Anat's attendant warrior) as Deborah is to Barak: a female leader who employs a male military assistant and executor. Deborah and Anat are charismatic leaders/patronesses who inspire warriors. Theologically, by identifying Deborah with God's power, this imagery claims that God has victory over Canaanite foes and is a dramatic and provocative depiction of Deborah's power in that war.[30]

One can also view Deborah's power via satire. Reading Judges as satire illumines Deborah's ridicule of Israel's tribal warriors, who failed to answer Yahweh's call. She uses humor to reduce the arrogant and parodies Dinah's rape amid Sisera's death. The diverse female voices range from gentle mockery, lethal irony, ridicule, and parody, to burlesque and reproof of disobedience. Abuse supports arrogance: Israel ignores God and suffers until Deborah arrives. She praises obedient tribes and ridicules the reluctant,[31] and her song exposes sexism in distinctive gender roles. Her song discounts the myth that women would engage in less war, fighting, competition, or violence when in authority. Her song celebrates power and courage and moves toward divine collaborative justice and freedom.[32] Instead of sexual appeal, Deborah uses language of vengeance and rejoicing over Sisera's annihilation. Such objectification in biblical texts begs the question of the morality of using sex as a weapon of death.[33]

Historically, eroticism and death coexist amid sex and violence: "Between her legs he knelt, he fell, he lay; between her legs he knelt, he fell/Where he knelt, there he fell, despoiled" (Judges 5:27). Jael is mother, lover, and killer. She is the nurturing, ruthless, heroic seducer/warrior and guerrilla assassin who uses erotic language and imagery as a "self-appointed female soldier." Sisera lying between her legs, euphemistically links his position and her sexuality; likewise, Sisera's mother hopes for "women booty," the product of her womb. Affection and war, conqueror and conquered compete, creating tension, discomfort, and uncertainty. This language of sex and sexual submission, of eroticism and ritual or sacrificial death implies vulnerability, petition, and inglorious defeat.

Jael and Judith

Jael, as depicted in the narratives, becomes an archetype that exposes a man's phobia of death and sexuality, symbolizes victory of the marginalized over the establishment.[34] In fact, both Jael and Judith seduce and kill through deception and lies. Yet Sigmund Freud and René Girard note that while sexual desire causes division within human society, religious rites have a unifying function. Successful sexual encounter involves an individual partner relationship; a "fascinating experience . . . [occurs on a] collective level if all evil aggression is suddenly projected upon a single evildoer. Blind rage is immediately calmed, deadly fear disappears. . . . [Miraculously] peace is restored to the deeply threatened community. . . . Sexuality is not able to structure either the social order or the religious and cultural world."[35]

Jezebel

Sexual prowess figures into but is not the seat of Jezebel's power. Despite popular tradition, the Jezebel of the Bible is not a whore, nor does she focus on sexual gratification. In the story, King Ahab sulks over not getting Naboth's vineyard. His wife, Jezebel, who panders to his greed, becomes the villainous, idolatrous foreign wife. Their marriage allies them with Phoenicia, alienates and exploits many of Israel's elite due to his family's monopoly in Samaria and causes resentment over the economy and his desertion of Israel's God and cult. Jezebel persuades the elders and other free persons to help falsely accuse Naboth. Jezebel becomes the Refining Fire, the very symbol of the ills of the Omride dynasty. Her female dominance in a patriarchal culture is abnormal, corrupting, and allegedly an ultimate cause for Israel's demise.[36]

The massive violence and power issues related to the downfall of the Omride dynasty also involve Athaliah, Jezebel's daughter. Her story relates to the death of many of Judah's princes, particularly in 2 Chron. 22:9-11 and 2 Kings 11:1-2. Was it a question of challenged authority for Jehoram after the death of his father? What was the role of Jehoram's wife, Athaliah? If Athaliah's ordering executions, even of her own offspring, is not myth or propaganda, what was her agenda? While it was customary to erase all members of an opposing family after an uprising and to leave no claimants to the throne or avengers, Athaliah has other concerns. Jehu probably comes to kill Ahaziah, because many opposed the Omride family. The people reject the house of Omri, especially Joram and his mother Jezebel.[37]

The major problem perhaps lay in the huge social upheaval of the Iron Age, when people had to shift from a tribal to a monarchical state, a change that affected religious, social, and ethical ideas. Perhaps because they could not cope with these changes, people focus on the activity and politics of their royal house. They react to Jezebel's new worship trends with greater nationalism and a monotheistic awareness of God. After Jehoram and Athaliah marry, they want to erase political opponents, including Jehoram's brothers, Judah's priests, and any Davidic household members. After learning of her son Ahaziah's death, Athaliah has to face strong Davidic opposition and hope to survive Jehu's reign, which explains her ordering the execution of her kin to advance herself.[38] Athaliah's strategy does not involve seduction or sex, but Judith's does.

Judith

In Judith, a fictional drama in two acts, the patriarchal norms are subverted: a female delivers Israel using beauty, not military might. These reversals occur amid recurring fear or its denial, sensual aesthetics, and the struggle over the utmost and true god. In both acts, the narrative moves from the campaign against disobedience and war preparations to the conclusion about Judith.[39] Is Judith a replacement for male leadership, a femme fatale meant to appease a male vision of femininity, or are both male and female voices speaking in Judith? As a Refining Fire, her character stands above all male actors; she may redefine reality; as a mother of Israel, she kills to give life to others; and her genealogy locates her as the ideal Israelite woman whose spouse gets his identity from his wife. Judith acts on her own and she orders the Jews to offer a counterattack.[40]

Judith's story involves a political scenario of exploitation and oppression, in which Judith's hand becomes God's hand in a quest for liberation. Judith laments her people's condition, but she presumes their problem is God's problem. Like Deborah, Judith takes charge and sends others out to battle. Like Esther, the Book of Judith involves feasting, sensuality, and sexuality as parts of her strategy. The banquet brings life to Israel and Judith and death to Holofernes and the Assyrians.[41]

The theme of sexuality permeates the Hebrew and Apocryphal texts, from Dinah's rape in Genesis 34 and Holofernes' lust for Judith to Judith's move from the prayer room to her preparations in the beauty parlor. Judith's beauty, sensuality, and sexuality tantalize Holofernes; her arsenal is her sex appeal, dress, and cosmetics; her sexuality is a military weapon. Judith's sexuality in a way embodies Israel and is Israel's glory, and she celebrates nationhood by being the one to destroy the enemy.[42] While her people do not have drinking water, she gets Holofernes to drink too much.[43] Judith possesses the alleged male traits of wisdom, bravery, forcefulness, independence, and the stereotypical female traits of physical beauty, guile, and sexual seductiveness.[44] Judith dances before all Israel and offers a psalm of thanksgiving; Israel is personified as a woman who sings the song, and she is only referred to in third person. After Israel's victory celebration, Judith returns home as an honored widow.

Judith and the Israelite community appear to be mirror metaphors for each other. In contrast to her brazen sexuality, Israel is the faithful, sexually controlled, holy community. Yet, as a widow, relegated to a private, proper place, she ceases to subvert the metaphor. The males appear to be castrated: they are ineffectual, impotent, or impaired.[45] In Judith, the politics of sexuality places Judith's chastity first in the incident with Holofernes and is the necessary component that lets Judith be the heroine. The politics of the double standard require that Judith be sexual and beautiful, yet simultaneously chaste and untouched. The figure of Judith reveals male ambivalence toward female sexuality as simultaneously "desirable and dangerous."[46] The story teaches that beauty and deceit are related, reinforcing the notion that female beauty and sexuality are dangerous to men because females use their beauty and charm to betray, seduce, and kill men. Scholars tend to focus on the politics of nationality, not sexuality, when analyzing Judith, Deborah, and Jael. Ultimately, both kinds of interpretations tend to carry an anti-woman message.[47]

Judith's story of faith and cultural paradox explores fear, power, and the ironic reversal of power when control shifts toward excessive zeal. Worship of the one true God is called into question when the Israelites' faith is tested. Both Judith and Holofernes act out of a sense of commission without direct orders from either of their gods.[48]

Herodias and Salome

Female will to power later costs another man his head in the story of John the Baptizer's death. Herodias and Salome, royalty by marriage, do not see their act of revenge as liberation, attaining authority, or covenant belief. The impetus of the Refining Fire of sexual activity that leads to John's death resides in the loins of Herod; he allegedly lusts after his stepdaughter, Salome. She so arouses him that he will give up half of his kingdom as a reward to Salome for satisfying his sexual desires. The question of sexual impropriety between Herodias and Antipas is also problematic. According to Lev. 18:16 and 20:21, if a man sleeps with his brother's wife, other than for levirate obligation, it is like him sleeping with his brother, thus implying same-sex incest, adultery, and fornication. Neither the Gospel nor Torah texts address the ethics of Herod's family's complicity in John the Baptist's murder; neither do the Gospels address the disregard of sexual boundaries within families. Further, Jesus' and John's disciples knew that John was in jail, but no concern is voiced about his well-being. Yet when John inquires if Jesus is the "one who is to come, or are we to wait for another?" (Matt. 11:2-20), Jesus sends John a reply and preaches about John, though the text records no intercession or visitations by Jesus on John's behalf.

What does John's death teach us? Does he need to die to foreshadow Jesus' death? Is he left alone because his faith is steadfast? Do the stories of Judith, Deborah, and Jael teach us to condone violence done in God's name? What does that make God? Do the vile mutilation and deaths of Athaliah and Jezebel appease the crowd? Asking "What's violence got to do with it?" awakens burning questions about conflict, sex, acquisitions, and idolatry, and how they collude to do great harm.

Violence against Women and Children

Violence—injurious physical, mental, emotional, or psychological action or treatment—works to restrict, thwart, or limit one's freedoms. Violence seeks to erase and obliterate the vitality of the self, and it destroys and annihilates total being. Violence is also woven into all our social fabric. As social, systemic oppression, it exists in structures and in the ethical, religious, sociocultural, and epistemological assumptions, standards, symbols, patterns, and habits that undergird the individual and collective life. Paradoxically, following societal rules and codes both forbids and foments oppression and violence.[49]

Violence against women and their children, for example, takes multiple forms: sexual harassment, child pornography, Asian sex-tourism, stoning, *sati,* illiteracy, forced prostitution, incest and sexual defilement, the silencing of women due to homelessness and isolation of older women, foot binding, female infanticide, date and marital rape, and genital mutilation. Most violence is intimate: Friends, husbands, prior sex partners, family members, or acquaintances are responsible for the murders of nine out of ten women slain in the United States. Often perpetrators are not held responsible, and society often assumes that women are at fault. Some female victims of male violence even internalize this guilt. Violence against women involves the fires of male control, dehumanization, and exploitation, multiplied by ageism, classism, racism, poverty, war, militarist colonialism, cultural imperialism, homophobia, and religious fundamentalism.[50] Individual and systemic violence negates the other, celebrates victimization, and reduces large segments of humanity to merchandise.

Full equality between women and men must occur before world peace and true social order can exist. Such equality requires education and opportunities for transformation of values and attributes. Then one can actualize new ones in his or her daily life and societal relations. More lip service has been given to gender equality than has actual change, and often the public discussion has trivialized the issues or made them "women-only" concerns.[51] Thus violence *by* women against men is something of a reversal, a decadent, provocative topic.

Biblical texts and Christian ethics often preserve the cycle of violence by hindering resistance to violence. The Hebrew Bible bears witness to the unfaithfulness and sinfulness of humanity, to God's judgment reflected through war, and to the faithful Lord who continues to work for humanity in spite of sin. God's continuing faithfulness occurs in God's promises to guide us toward peace. Biblically based Christian faith and theology often support the victimization of women and children by denigrating their status, although Jesus suggests that justifying Hebrew biblical retributive justice is antithetical to God's love (Matthew 5–7). Christians cannot overcome their own violence-producing action, exploitation, or objectification unless they also condemn the systemic evil that harms those who struggle at the bottom of the socio-political, economic, and cultural barrel of domination.[52] Says Joanne Carlson Brown of the complex ramifications of Christianity's central motifs:

> The image of "divine child abuse" is the central image around which all theology, worship, and ritual are developed. [Stories about] God and father-daughter incest . . . stories we tell in church, especially around the passion of Jesus, are imbued with violence. [These alleged] stories about a loving god and how [God] cares for [God's] children. . . are stories about a God who . . . requires that [God's own] children suffer, and punishes them when they fail. Furthermore, [God may sacrifice a child] whether it is [God's] own son or an eleven-year-old girl.[53]

Mimetic Desire and the Scapegoat Mechanism

Some further light on these complex relationships comes from notions of scapegoating and mimetic desire.[54]

Communities rely on the scapegoat mechanism to avoid engaging in destructive rivalries. For René Girard, unconscious hiding of violent impulses and the desire to avoid violence produces religion. The major tool of religion is the sacrifice or violation of a randomly selected victim or scapegoat. Violence arises out of mimetic desire, the impetus to imitate a model, which always puts the "disciple" in a double bind. Uncontrolled mimetic desire can lead to complete societal chaos. That unbridled desire is instead channeled into ritualized violence against a sacrificed "scapegoat." Most societies use scapegoats to impute the community's ills to the victim. For Girard, human communities sustain order through a system of differences, but violence threatens to erupt from these very differences or rivalries. Sacrifice helps maintain and yet diffuse the differences. For the disciple or subject, desire is directed toward the other's desires, not toward the one the subject most resembles. With mimetic desire, the model is the rival/disciple and the rival is the model.[55] To locate the mimetic rivalry in the case of women who are murderers, accessories, or instigators involves examining their status, context, locus of power, and desires, to determine whether each is model, disciple, or both.

The Language of Women Warriors

When talking about women warriors, the *warrior* metaphor gives these women a more typically male quality: entitlement. As internal metaphor, *woman warrior* means she has attributes, skills, and characteristics of a warrior. Since warrior historically is male, and binary oppositions exist between man and woman in society, the woman warrior shares certain of his features. As an external metaphor, *woman warrior* refers to her social role. Both warrior and woman are part of the human domain, and the woman warrior takes on male status, although she is female; she appears to threaten a man in patriarchal systems and becomes entitled. Entitlement means status and also the authority to maintain, condemn, or modify ways of experiencing genders.

Deborah and Jael

In the case of Deborah and Jael, the metaphor of woman warrior has strong possibilities because pre-monarchical Israel had no central bureaucracy. Israel consisted of independent tribes based on strong blood and residential ties. Deborah could lead in war because of the domestic nature of military organization. Though women did not normally lead at this time, Deborah exemplified the tensions regarding gender roles. The writer of Judges uses Deborah as a Refiner of Fire—a warrior to shame the weaker males around her, which works if war is for men only. The voracity syndrome—the implied sexuality in the tent scene—allows Jael to emasculate Sisera in the "sexual privacy," as the "tent peg in Jael's hands becomes synecdochically the ravaging phallus," the reversal of rape.[56]

As a warrior woman, why does Deborah disappear in Judges 4:14b-15? Some theological reflections see Deborah and Jael as metaphors for Yahweh. Displacing Deborah, Yahweh the protagonist acts against the cults of Asherah and Anath, Canaanite goddesses. Our questioning of Deborah's role often assumes that women in twelfth-century patriarchy were unaware of their own oppression and therefore assumes a gender and ethnocentric bias and reduces the scope of questions one can ask the text. In Judges 4, who will give up Sisera—Deborah or God? Until the battle, Deborah's and God's presence and speech are one. When God's actions silence Deborah, as the main character and woman warrior, she may echo the Canaanite divine female warrior goddess, Anath.[57] In Judges 5, the motherhood of Deborah and Sisera's mother accentuates loyalty to other women. That Deborah disappears and Yahweh gives Sisera up to Jael tends to make women less important in their own story.[58]

Some scholars contend that Deborah subverts submission, which creates a pseudo-pacifism, justifies the authority of violence and use of force, and finds problematic an aggressive, warrior woman. Is all violence wrong? Is any violence acceptable? Some scholars laud Deborah as a source of empowerment; others find her instigation of violence difficult. Some scholars contend Sisera got what he deserved and that Jael was courageous. Others find her violence disturbing.[59] While Jael's action breaks hospitality laws, the text does not condemn her or mention hospitality. Perhaps, given the stories of Genesis 19 and Judges 19, where hospitality dictates that "male hosts offer the women of their households to rapists," commentators read Jael's actions negatively.[60] My Girardian reading of the Deborah-Jael story is a complex web of mimetic triangles set in the context of a young community shifting from a tribal confederacy with weak leadership supposedly on a quest to take the land Yahweh promised Abraham—notwithstanding that other people already occupy the land. In addition, several critical issues are at play:

1. Yahweh told Israel to drive out the inhabitants from the land; Israel grows strong but does not drive the Canaanites out (Judges 1:28).
2. The angel of the Lord reminds them about the covenant made in Egypt: since no covenants with the Canaanites are allowed, they must tear down Canaanite altars. Because the Israelites remain disobedient, God makes the Canaanites their adversaries (Judges 2:1-5).
3. After Joshua and his whole generation die, the following generation does not know the Lord nor what the Lord did for Israel. Subsequently, Israel does what is evil in the sight of the Lord: they abandon Yahweh and worship Baal and his female consorts, Astarte and Asherah (Judges 2:11-15).

Repeatedly, the Lord brings Israel misfortune and raises up judges, that is, charismatic leaders, to free Israel from oppression. In and around Deborah's story, the following mimetic or imitative triangles unfold: Canaan and Israel vie over land; the people worship Yahweh or Baal; and Barak and Jael both confront the challenge of Sisera. This mimetic crisis also collapses into the double bind as Jael brutally murders Sisera, Barak comes later, and the text claims that God subdued King Jabin, where Sisera serves as the scapegoat for

Jabin. Later, the Israelites finally destroy King Jabin. In the poetic version of this saga, Deborah, as model with Barak, and the selected tribes of Israel, as disciple, fight the Canaanites. Jael kills Sisera, Deborah is mother of Israel and model, and Sisera's mother is disciple. Yahweh has the victory over Sisera; the mimetic mechanism is skewed but accomplishes the task: the land rests for forty years.

Girard: Killing of the Scapegoat

Jezebel's story has a different track. One Girardian reading of 1 Kings 18 would see their societal, collective crisis brought about by drought as resolved by killing and making explicit this scapegoat. The need for water diminishes social distinctions. The curse on the king, his people, and society creates a leading societal mimetic crisis. Killing or expelling the scapegoat keeps the society intact. Societal continuity requires that everyone sees their social responsibility in killing the scapegoat and that the scapegoat be from their own community. This drama has two scapegoats: the Baal prophets and Jezebel (1 Kings 18:22-24).

When the 450 Baal prophets are unsuccessful in calling their god to render sacrifice, they themselves become scapegoats. The people, as Yahweh's agents, grab the Baal prophets, and Elijah slaughters them. This is a sacrifice since the prophets are slaughtered, but also an anti-sacrifice, because the Baal prophets are butchered at a distance from the altar, not sacrificed to Yahweh. In the second cycle, the text blames Jezebel for introducing Baal worship to Israel, for offering hospitality to 450 Baal prophets and 400 prophets to Asherah, and for ignoring Yahweh's covenant, traditions, and justice. While Ahab dies as a tragic hero, one can see Jezebel as heroic as a double of Ahab, or see her death as unheroic, since she tries to handle the crises through seduction. Using cosmetics to distract and control Jehu hints at Jezebel's symbolizing Asherah (portraying the goddess as a sacred prostitute). Does this heroic queen's attitude express tragic, passionate, but untimely pride? If Jezebel is judged harlot, her words ("Is it peace, Zima, murderer of your master?") may be an effort to reach Jehu and Yahweh's male pride and machismo, with Jezebel becoming the scapegoat herself:

> Yahweh is the victor, [via] . . . male activity: violence, cynicism, aggression, and mercilessness. . . . Jezebel is eaten by the dogs, so that . . . she becomes dung on the field. . . . The death of Jezebel is consummate humiliation and the outcome of her double responsibility: she seduced Ahab to institute a foreign cult, . . . and she seduced him to ignore the traditional maintenance of coherence between property and family in a Yahweh obeying society. . . . Her death became the death of the scapegoat, killed by the word and faceless mob.[61]

This collective violence by a mob, sanctioned by God, depicts a Girardian cosmology that connects the mob, lynching, collective responsibility, and sacrifice.

Jezebel and Her Daughter Athaliah

Jezebel links the Deuteronomistic history of Elijah and his two mountain-top experiences: the contest with the Baal prophets at Mount Carmel (1 Kings 18) and his experience on Mount Horeb (1 Kings 19). Jezebel both advances the Baal cult in Israel and through her daughter, Athaliah, in Judah. Jezebel is the scapegoat, the desired object for Yahweh and Jehu. That Jehu comes for Jezebel echoes Canaanite mythology, in which the god of Death, Mot, enters Baal's palace via a window (2 Kings 9:30). Jehu commands her eunuchs to throw Jezebel out of the window, which mirrors Sisera's mother awaiting her son and foreshadows Athaliah's death (2 Kings 11:16).[62] Did this kind of refining of the fire of violence begin with their deaths?

The violence begins with Jezebel's helping to create false testimony against Naboth following Deuteronomic law. While Jezebel is the instigator, the text views her husband, Ahab, as a coconspirator, and he is ultimately held responsible for Naboth's death (1 Kings 21:19; 22:38; 2 Kings 9:35). Ahab dies trying to use the land he and Jezebel stole from Naboth. The initial lies foreshadow Ahab's family being consumed by dogs. Retributive justice of an eye for an eye is the fate of Jezebel and Athaliah.[63] Athaliah's desire for power and the monarchy causes her to sacrifice her kin. The text vilifies and demonizes Jezebel by ascribing the whoring metaphor to her, a vehicle which the patriarchy uses to shift blame and bolster male control: "as the quintessential foreign woman of power she is for the patriarchal subject the quintessential Other, to be feared and blamed."[64] Though Jezebel, the one who had scapegoated, gets sacrificed by Jehu and Yahweh for the crimes of idolatry and murder, these acts of violence do not cause lasting peace, given the demise of Israel in 722 BCE and Judah in 587 BCE.

Violence was a dominant motif in all the biblical texts during the ninth century BCE. Eighth-century prophets critique the earlier reliance on kings and the mistaken political calculations of Elisha. Thus Jehu's murders and Athaliah's uprising minimizes the monarchy's legitimacy, and God cannot be used to support such a political agenda: "Name him [your son] Jezebel, and I will put an end to the kingdom of the house of Israel" (Hosea 1:4).[65]

Judith and Holofernes

In Judith's story, the mimetic rivalry in Judith takes yet another twist. Nebuchadnezzar, King of Babylon, who caused the fall of Jerusalem (587–586 BCE), attacks Arphaxad, the alleged but unknown king of the Medes, in the northern part of Iran. Nebuchadnezzar desires power and land and swears to take revenge on all who do not join him in war. He orders Holofernes to punish the disobedient through terrorism and military campaigns. Holofernes destroys their shrines and bids all to pay homage to Nebuchadnezzar alone. Holofernes and his men make the people of Israel/Bethulia surrender (1–7). As Holofernes dries up their water supply, Israeli cries out to God, echoing Exodus. Judith suggests that they remember God's acts in history, be thankful, and that she, Judith, has a secret plan.[66]

Seeing the story of Judith and Holofernes as symbolizing the fear of castration, with a female foe or rival, where the head not the sexual organs are cut off, recalls the scenarios of intriguing refiner's fire of Salome and John the Baptist, and of David and Goliath. Judith masterminds the plan, participates in seduction, without removing her garments, and saves her people from Holofernes. Judith desires peace for her people; Holofernes's desires to conquer them. The mimetic crisis, which ends with the beheading of Holofernes, diminishes the Assyrians, builds up the Israelites, and honors Judith. European artistic renderings show Judith either before the murder, or in the midst of the decapitation with her maid, or alone putting Holofernes's head on a dish or in a bag. Donatello's statue has Judith standing, between blows, transfixed with her mouth open, posed in a sexually provocative manner with her right leg between his thighs while her own left leg encircles his back. Late Renaissance and early Baroque painters tend to focus after the decapitation; later Baroque depictions focus on violence, revenge, and sexual activity. Judith reemerges in nineteenth-century art amid violence and heroism. Twentieth-century artists depict Judith as femme fatale during orgasm, as seductress.[67] All these depictions seek to make sense of "the volatile vapor of meaning" that is Judith's legend.[68]

Salome and John the Baptist
Salome's dance and the decapitation of John the Baptist have been immortalized in a fourteenth-century mosaic in St. Mark's of Venice, Italy; in a fifteenth-century fresco by Fra Filippo Lippi; and in Richard Strauss's opera, based on Oscar Wilde's play *Salome*. The mimetic, refining entanglement involves Herod's lust and Herodias's revenge, embodied in the desire of Salome's dance. While the biblical text remains quiet regarding the import of this sacrifice on peace to Herod's kingdom, the murder fails to silence John's disciples and Jesus.

Readings, Rejections, Challenges
René Girard's scapegoat scheme does seem to shed light on the dynamics of biblical violence. But it is not invulnerable. Christine Gudorf opposes

Girard's thesis and claims surrogate victim sacrifice does not silence, contain, or break cyclical violence. Sacrifice rechannels violence and actually protects those in power from the protest of those whom they oppress, she argues. For example, ritualizing Jesus' suffering and death and calling the powerless to imitate Jesus' obedience and self-sacrifice lets Christian ministry and theology maintain the violence of social, ecclesiastical, cultural, and political structures and discourses. A theology that remains mute on the socio-political causes of Jesus' execution and fashions him as the model sacrificial victim whose death God willed or needed continues religious violence rather than helps believers resist and transform the violence.[69]

In sum, biblical women usually have little power, are usually controlled by men, and often end up being cast as the one who betrays others. At other times women play a salvific role as God's instruments.[70] Women excel and show strength in arenas of moral courage, mercy and sympathy, philanthropy and responsiveness toward those who suffer and are in need. These women show more strength than men and refine the fires of violence for a divine good—or human greed. Like the ancients, we have tended to accord certain qualities disproportionately along gender lines until they have become gender role identity. We acknowledge that relationships need to be models of unity and equality; we must teach spiritual skills and values to children, especially about equality, which is critical for building self-esteem of girls.[71] In light of our contemporary situation, how do we read women who kill, especially Jael, Jezebel, and Judith?

Women Who Kill: Biblical Women in Modern Perspective

Readers tend to be repelled by Jael's murderous act. Why? First, she holds the hammer in her left hand and the tent-peg in her right, reversing the order. Sisera had already been defeated and comes to Jael in a moment of weakness. She takes him in, is victorious, and breaks the sacrality of Bedouin hospitality by giving him warmth, milk, and near-maternal care: the primal human bond between mother and child, mother and son.[72] In contemporary courts, Jael might be tried for premeditated murder, or at least manslaughter. The text does not tell us what happens to Jael. She might have considered her sacrifice of Sisera to be a well-being offering without blemish before the Lord, a covenant meal where one sacramentally relates to God and to Israelite community (cf. Leviticus 3).

While the biblical texts praise Jael, they vilify Jezebel. The biblical text rejects Jezebel by using the metaphors of harlotries and sorceries, implying the Canaanite fertility cult and its sexual and mantic manifestations. As a foreign woman, Jezebel symbolized the Omride's politics and idolatry. When Jehu approaches Jezebel, he does so as a religious quest out of loyalty to God.

Jehu and Yahweh desire Jezebel's ruin. Jehu, regardless of his possible motives, aligns with Yahwists, who see him as the voice of hope over against Jezebel.[73] Elijah's prophesy against Ahab's house and the actions Jehu takes against that royal dynasty (1 Kings 21:19-27; 2 Kings 9) concern a promise that calls for the elimination of the house of Ahab like that of Jeroboam.[74] If Jezebel had a trial today, she would be convicted of accessory to murder and conspiracy and might be tried for orchestrating organized crime. Jezebel may have been obsessed about her man, but her acts of idolatry convict her. For all intents and purposes, Jezebel got the death penalty—more heinous and barbaric than the electric chair or lethal injection.

And what is Judith's sentence? Judith's story challenges us to wrestle with tradition amid theology, religious institutions, and socio-cultural constraints on women. Judith's story turns tragedy to triumph as she accomplishes her task without direct help or promises from God. Judith is the independent subject within a patriarchal, male-dominated society. In one sense her deceit against Holofernes serves the covenant tradition, as Israel seeks its true God amid a loss of faith and then reclaims that faith after being tested. Judith's trust in God ultimately helps renew communal faithfulness. God answers Judith's prayer and helps her incapacitate the Assyrians, Israel's enemy. Judith's Refining Fire does not let a patriarchal system impede her progress. She knows that her status and gender do not remove her communal responsibility, and that genuine lament requires unfaltering trust. In the Book of Judith, the lament begins (chapter 4), climaxes (chapter 9), and resolves in a hymn (chapter 16). The political intrigue shaped by seduction, sexual desires, and innuendo lets Judith press societal conventions and acts in a "male" way—that is, aggressive, bold, and confident.[75] Today, Judith would be tried and probably found guilty of premeditated first-degree murder.

"What's Violence Got to Do With It?"

Sometimes everything. Mimesis run riot often results in more chaos, more pain, and a broken society. When women do violence, their acts may or may not be read in the same manner as when men do. Society tends to be surprised that women are capable of murder. Women as refiners engage the fire, the violence of murder; some women kill in the name of God, desire, passion, revenge, and self-defense. Women abuse, women batter; women kill others; women kill themselves. Violence is no respecter of gender, class, race, time, or beauty. How dangerous it is to take lightly biblical texts, dubbed the Word of God, that at once require humans to "do justice, love kindness, and walk humbly with your God," (Micah 6:8) but allow a divine service through evil, murder, and sacrifice.

Women kill with words
Women kill with kindness
Refining the Fires of murder
Blood runs
From the wounded soul.
Violence begets not Grace
Oft fails to bring peace;
Birth embodies violence
Violence that wrenches away life
Creates Death
Where is your God
Does your God require violence:
Refining Fires of pain and desire?
What does your God require of you?
What do you require of your god?
Of yourself?
Is violence a prerequisite for life?
Does your Eucharist need that much pain?
Who are You?
Whom do you serve?

3. Lay My Burden Down:
Spirituality Transcends Antebellum Violence

Ev'ry time I feel de Spirit
Movin' in ma heart, I will pray.
Ev'ry time I feel de Spirit
Movin' in ma heart, I will pray.
Upon de mountaun, ma Lord spoke,
Out o' His mouth came Fire an' smoke.
De Jerdan Ribber chilly an' col,
Chill de body, but not de soul.
All aroun' me, look so shine
Ask me Lord if all was mine.
Ain't but one train dat runs dis track,
It runs to Heaven an' runs right back.
—Traditional African American Spiritual[1]

The Refining Fire of African American Spirituals

"Ev'ry Time I Feel de Spirit," an African American Spiritual, celebrates African American spirituality and ritualistic, sacred overcoming. African American Spirituals, living texts by enslaved Black folk, offer protest, praise, and proclamation. The Spirituals, as chants of collective exorcism,[2] are Refining Fires that protest injustice, express praise and knowledge of God, and proclaim true, universal humanity. These Refining Fires, as liturgical psaltery, saved African Americans from utter hopelessness during antebellum slavery through the Civil Rights Movement. These litanies of hope signify—rename or revise—when they name a social location of oppression due to the evils of slavery and racism. These sacred texts are conscious of the quest for liberation from slavery, and like the Psalms, from which many take there words, imply a certainty of hearing by God. Slavery, America's Original Sin, was part of the Spirituals' maieutic or midwifery process. Slavery and its kindred spirit, racism, are processes that permeated and continue to permeate the entire nation with moral malaise, xenophobia, and violence. Racism, America's concupiscence, annihilates and denies love and Refines the Fires of compounded hate, fear, and a need to wield power. The Spirituals champion "an advanced, effective psychological method . . . reflected in such current

terminology as post-traumatic stress," in which "the experience of emotionally expressive singing is transformative."[3] Celebrating the existence and aesthetics of love, the Spirituals Refine the Fires of beauty and elegance while
inducing a theodicy, that is, a theology of justice, and grounding the individual in a cornucopia of renewal that provides a eucharistic, healing power.

My theology of justice confronts a notion of divine, aesthetic benevolence
amid human perceived evil within an African holistic, religio-musical worldview and the Eurocentric Protestant biblical and hymnic traditions. My
inquiry calls for a cultural revision of human transformation[4] and asks how
the Spirituals provide the oppressed with a relationship with God and their
sanity amid a brutal, paradoxical, existential, and ontological context.
Singing the Spirituals provides a prescription for well-being, praise, worship,
belief, and sources of authority that embrace eschatological issues of life,
death, hope, despair, freedom, and transformation within all life's essences: a
vibrant spirituality. This chapter explores the inherent spirituality in selected African American Spirituals, the language of the antebellum protest era
and of the Civil Rights Movement: Fires constantly being Refined by the
Divine and the divinely ordained to construct beauty out of the chaos. After
surveying the context of the Spirituals, this chapter: (1) explores the beauty
and elegance or aesthetics of the Spirituals via rhetorical-musical critique, (2)
explores their philosophical and theological dynamics, (3) reflects on a contemporary ontological spirituality of "I-amness" and "We-ness" towards an
experience of *imago dei,* and (4) locates aspects of this spirituality as reforming, transformative Fires in selected Spirituals.

Socio-cultural and Historical Imagery

That the Spirituals Refine the Fires of empowerment and affirm African
American personhood, freedom, and God "with us" becomes apparent via an
evaluation of slavery, racism, mimetic violence, myth, and ritual. Slavery was
vindicated as an American institution by biblical, scientific, political, economic, and psychological mythologies. Although the first slaves on North
American shores in 1619 were European indentured servants and Indian cap-
tives, slavery became institutionalized and Africanized in 1640, although the
first Blacks arrived in South Carolina in 1526. The South Carolina Blacks
rebelled, the colony failed, and the putative and unsuccessful white slave
owners sailed away, leaving the Blacks behind.[5] The fear of slave insurrections[6] spawned coercive laws, inhumane punishment, and opposition against
slavery itself.

Abolitionists opposed the insidious structure and argued for manumission
on ethical grounds,[7] even though the U.S. Constitution regarded slaves as
three-fifths of a person in apportioning members of the House of Representa-

tives to ensure protection for the "peculiar" institution by overrepresenting the white male property owners of the slave states.[8] Stereotypes, language games, and unstable opposing compounds expunged Black existence,[9] but oral slave narratives collected during the 1930s show the vital, aesthetic Black self as nurturer, survivor, and freedom seeker within the family and the Black church.

The Spirituals' Message of Freedom

Many Spirituals signify that freedom is a God-given right.[10] Slave bards and 1960s Freedom Fighters created "Freedom" Spirituals, which celebrated and camouflaged their strategies and defiant acts. The "Freedom" Spirituals aided and uplifted extended families in coping with and surviving family separations and dissolution by plantation owners.[11] The Black Church, a diverse institution,[12] used the Spirituals to sustain Black folk, to preserve their African past, and to urge them to find freedom in Jesus.[13] The Spirituals sustained Black folk as their protest and quest for social justice created a tolerance and temperament in this country that allowed for the 1954 U.S. Supreme Court decision of *Brown v. Board of Education,* which hurled the United States into a modern revolution and ended legalized, institutionalized Jim Crow, a twentieth-century institution.[14] The Spirituals represent one genre of Black protest that began decades earlier with intellectual thought, pan-Africanist work, and organized social protest.[15] The Black church housed the 1960s protest meetings, which continued the effort of eradicating legalized institutionalized racism.

Racism, a destructive Refiner's Fire, denies total communal wholeness and creates a dialectic of power-based relationships. Racism is a system of belief and meaning shaped by White supremacist dominance and a type of chronicled, idolatrous faith that questions God's creation, offers an alternate deity of nature or biology.[16] By the 1960s, racism evinced marks of the demonic:[17] a fanatical assertive effort to place all reality in its dogma and bar other voices that challenged its ultimacy. Slavery and racism are historical pathologies shaped by demonic idolatry, dominance, and the fear of economic competition. Racism destroys the body politic[18] and halts freedom.[19]

Ideas of freedom pertain to God's justice, race, and the relationships between God and humankind. Negative racial attitudes castrate God's justice and communal mutuality and exhibit idolatrous aspects of American civil religion,[20] those cultural experiences and institutions with religious, nationalist tendencies in the United States. The American concept of the alleged "one nation under God" leads to "spiritual and cultural schizophrenia,"[21] which creates racist laws and customs transmitted through legal myths, sacralized faith, stereotypes, and rituals. In the 1960s, lines blurred between the sacred and secular gods of intelligence, science, and technology.[22] This fuzziness supported the Spirituals' call for action against victimization, a Refining Fire of faithful protest and praise of God. Their call for freedom tempers the schizophrenia and appreciates differences. Just as violence is difference itself,[23] racial differences trigger racial violence, in which "ethnic and religious minorities tend to polarize the majorities against themselves."[24] The victims' physical, religious, and cultural criteria tend to make them substantial targets.

The oppressed is the scapegoat, a product of collective violence and mimetic desire, in which one imitates the desire or the will of another, therefore pitting persons against each other. Collective, oppressive violence scapegoats and fuels the Refiner's Fire of dehumanization, making African Americans a collective "It." Racism—indeed, all oppression—is desire, a form of acute mimetic rivalry with the other. Desire always looks for something it imagines to be most irreducibly other.[25] In America, many Whites desire the perceived biological or sexual prowess, physical stamina, earthy resilience, and exotic coloring of Blacks. Blacks desire the perceived freedom, justice, and pursuit of happiness of Whites. In setting Black chaos in opposition to White orderliness, racism represents conflicts between modernity and tradition.[26] Nonviolent religion of traditional African American Christianity is mimetic intimacy[27] and gratifies desire that embraces the other. This experience of *imago dei* (imitation of God) is a profound desire[28] that advances toward reconciliation.

Myth, Ritual, and Oral and Written History

Racist myths opposed to reconciliation live via rituals. Myth reveals consciousness;[29] it lets one be, think, and experience truth, while shaping belief systems.[30] Myths and rituals shape racism and power and perpetuate racial dominance. Myths give meaning, and rituals give purpose.[31] Rituals sacralize belief systems internalized by myths, and both preserve racism. The Refiner's Fire of racist myths view Blacks as inferior, abnormal, and unethical.[32] Racist myths and rituals are inherently arrogant, for they infer that an illicit superiority exists in those who possess such beliefs. Spirituals, as rituals grounded in rich African cultural myths, refute racist myths produced by greed, selfishness, and the quest for privilege.[33] Even after slavery ceased,[34] racist arrogance persisted along with racial pathos—an artistic, racist representation or experience that summons pity, compassion, or sorrow—the polar opposite of arrogance.

The pathos of racism is a reaction to gross victimization and injustice. Racism, a pathological will to power[35] like other modes of oppression, warps personality and impairs the psychology of the rejected. With the pathos of the ego, no power can disguise one's basic inner powerlessness. Legalized Jim Crow, the arrogance and pathos of racist power, existed as officially recognized and endorsed segregation from 1877 to 1954.[36] Patriarchy, the arrogance and pathos of sexist power, keeps women from experiencing their full self-actualization. Elitism, the arrogance and pathos of class power, forges a poverty of economics and self-esteem. Human pathos aroused the anguished cries of 1960s Black Power extremists and the racial crudities of white supremacists as both groups tried to fill or obscure the internal void. The outpouring of the Holy Spirit in the 1960s made room for the *aggiornamento* of Vatican II, the feminist movement, and Lyndon Johnson's Great Society project toward helping the poor and planting seeds of populism. The redemptory pathos of power[37] requires people to champion the sacredness of human life. Ideally, one can relate interracially without having to be undifferentiated, sequestered, or annihilated. Racism, sexism, and classism respectively entail the arrogance and pathos of a racial, gendered, and economic self. African Americans deal with the arrogance and pathos using the Spirituals as documents of power.

The Spirituals confirm God's benevolent justice, African American oppression, the European oppressor, and an American use of power. This rhetoric of resistance functions as a flight *to* and *for* sanity.[38] An Afrocentric aesthetic depicts how Blacks redress their oppression and know empowerment via song.[39] The more the Civil Rights activists sang, the more social reality changed; even their jailers could not stop the singing.[40] Black slaves created the Spirituals in response to oppression; a century later the Civil Rights workers used these songs to contest racism. Grassroots leaders and communal groups Refined the Fires of justice as they sang. "They were on fire for freedom. . . . It was so powerful."[41] This socio-historical setting provides the context for examining aesthetic power via rhetorical-musical analysis.

Rhetorical-Musical Analysis of the Spirituals
A Black Aesthetic
My musical critique explores the personal and communal dynamics and the musical and literary rhetoric of the Spirituals to uncover a rich aesthetic vocabulary.[42] I develop a protest hermeneutic of survival and hope toward societal healing, beginning with an inquiry into Black aesthetic criticism. A Black aesthetic engages the diversity of Black people, of the folk and the formal that name and characterize supportive aspects of a free, political life.[43] Performed Spirituals celebrate a rich African socio-cultural heritage; reveal primordial, exilic harmonies; and blend African, American, and African American music, creating a new music that reflects divine and human justice, woven as a Black aesthetic of freedom.

This aesthetic involves music as vital art, not trivial amusement: the gathered Black folk aesthetic within the DuBoisian veil and the African American tradition since 1800. The DuBoisian veil signifies the Black experience as "double consciousness, the divided self."[44] Music as living art involves active engagement, has depth, inspires as functional art, and makes an enduring impact that reinterprets the American ideal.[45] Black music, particularly the over six thousand existing Spirituals,[46] reconstructs reality and knows art as life duplicating life.[47] Such art forms need a hermeneutic that can disrupt partisan opinions, favor discovery,[48] and create change.

Discovery and change afford prototypes that indicate a descriptive motif questioning the basic concepts or discourse at the level of actuality.[49] In African American aesthetic motifs, one sees linguistic functions that act as basic themes or units of linguistic gestures in the Spirituals, from the verbal to the artistic and graphic.[50] These include "Freedom," "Dry Bones," "Light," and "Wheel in the Middle of the Wheel," during the 1860s and "Eyes on the Prize," "Freedom," "We Shall Not Be Moved," and "I Am Somebody" during the 1960s. Refined by the Fires of a freedom quest, Blackness becomes a central, organizing principle of Black folk life expressions and beliefs that reflect the import of America, race, the failure of Black power, and the significance of culture, consciousness, and society.[51]

Signifying and Black Double Voicing

One imaginative metaphor that captures the Black aesthetic is *signifying*. Signifying reveals Black double voicing—the revising or renaming in Black and White literary traditions that involve responses to the world by Black texts.[52] Double voicing brings new semantic bearing to a word that has and keeps its own meaning.[53] Critical to the socio-musical roots of Black language systems, signifying texts are the formal language systems of difference that people convey in ritual gatherings of beauty parlors or barbershops and family gatherings as they talk about talking. This unique vernacular is an African American's sign of difference and identity, filled with personal but communal cultural rituals.[54] Doubles conceal and disclose the other.[55] Thus in the Spiritual, "Oh, Freedom," freedom exorcises evil and calls for mutuality, self-actualization, and communal peace. Freedom speaks yes to life and no to coercion, death, and thus the need for mourning.

> Oh, Freedom Oh, Freedom
> Oh, Freedom, over me;
> And before I'd be a slave
> I'd be buried in my grave;
> And go home to my Lord, and be free.[56]

Signifying, a meta-discourse or dialogue about language traditions itself, and the Signifying Monkey,[57] a meta-figure, symbolize Black indirect argument or persuasion. Black bards and Griots signify in the Spirituals as they Refine the Fires of communication, as they hear/read, repeat, imitate, and revise each other's texts. Blackness in the Spirituals is Black signifying difference.[58]

This difference reflects the semantic and political dispute between parallel Black and White linguistic circles. Signifying excludes everything that disrupts coherent meaning and depicts meaning through Black language style and the Black rhetorical difference. Signifying engages the in-group information with—not on—the transcendent signified[59] with God. Signifying portrays Black vernacular rhetoric, and double voicing represents or reconstitutes a subject. Signifying, a metaphorical process of shared knowledge, reveals to speaker/singer and hearers the signifying, a second, encoded, hushed, multifaceted vitality,[60] and ignores the dictionary-syntactical meaning. Signifying hides and intensifies to recreate the aesthetic.

Aesthetic influences frame and illumine justice in the midst of power and desire, and they galvanize people toward change and right relations. As liberating artistry inspired liberation politics,[61] these Griots, or "cantors of people's agony, vision and hope,"[62] make public the price of democracy. Song evoked healing and created and later revived the call to live or die for freedom.[63] These songs Refined the Fires of oppression and permanently changed people's consciousness toward conversion, new thinking, new actions about beauty, justice, and life. A focus on the musical aspects of the aesthetic analysis affect musical critique.

Theomusicology

Musical criticism surveys the mingled textures of sound, silence amid performance. Musical style—the complex human action of song and behavior patterns—includes all aspects of musical production, from participation and psychosocial function to formal ambient factors. Songs identify and reinforce cultural structures and practices. Musical analysis of the Spirituals generates human experiences, cultural designs, and values[64] and involves theomusicology.

Theomusicology is a "theologically informed discipline" that studies the sacred and secular actualities and musics, including their therapeutic values (theomusicotherapy).[65] Theomusicological analysis of the Spirituals involves decoding music that illumines the archetypes of meaning and takes a holistic view of human spirituality, affecting healing and accord. In theomusicology, God speaks through people to self-communicate via the graces, the aesthetics, the incredulities, and the hopeful imagination in secular life in which the Ultimate Being discloses Itself through human beings.[66] Critical listening reveals the challenges, the evils in the church and the world as they fail to respond to these "hidden cracks beneath the social surface."[67] These fissures occur midst the desire for hopeful change. The Spirituals see the cracks, lessen the incongruous vision, and create a harmonious conversion. Theomusicology champions the quest for freedom, seeks to erase intellectual arrogance, and invites an ethics of accountability.[68] When societal problems belong to all, they become important enough to treat. An Afro-sensitive theomusicological study of the Spirituals interprets through cultural exegesis, understands Black religion, which shapes all Black existence, correcting for errors affixed to Black culture by others, and creates harmony.[69] Theomusicology warns against Eurocentric scholarship when such scholarship results in cultural idolatry, noncreative conceit, and negation. Co-participation in social and self-rule is the goal.[70]

Ethnomusicology

Both theomusicology and ethnomusicology relate to music as culture. Ethnomusicology studies the behavior of all participants in musical production and reception and the shared cultural meanings of musical sounds,[71] unique functions, and practices by analyzing the oral tradition and socio-cultural context.[72] In short, ethnomusicology focuses on cultural questions with no predetermined agenda to deal with the sacred; theomusicology studies the socio-cultural via the sacred or theological. How do we value human subjectivity and the human ear while searching for objective authenticity, dealing with biases, assessing acculturation, weighing patterned versus spontaneous behavior, and pondering ethical concerns?[73] One response is to examine the transforming powers of performed text and music.

Musicking

Musicking, the vital social activity of creating and recreating music, mirrors the Black theomusicological environment. African American music sprang from African musicking and involves a culture affiliation and religious ethic that assign an African's devoted musical sense of being and behaving. The musicking of Spirituals produces social action music that archetypically relates human experience toward wisdom, direction, and healing.[74] Within musicking, "feelings of acceptance occur through effective Reacting, Perceiving and Producing that constitute the core of selfhood."[75]

Communicating universal access to the self and the human condition, Black music has nurtured the seeds for freedom, unrest, and protest signifying, planted during the nineteenth century.[76] The height of the 1960s freedom struggle parallels the apex of singing freedom songs, as a weapon and viable catalyst for inducing social change, as sound and silence[77] mobilized masses, dramatized injustices, and signified liberation. "Silent dissonance" parallels the emergence of Black power and nonviolent direct action.[78] Black music idioms recite the human struggle-fulfillment,[79] and allows listeners to perceive, appreciate, and personally appropriate that experience. Spirituals embody *nommo,* or word-power, that rebels and resists, as it names, hears, calls, embraces, penetrates, causes all life,[80] and affords daily communion with God and community through prayer and praise as songs in motion.[81] The feelings and emotions evoked within the Spirituals lead toward issues of thought and logic, in which performer and audience are one in experiencing the message. The communicative, healing power of the Freedom Songs emanates from traditional Spirituals: aesthetic, living texts—songs of protest that Refine the Fires of musicking and conversion, where slaves lived unchained:[82] their thought and belief, the God-talk.

Spirituals are liturgical songs of reformation as they unite the communities of slaves and freedom fighters in the worship of God and the promises for liberation in the United States. They soulfully celebrate and ritualize God and declare discontent against oppression, call for emancipation and equality in voices to awaken American collective consciousness. These reformation chants challenge America to think about God, humanity, freedom, and evil with passion, rhythm, and motion. Spirituals champion the Refiner's Fire, the covenant of Black liberation with divine revelation in which grace heals alienation and brokenness. This synergy for reformation within singing fuels the resistance and the reform because these songs garner support and indelibly mark humanity in a way only available through communal song. Most traditional Spirituals imply a philosophy and theology of self and communal actualization, of divine liberty and justice for all. Theological-philosophical analysis exposes oppression as collective possession that Refines a Fire of mass psychosis as the Spirituals become a ritual, collective exorcism toward reconciliation and justice. Their call for justice names and demands redress for the evil.

A Quest for Justice amid Life and Power

Slaves contemplated and lived justice as they differentiated between universal, applied, and historically contingent justice. A universal justice criticizes society for privileging some but oppressing others. Spirituals call for a public, dialogical quest for justice of solidarity and individual freedom that extends the "we" to those previously dubbed "they."[83] Other Spirituals proclaim that "we-ness" requires transformed thought and socio-political structures that produce new forms of justice and equality, taking seriously human ultimacy, intimacy, sociality. These tenets of a prophetic Christian tradition[84] celebrate the dynamics of life and the philosophical historicism midst African philosophies. Most African people think and experience no distinction between the sacred and secular, the material and spiritual. Africans exist as religious beings framed by unity with self, progeny, and ancestors dynamically connected to a central, powerful creator God. Africans paradoxically know and relate to God through ritual in a religious, social ontology expressed anthropocentrically.[85] Such just, communal, theological humanism that exists in the Spirituals emerges in the complex language of these songs.

The coded dialogue of the Spirituals epitomizes the ontological and existential complexity of Black life in the United States. W. E. B. DuBois's concept of the veil[86] expresses the multilayered socio-political African American experience of double consciousness or two-ness of being and symbolizes an interpretative or hermeneutical horizon where the two-ness exists in tension: the socio-historical contextual doubles of two races, their interrelated stories, the two-ness of words and music, the two-ness of relatedness between the divine and the community, and the community itself. A doubled existence was par for the course for folks who were free in God and enslaved to humanity. The Spirituals embody these doubles and tell the story of a way of life, provide a cultural inventory, and offer social commentary on a lived reality.[87]

Spirituals document human life and use of power; they exude vitality, foster pride, and spontaneously conserve related traditions and memories. They ponder blessings now and the riddle of slavery midst the themes of prophecy, penitence, praise, fellowship, faith, aspiration, and advice. Spirituals communicated and reaffirmed the displaced African's status as *imago dei:* an engagement of active, loving relationship in which all God's creations stand equal before God. During the Movement, Spirituals helped unify disparate groups as they confronted legalized collective racist evil via moral, nonviolent organized protest and paradoxically exposed the United States' denial of moral and legal rights to persons of color. This denial signifies the contradictions within American law, cultural mores, and practice. The "all men are created equal," clause in the Declaration of Independence historically referred to all white (Anglo-Saxon) male, Protestant landowners. Equality was not for African Americans, women, non-Protestants, non-Whites, and White males who owned no property. (A white male who owned a slave but no land was included, since a slave was "property." The slave being "property" was excluded.) Despite these paradoxes and inequities, the Spirituals embodied African Americans' sense of self, God, and relationship with God. They incubated and delivered Black folk from total despair in the antebellum and 1960s eras.

While justice is possible, human sin, alienation, and rebellion require that talk about justice begins with talk of injustice.[88] The institutional church, aided by American-Biblical-Christian mythology, often continues to support racist oppression. The power and justice of God alongside those church folk who want to do good indicates the option to choose to change. The God on the side of antebellum and Civil Rights activists presses for a praxis-based justice. A working definition of justice concerns just distribution of goods, opportunities, and powers, including access to basic processes and structures, with mutuality and respect for human life and experience.[89]

The Composite God

Such an experience undergirds the message of the Spirituals. These sacred/secular melodies honor a compassionate, benevolent God who Refines the Fires of creativity and wisdom and embraces the oppressed. Blacks are actualized offspring created *imago dei* by a liberating, compassionate God. The Spirituals include historical and recent experiences, from relationships with God and Jesus, the freedom quest, and the absurdity and contradictions of reality to life, death, and love. God's compassionate love empowers and redeems as liberating love that changes the present moment. The composite God delivers and brings freedom. "God the Creator-Revelator (Maker), God the Freedom-Fighter (Christ Moses), God the Redeemer-Comforter (Holy Spirit Jesus)—God the Revelator, Freedom-Fighter, Liberator . . . the godhead [is] one."[90] This oneness in the Spirituals produces a reconciliation that affirms an existential, communal, and subjective experience of double relatedness: a twofold attitude, the Buberian I-Thou, I-It.

I-It generates injustice, separation, subjugation, objectification; I-Thou speaks life, relationship, and ultimate, responsive, mutual encounter with grace. Evil destroys the true relationship and occurs when mutual respect and dignity exist between two beings.[91] Evil happens when idolatrous power supersedes the good of the whole.[92] Though all people must function as I-Thou and I-It, one who knows freedom moves between both worlds of causality, relation, and reciprocity with God and humankind. The Spirituals and other slave narratives show that the slaves knew freedom and mutuality in God, the balanced I-Thou, I-It scenario. Thus, the theoretical issue of the existence of evil per se did not bother the slaves. God did not cause slavery; slave masters insisted on reducing relationship to I-It. Slaves held evil in a context with God's freedom and justice: they knew suffering but did not find God's justice and goodness dubious. In faith, slaves and their 1960s counterparts developed a "soul theology" steeped in grace and goodness that empowers and gives psychic healing and spiritual survival. Soul theology, a distillation of African American theological and anthropological beliefs, posits the majestic ultimacy of God, the goodness of creation, and the communality of persons where divine justice prevents exploitation and helps one to make sense out of a powerless existence. Soul theology champions the communal "I-Thou's" as God's just rhetoric of impartiality.[93] This impartiality calls the oppressed and the oppressor to conversion: from slave and enslaver to free, transformed, whole beings, evoking a now and forthcoming eschatology.

Black Eschatology

Theologically, Black eschatology in the Spirituals helps shackled persons view their reality as rising above present historical boundaries. Eschatological singing puts the future in the present, juxtaposing historical liberation—

past, present, and future.[94] This triadic history awakens a concept of heaven
and helps Black people affirm their humanity while viewed as nonpersons. In
response, the Spirituals indict slavery and racism via God's freedom, claim
that Christ redeems from sin, and call for a radical conversion of all relationships. Today, that call, for a relational, just encounter, must include racism,
sexism, classism, ageism, and homophobia. The call for exorcising these evils
can assure the victimized the reality and triumph of divine good. The Spirituals as living, performed, artistic texts call for a holistic, spiritual-based life
of ultimate intimacy with God: a universal, vibrant spirituality. The creative
signified spirituality in the Spirituals is rich in much imagery, stylistic components in the rhetorical-musical and the philosophical-theological analysis.
After presenting the larger contextual structures of communicative spirituality, I cite particular instances of spirituality in selected Spirituals.

Synthesis: Creative Spirituality Signified

The Spirituals reflect holiness, with a heritage from the past and a vision for
relevance today. The qualities of that holiness make clear that the dynamics
of that spirituality involve well-being, praise, worship, and knowledge of
God/Spirit, belief, authority, and celebration of one's own reality, which has a
universal or Jungian archetypal "significance beyond the person"[95] who experiences the spirituality in the Spirituals. Well-being concerns the total welfare, health, and blessedness of an individual and a community. This well-
being Refines the Fires of holistic freedom from "dis-ease" and produces
soundness of body, mind, spirit, and contentment: The Spirituals couch well-
being in a personal, social, and communal context of relatedness to God.
These reformation songs, similar to the Psalms, inspire, renew, and know a
certainty of hearing from God. These therapeutic litanies, cultural products
that relate human experience as living art, unveil the complexities and paradoxes of survival as they champion the Black aesthetic. These therapeutic
rebirthing processes destroy the racist theme of scapegoating Blacks and
Blackness by thwarting bigots' myths and rituals. The rebirthing process
involves a liberatory procedure wherein both oppressed and oppressor experience transformation. The masterful poetic and musical symbols forge a collective integrity that relies on humor for healing while they promote personal fortitude and emotional growth.[96] Spirituals effect an empowering,
aesthetic event couched in a historical musical recital as they promote self-
esteem and communal hope, freedom, mental release, and reaffirmed faith.[97]

Faith and the Spirituals

Faith is germane to well-being and to the adoration and sense of God present
in the Spirituals. Faith sustained the downtrodden's belief that God is for

them, that God cares, and that God is just. Thus the covenantal relationship between God and these oppressed downtrodden means that God and Black folk can freely participate together in a society to exorcise evil, now! The Spirituals express life amid injustice through the beauty of human speech, sound, and passion, as the mutual love between God and the oppressed redefines and transfigures all structures and values toward healing. Such loving power is salvific and exudes a creation theology that affirms the good, in spite of the bad choices humans often make. These liturgical chants honor the goal of justice: right relationship linking God and humanity, embracing diversity and difference. Anchored in faith, the songs honor blessed reconciliation and joy. In a performed arena of rhythmic discord, metrical ambiguity, percussive playing, and singing with contrasting timbres, the spirituality of the Spirituals embodies the Refiner's Fire of theological, epistemic, eschatological, ontological, and existential reality of God and humankind in a belief system and ethics of love and answerability.

Spirituals affirm beliefs that signify freedom, mutuality, and life as gift in a power zone of political protest. That protest brings new meanings among language and musical systems. New forms and structures create a reciprocity and redress that build self-esteem and social equanimity. The Spirituals recite an everyday religiosity and spirituality that integrate apparently contradictory tasks of inner solace and meaningful action with an exceptional world vision and power for wholeness.[98] Freedom, tied to a critical notion of spirituality and accountability to God, self, and neighbor, undergirds the notion of authority present in the Spirituals.

Empowerment of the Spirituals

This authority evokes empowerment. The Spirituals declare the rights of shared justice and disrupt injustice. They embrace key motifs that identify and reinforce a value system that holds every individual as important and loved, championing reconciliation. The chief authority is a compassionate, benevolent, liberator God. Pedagogically, the Spirituals authoritatively declare God as the One who is on the side of the oppressed. A relationship with this God who acts, knows, and responds best is with a God who authorizes one to rebel and resist injustice, moving towards solidarity within the self—an inner connectedness—that celebrates "I am a child of God" and "We are children of God." Such awareness creates a holistic and functional sensibility of healthy "I-Thou" relationships. This spiritual dialogue involves an engagement of emotions, images, ideas, thoughts, and ideals, set in sound that reflects coherence and a common life pattern.[99] This engagement extracts an irrefutable authority for all those who suffer or who cause suffering. The music heightens awareness and opens people to the need to protest, as music arouses social cognitive and affective comprehension.[100] Babies are not born racists but are taught to hate; archetypal songs, like the Spirituals, can teach people to love.

Analyzing Individual Spirituals

In exploring the possibility of embracing the spirituality found within the Spirituals, we Refine the Fires of hope and change, made clear when examining individual Spirituals. In the volumes edited by James Weldon and J. Rosamond Johnson, *The Books of Negro Spirituals,* the elements of spirituality are apparent in a broad reflective sense within the songs' components of wellness, liturgy, belief, and authority. Time and space prohibit citing full verses of each song. My comments reflect the Refiner's Fire of transformative exuberance, of spirituality within the lyric and musical texts of these sacred songs—only a sampling of this rich compendium of Spirituals.[101]

Several songs anchor their spirituality in the Hebrew Bible or Old Testament. "Go Down Moses" Refines the Fire of divine, majestic movement in a minor tonality that confronts civil authority, orders retributive justice, and evokes prophetic intervention. The ascending lines connote transcendence as the sustained tones and pedantic exhortation reflect a contemplative liturgical moment where liberation means wellness, which begins when the oppressed thirsts for freedom and the perpetrator "let[s] my people go!" "Joshua Fit the Battle of Jericho" uses syncopated, moving notes to echo footfalls and Refines the Fire of resistance in battle. The close-knit movement of the notes declares war against the enemy and goes on record showing apparent victors are not the true winners. The trumpets and horns symbolize the weapons of battle and signal an overcoming power with implicit hope and faith. "We Are Climbin' Jacob's Ladder" Refines the Fire of quiet dignity in a communal procession toward God. The ascending and transcendent movement in a major, bright tonality makes an eschatological jump toward a Christocentric defense of the cross; the chordal movement depicts one overcoming obstacles, making a commitment, and determining a resolution. "Swing Low, Sweet Chariot," which comes from the Elijah/Elisha sagas, Refines the Fire of a divine carriage and support of humanity. The slow, swinging, rocking motion depicts life as divine gift. One actively seeks the chariot that carries one home to wholeness with family, safety, and love. Freedom Fighters often used this song to announce the arrival of an underground railroad or a time for a meeting, signifying an eschatology of both now and not yet.

"Little David Play On Yo' Harp" Refines the Fire of healing as it mirrors the therapy that David's harp playing accomplished for King Saul as well as the inherent contrast between David as shepherd to sheep and David as challenger to gigantic Goliath. The playful music uses irony to show that apparent strength and size do not guarantee victory. David's victory elicits "Hallelu's" of celebration and overcoming. "Didn't My Lord Deliver Daniel?" Refines the Fire of humor as it mischievously and proudly asks and confirms that God's deliverance of Daniel assures the liberation of all. God delivers Daniel, Jonah, and the Hebrew children within theophanies of a moon's purple stream and later, when the stars disappear. The moving notes and syncopated rhythms highlight eschatological judgment and celebrate prayer and the mission of the Gospel ship that ushers humanity to the Promised Land.

Other Spirituals focus on New Testament texts of transformation. "Calvary" Refines the Fire of Jesus' passion and suffering as analogous to the suffering of the oppressed. This liturgical Lenten-type Spiritual shows a prayerful, reflective, pensive witness and confession of pain. The minor tonality establishes the reality of anguish, the first step in healing, along with concern for self and others. This song neither denies nor minimizes pain, neither celebrates victimage nor asks for pity. "Steal Away to Jesus" signifies that God/Lord/Jesus Refines the Fires of freedom, wholeness, and home. Slavery and oppression are no longer the only option. The step-like melodic movement suggests that life has afflictions that cause one to tremble, but the trumpet calls one to steal away, physically, emotionally, mentally, and spiritually. "My Lord's A Writin' All De Time" uses themes of praise, rejuvenation, renewal, and consciousness, set in a major key, to Refine the Fire of God's omniscience. One can meet God and Jesus in the middle of the air, as God calls sinners from everywhere. The divine calls humanity to prayer and liberation because Satan is within close proximity. A lively, jovial march-like melody creates an invitational mood of possibility and transformation.

"Somebody's Knockin' at Yo' Do'" presents a vivid, steady, hymn-like scenario that Refines the Fire of dialogue. The appeal to the hearing senses is a pressing call to the sinner, one separated from God, to experience redemption and salvation. The knocking that sounds like Jesus is an opportunity to conversion, grace, and metamorphosis. Musical intervals of thirds and fourths create a sense of resolution mixed with vital awareness as a door symbolizes heart, being, and one's mental and spiritual center. "Give Me Jesus," a psalm-like prayer of devout piety and contemplative fervor, Refines the Fires of hope and Christocentric intimacy. The verses state that with death, at the plea of dark midnight, in the morning at rising, and when visiting with mourners, one wants Jesus. This desire to be with God incarnate reiterates the need for spiritual well-being. The sustained lines of the refrain musically rise to a heightened tension and then resolve twice to a sense of completion. "Peter Go Ring Dem Bells" uses a major tonality in cut time to Refine the Fires of praise and exultation that celebrate communication with God (heaven) today. This jubilant Spiritual wonders where "my Mother" and "Sister Mary" have wandered, because the singer wants to share with them the good news that God cares and responds. The Gospel message evokes an immediacy with God that supports a vital spirituality of response and responsibility. Some Spirituals combine themes from both Testaments along with religious, theological, and ethical motifs that shape Black aesthetic spirituality.

"Git On Board, Lil' Chillen" uses a fast-paced energetic music to call individuals and communities to Refine the Fires of improvement, freedom, and salvation. The phrase "room for everyone" signifies the mutuality between rich and poor, first and second class, and implies the inclusivity of other categories of difference. Often used to announce the Underground Railroad, this reformation song uses the "gospel train" as a metaphor to celebrate sensory experiences of spirituality, in which one hears, knows, and affirms liberation. The fare is cheap, but one still must pay; in other words, in life everything has a price. "My Lord, What A Mornin'" Refines the Fires of amazement and awe of creation. Contrasts and juxtapositions occur in created order, in nature, as the trumpet signals that sinners moan and Christians shout. The allusion to God's right hand implies final judgment, separation between the sheep and the goats. These contrasts, set with loosely sustained, simple rhythmic-melodic lines, offer confession and belief in God's ultimate authority.

"Listen to De Lambs," in conversation with "I Couldn't Hear Nobody Pray," reflects the vast dichotomy and paradoxes within the body of Spirituals. "Listen to De Lambs" Refines the Fire of vulnerability, beginning as a slow, plaintive pastoral litany that entombs the defenselessness of lambs who need a shepherd; that is, one needs to be attentive to and concerned for communal suffering, for those who cry. The desire for Heaven reflects the need for completion and acceptance when the slave is released from physical death in actual life and the psychological death that slavery breeds. Though life gets bad, angels or messengers affect change and give honor to humanity as people experience grief, are attentive to behavior and ethics, and avoid sin, as one focuses on oneness with God and freedom. The paradox of not hearing when told to listen intensifies an environment in which people do pray and Refines the Fires of life cycles, as it celebrates a spirituality of liturgy, baptism, salvation, and creation theology. The musical line of horn-like clarion calls places one in numerous settings of geography, emotional and physical states, and existential and eschatological realities. The pedagogical, dialogical tone implies that the performer says she or he cannot hear someone pray as an invitation for them to pray. Other Spirituals specify a particular physical or emotional reality or time frame as the catalyst for individuals to get in touch with their spirituality.

"De Blin' Man Stood on De Road and Cried" Refines the Fire of fragility in an uplifting, hymn-like setting, claiming it is all right to be vulnerable and ask for healing and salvation. Vision concerns the desire for awareness; shoes indicate a concern for direction, and gospel shoes reflect looking toward the kingdom of God, as one deals with pain, through faith. "I'm Troubled in Mind" Refines the Fire of hopeful incarnation, as it reveals that without Jesus, one has no life but worry and mental and emotional anguish. The somber tune contrasts with a hopeful message of Jesus as savior, source, friend, confidant, and intercessor. Life without this source is full of grief, burdens, and death.

"Deep River" Refines the Fires of the depths of God in celebrating the richness and profundity of life as an ongoing process. This ballad's music includes wave-like motions of the river, symbolizing the heights and depths of life and the freedom that comes beyond Jordan. The desire to get into a campground echoes revival, freedom, and communal fellowship in God's presence. "By and By" builds on the general idea of "Deep River" and Refines the Fire of hopeful, majestic victory. In time, one can release burdens, heavy loads, and suffering and put away troubles. The song warns one that hell, separation from God, is deep, dark despair. The salvific intent implies grace and the possibility for self-actualization. "All God's Chillun Got Wings" in an elated, high-spirited, dance-like, quick time Refines the Fires of human choice, as it enumerates what people do and have in Heaven: put on a robe, fly with wings, play a harp, and walk in shoes. The double entendres reveal that the oppressed will ultimately have what they do not have now but those who do have robes and shoes on earth are not necessarily going to heaven. Those who oppress and exclude will one day be excluded. Heaven, the panacea, means now, and if not now, soon freedom and wholeness will happen for those who remain true despite their circumstances. "Gimme Dat Ol' Time Religion," also set in a quick tempo, Refines the Fire of an original grace— an old-time, covenantal, transformed, and immediate relationship with God. The old-time religion is not that of oppression. The hope for revival, renewal, and wellness produces possibility for true association with God: an eschatology of present desire.

The Spirituals as Creative Change

Spirituals creatively signify a rich spirituality that teaches, moves, and inspires performers and listening participants in different ways at different times and different places. Music moves one through its poignancy, its implied and embodied beauty, in ways that most people do not understand but leave to divine mystery.[102] The Spirituals Refine the Fire of change and express relationships and intimacy with God, self, and the neighbor, as they affirm total health, freedom, aesthetics, and holistic belief systems; celebrate God's love and authority; champion freedom; and blame human choice for personal and institutional evil. These reformation songs use humor and balance to achieve a society in which "I" and "Thee" become "We" as *imago dei,* the epitome of spirituality. In the 1860s, in the 1960s, and today, one marvels at the embodied genius in the Spirituals and appreciates their inherent love for the consummate human spirit. The Spirituals honor God, life, and freedom and ask, "Do we want to be well, spiritual human beings?"

4. Sojourner's Sisters:
1960s Women Freedom Fighters Right Civil Wrongs

The women
In the chorus
Provide solo voices,
Calling the shots,
Not fired from guns;
Fired midst hope.
Outrageous women:
Fired up resources and ideas,
Organizing,
Them loving men and women.
Alto, soprano, high-low voices
Choruses, choirs, ensembles
Singing songs
Causing earthquake tremors of protest.
Whirlwind ideas,
Views of possibility:
Go 'head!
Ella, Fannie Lou, Septima,
Daisy, Jo Ann, Modjeska,
Gloria, Doris & Denise
Rosa, Zilphia, Bernice.
Many thousands unnamed:
Sing, baby, sing.
Sing the songs of life,
Sing streams of steady support.
Singing women,
Walked in Montgomery,
Sat-in in Albany,
Were fire-hosed and bombed
in Birmingham.
Crossed barriers in Little Rock
Studied at Highlander
Worked Freedom Summer
in Mississippi.

Songs and Sisters,
Hand in Hand,
With and without the drum major:
Sang and
Moved the Movement!

African American Women Activists of the Nineteenth Century and the 1960s

African American women have worked, individually and collectively, for the empowerment and survival of their people since landing on these shores. They have Refined the Fires of love, empowerment, and faithful community-building, making nutritious cuisine out of leftovers and warm quilts from clothing scraps and helping Black children, Black men, and themselves feel like "somebody" when the dominant culture said they were "nobody," nothing. Throughout the nineteenth century, women like abolitionist Maria W. Stuart, underground railroad conductor Sojourner Truth, and educator Anna Julia Cooper offered protest. Nationally, organized Black women's groups relied on the work of these nineteenth-century women to acknowledge the victimization of Black women and the connection between Black sexuality and White violence, particularly lynching. Cooper saw the connection between American racism and African American sexism.

Ida Wells-Barnett documented countless incidents of Southern lynchings of Blacks and Whites and showed the economic and sexual reasons for lynching.[1] Wells-Barnett used a moral standard and found the Black clergy wanting; in addition, she often fell victim to Booker T. Washington's avaricious opportunism and found herself abandoned by the same organizations she helped found and build. Wells-Barnett's career ended with a combative pessimism similar to that of Martin Luther King Jr. Her Refining Fire is directed not only at the sicknesses of larger American society but at the sexism of Black culture.

Though different as individuals, these women had a common denominator: the prolonged struggle against the effects of race, gender, and class oppression in the United States and those of class and gender combined in Afro-America.[2] These women persevered and were instrumental in creating change at home and in society. Often women's work and women's revolutionary acts of transformation go unrecorded in mainstream historical documents. This chapter celebrates 1960s activists Sojourner's Sisters, women like Sojourner Truth who have Refined the Fires of justice by challenging systemic and personal violence. After giving a brief biography of each woman, I will assess the impact of recent women activists—Ella Baker, Septima Clark, Fannie Lou Hamer, Coretta Scott King, Bernice Johnson Reagon, and Joanne Robinson—and their relationships and interactions with Martin Luther King Jr.

Collectively, one of the first organized efforts to bring African American women together across religious, socio-political, and ideological lines was the Black Women's Club Movement, particularly the National Federation of Afro-American Women (1895). These groups worked to change the incapacitation created by Jim Crow and the constant humiliation of domestic service work by Black women. Like their counterparts in secular clubs, Black church women combined their Christian commitments with their approaches to action in Refining the Fires of oppression.

This Little Light of Mine: Those Who Accomplished in Spite of

Hundreds of Black women participated in the Civil Rights Movement through sit-ins, Freedom Rides, prayer marches, and voter registration drives. They saw the 1960s coalition-building with Black men and other ethnic communities as central to their ongoing denominational service and mission work.[3] Female members of the Student Nonviolent Coordinating Committee (SNCC) demanded that the organization explore sexual discrimination within itself. Women claimed they usually had to do mundane work and rarely had a chance to take leadership roles in meetings or policy making. Many within the Movement and in larger society did not and still do not comprehend this message. Like other civil rights groups, SNCC did not have an egalitarian policy regarding sexual relations. Stokely Carmichael's less than humorous faux pas, that "the place for women in the Movement was prone," showed a lack of consciousness by the male civil rights leaders of the 1960s concerning women's rights. Carmichael said in public what the other male leaders then and now hold in public and in private.[4] This ongoing oppression of women has not silenced the Refining Fires of commitment and work for change.

Ella Baker

One of the places that served as a catalyst for organized social activism was Montgomery, Alabama. The Civil Rights Movement in Montgomery grew out of the organized efforts of the Women's Political Council, a Black professional women's organization that had organized to protest injustice prior to Rosa Park's arrest and used Park's arrest to launch an all-out protest. These powerful women with prophetic vision invited ministers of the city to fall in behind them.[5] Other activist women decided the time had come to act, to Refine the Fires of change, and they did in their own way, notably, the fiery activism of Ella Baker.

A North Carolinian, Baker (1903–1986) heard slave stories from her former-slave grandmother. After graduating high school valedictorian, Baker attended and graduated from Shaw University and worked with the Works Progress Administration (WPA), in which she helped form consumer cooperatives in the Midwest. She spent six years as a field secretary for the National Association for the Advancement of Colored People (NAACP) and worked with Black writer George Schuyler and the Urban League to organize the Young Negro Cooperative League to promote consumer cooperatives. Baker left the north to help organize mass meetings for the Southern Christian Leadership Conference (SCLC). After helping set up the SCLC's Atlanta office and serving as executive secretary, Baker decided that student sit-in leaders should be organized. Baker persuaded her alma mater to provide the place and SCLC to give seed money. With student enthusiasm, some funds, and Martin Luther King Jr.'s backing, the Student Nonviolent Coordinating Committee (SNCC) came into being in April of 1960. Over two hundred people representing fifty-eight different Southern communities came together. (Forman notes that there were over three hundred people representing fifty-eight different communities and fifty-six colleges.) The students decided to remain friendly with SCLC but to be an independent organization.[6]

While in New York, Baker served as the president for NAACP and worked for community activism against public school system segregation. She Refined the Fires of change as she worked wherever there was a need, especially to help people see that only they could protect themselves from injustice and the ravages of violence. Her locus of action was always community empowerment. Baker thought oppressed people would be hindered if they had to rely upon a single leader. Single leaders may think they are indispensable, especially when they begin to believe their own press. The media likes to take one person who has come to the forefront and then make her or him into an icon, a living legend; hence the propensity to develop a Messiah complex. Before long, the individual may think that he or she is the Movement. The true grassroots Movement was largely carried out by women in churches.[7] Baker, an articulate, intelligent woman, shared history with many more public and unsung workers in the Movement and had a broader perspective on the Civil Rights Movement in devotion to the liberation of all people.[8]

Baker was so adamant about following the collective will of the people and not having one leader that she helped people organize by doing the publicity and menial tasks that others did not want to do. Baker Refined the Fires of opposition to oppression by being a behind-the-scenes "generating force" for SNCC. At the organizing conference of the SNCC-SCLC leadership, King, Ralph Abernathy, and Wyatt Walker tried to convince Baker to encourage the students to become an arm of SCLC. Baker felt that it was too soon for the students to solidify their structure and that they had the right to decide such issues for themselves; after all, the students fueled the sit-in movement. Baker rejected the idea and left the private meeting. The students voted not to become a permanent organization at that point, so they declined SCLC's offer, particularly given that the students had harsh criticism for adult civil rights activities. During a fall 1961 meeting in Mississippi, King and Abernathy said they had funds for the Southern student movement; Baker questioned SCLC's integrity in regards to such funds, which never reached the students. She also questioned the tactics of King and Abernathy, which made it seem that the two men were more involved than they actually were.

In 1963, Baker helped organize the first annual benefit for SNCC at Carnegie Hall.[9] Baker was astute and saw the larger vision. In 1962 in Hattiesburg, Mississippi, she noted that the end of segregation was not the only goal, since all people needed jobs, education, and freedom. Even with the vote, people in poverty are not free. Later she reminded SNCC members that they needed to "penetrate the mystery of life and perfect the mastery of life, and the latter requires understanding that human beings are human beings."[10] Baker helped SNCC stem several crises, because she listened and could offer acceptable compromise, something beyond the ken of the male Civil Rights leaders.[11]

Like other Black women, Baker acted as a moral agent who Refined the Fires of ethical living as she helped create and communicate a positive moral standard that critiqued the hegemony and elitism of dominant, Eurocentric ethics, which systemically oppress and shape the Black community and larger society. She critiqued any sense of dominance within the Black community as well. Baker knew that the rich experiences of Black women could help challenge this dominant male worldview. While such women must never forget their Blackness, they also should never idealize or romanticize their identity or let their diverse experiences be reduced to a single ideal. A Black woman then and now must be aware that over against the power, determination, and healthiness of her heritage lie the sickness of Black women's suffering, the stereotypes, the historical and ongoing instances of being misused and abused.[12]

Baker did not support singular charismatic leadership like King's. She was a subversive who organized people for their own empowerment, to help them see their own strength in unity; she also understood the significance of student participation in the sit-in movement. Ella Baker gave personal witness to participatory democracy as a new abolitionist who worked tirelessly, with modesty and wisdom for the cause of human rights.[13] Baker is best symbolized by the Swahili concept of *fundi*: "one who hands down a craft from one generation to another."[14]

Septima Poinsette Clark
Baker's kindred spirit to the South helped give others agency via liberatory classrooms. Septima Poinsette Clark (1898–1987), educator, humanitarian, and civil rights activist, also left a legacy to future generations. King referred

to this South Carolina native as the "Mother of the Movement," one who Refined the Fires of activist change. During childhood, Clark's later activism was aroused as she watched Marcus Garvey's ships in Charleston's Harbor. Clark began her teaching career on Johns Island, because Black teachers could not teach in Charleston's public schools. Married in 1920, Clark was widowed in 1925 with two children. She taught in the Columbia, South Carolina, school system for seventeen years, while taking classes at Columbia University in New York City and Atlanta University with DuBois, eventually graduating from Benedict College and with a master's from Hampton University.

While in Columbia, Clark began to participate in citizenship education and later designed similar classes for the Highlander School and SCLC. Clark worked toward equalized pay for teachers, where equal education would receive equal pay.[15] After moving to Charleston, Clark participated with the YWCA and taught in the school system from 1947 to 1956. Clark lost her job in 1956 because the South Carolina legislature banned teachers from NAACP membership and she would not relinquish hers. Four years shy of retirement, Clark was terminated after four decades of teaching and lost her state retirement benefits. She then went to work for the Highlander Folk School. In 1976, after making her case with the support of the National Education Association and legal representation, South Carolina Governor James Edwards noted her wrongful termination, and she received her pension.[16]

The Highlander Folk School, founded by Myles Horton as a planning and retreat center for community activism, did not follow segregationist mores and laws and was an ideal place for Clark. She became the director of workshops.[17] Rosa Parks, who greatly admired Clark, met her at one of the workshops. The state of Tennessee eventually was able to close Highlander school and sold its property without giving Horton any compensation. Sensing the possibility of the state's action before it occurred, Horton contacted Martin Luther King Jr. and negotiated SCLC sponsorship of the citizenship programs. In Georgia, Clark used her forty years of experience to help train staff, leaders, and students, including Dorothy Cotton, Hosea Williams, Fannie Lou Hamer, and Andrew Young. At sixty-three, Clark traveled throughout the South Refining the Fires of broadened citizenship by directing SCLC citizenship workshops on basic constitutional rights, the American political system, and organizing for change. The workshops had films or lecturers, ranging from Eleanor Roosevelt and local university professors, to ministers like King, who put social problems in a theological context. They sang songs familiar to Southern folk, often fitting new words to old tunes.[18] While her skills and leadership were outstanding, Clark was not fully accepted on the SCLC board, although she was the first woman elected to it. Like Baker, Septima Clark had to face male chauvinism in the Movement.

Clark complimented as well as critiqued King's leadership. She found him a nonviolent person who showed this method could work and he helped people celebrate rather than be ashamed of their Blackness. Male leaders seemed to think women were incapable of leadership, and Ralph Abernathy asked King point-blank why Clark was on the board, despite the fact that she designed the whole citizenship program. Clark observed that neither Ella Baker nor Rosa Parks in particular nor women in general could ever have their rightful place on the executive board and in the Movement. Clark further observed that Coretta Scott King only came into her own after Martin Luther King Jr. died.[19]

A keen observer, Clark wrote King about her frustrations concerning those who seemed more interested in the limelight associated with the Movement than doing the daily empowerment work with people. She continued to Refine the Fires of a social activism after retiring from SCLC in 1975 and served as a school board member, was awarded an honorary doctorate by the College of Charleston in 1978, and was honored by President Jimmy Carter with a Living the Legacy Award in 1979. Clark felt a moral obligation to serve God by serving humanity, for she wanted to combat "the greatest evil in our country . . . not racism but ignorance."[20]

Fannie Lou Hamer

Another trailblazer for the cause who fought ignorance and racism was the warrior, Fannie Lou Hamer (1917–1977). A civil rights activist and sharecropper, Hamer was "sick and tired of being sick and tired," but she Refined the Fires of faith as she believed everyone should work until all people could safely live in America. Her epithet of being sick and tired echoed the exhaustion, weariness, and frustrations of Black Mississippians in their quest for justice.[21] Hamer became active in the Movement without hesitation in 1963 at age 47, with her husband and two children, as Mississippi sharecroppers. With her characteristic limp from a childhood bout with polio, Hamer sang as if she were sobbing to the heavens. She became a field secretary for SNCC when she was fired and thrown off the plantation for her activism. Hamer lifted her voice toward the sky with the songs of Spirituals and hymns. In 1964, Hamer and other African Americans from Mississippi ran for U.S. Congress, a first since Reconstruction.[22]

Hamer's question "Is this America?" thundered and resonated during the year before the national credentials committee for the Democratic party convention. "Is this America?" was her challenge to America to deal with its ongoing hatred and hypocrisy, bigotry, intolerance, and racism. Coming out of a pseudo-slavery system of sharecropping that kept tenant farmers indebted to their plantation owners, Hamer became one of many Black women, grassroots

Refiners of the Fires of liberation, who were key participants in the organization, mobilization, and determination of the Black activist Movement. That
same determination gave her the strength to keep her name on the voting
rolls, despite threats of eviction from the plantation owner. Despite persecution, death threats, arrests, job losses, and brutal beatings that left her with
permanently impaired vision and kidney damage, Hamer kept on protesting
and fighting for justice.[23]

Hamer's stamina was rooted in biblical faith, indicative of two of her sig-
nature songs, "This Little Light of Mine" from the Sermon on the Mount and
"Go Tell It on the Mountain" from the Exodus narratives. Hamer's biblical
faith sustained her work for SNCC throughout the Mississippi cotton fields
during the day and as she inspired mass meetings at churches during the
evening. That faith empowered her to sing the songs that were integral to the
founding of the SNCC Freedom Singers. During one bus ride returning from
voter registration, it was Hamer's singing that calmed everyone on the bus.[24]

She calmed and inspired people with her voice, especially during Freedom
Summer, 1964. Hamer Refined the Fires of strategic organizing by helping
found the Mississippi Freedom Democratic Party (MFDP) to show the nation
the racist practices of the "regular" Democrats and to register as many voters
as possible. Initially, the MFDP wanted to work within the convention systems, from precinct to state, but they were not allowed to attend meetings or
had restrictions levied against them. At the Democratic National Convention, hoping to get leverage with the national party, Hamer addressed the
credentials committee and told of the horrors perpetrated against Black citizens in Mississippi. Fervently she exclaimed, "If the [Mississippi Freedom]
Democratic Party is not seated now, I question America. . . . Is this America?
The land of the free and the home of the brave? Where we have to sleep with
our telephone off the hook, because our lives be threatened daily?"[25] Despite
the finagling by President Johnson to steal the thunder of the MFDP by calling a press conference in the middle of Hamer's speech and the compromise
tactics by Walter Mondale and Hubert Humphrey to secure Humphrey's vice
presidential nomination, the MFDP rejected the compromise to seat only two
MFDP members selected by Humphrey. Hamer led the MFDP delegation in
singing Freedom Songs on the convention floor.[26]

Even King was a behind-the-scenes culprit seeking to placate MFDP
members. King had engaged in prophetic Christian leadership to transform
American life and culture, but toward the end of his career, his optimistic,
eschatological hope about a changed American cosmology stood over against
the tensions that resulted from his complicity in excluding Fannie Lou
Hamer and the Mississippi Freedom Democratic Party from being seated, his
commitment to Black Christian morality, and his somber pessimistic view of
America.[27] Hamer was not threatened. Though disillusioned,

this strong, invincible woman, without benefit of formal education, showed the country that knowledge, wisdom and organization skills did not come with the acquisition of academic degrees. . . . As Hamer stated, "whether you have a Ph.D., D.D., or no D., we're in this bag together. . . . And whether you're from Morehouse or No house, we're still in this bag together."[28]

The MFDP kept challenging injustice, poll tax, and literacy tests as voting requirements as well as disenfranchisement. Although the MFDP disappeared into obscurity, it shaped the 1968 Democratic National Convention with some of its former members unseating the "regulars." Most important, the MFDP catapulted Fannie Lou Hamer into the public arena, where she helped shame America into acknowledging its institutionalized racist, hostile, evil environment.

Hamer Refined the Fires of change and justice as she helped organize Martin Luther King Jr.'s last dream, the Poor People's Campaign. Although suffering from diabetes, heart trouble, and later breast cancer, Hamer organized a farm cooperative to aid plantation workers in getting land. Hamer worked to bring about economic justice, though she remained poor. Buried on the same cooperative she helped to found, her grave lies near a flowering cactus plant that appropriately symbolizes her life. The environment she lived in was just as harsh and unwelcoming as any desert. Despite this terrain, Hamer managed to rise up, become tough, survive, and blossom, offering hope to countless others who toiled without hope. Once Hamer countered, "I'm never sure any more when I leave home whether I'll get back or not. Sometimes it seem like to tell the truth today is to run the risk of being killed. But if I fall, I'll fall five feet four inches forward in the fight for freedom."[29]

Bernice Johnson Reagon

Of the thousands inspired by Fannie Lou Hamer stands another woman short in statue, but a giant in social activism and song: Bernice Johnson Reagon (born 1942). Reagon is the daughter of a minister who pastored in Worth County, Georgia, and of a faithful, supportive mother. At age five, Reagon felt the power of congregational support when she and her sister Refined the Fires of participatory song by singing for the entire congregation. She blossomed in a church in which women opened up meetings, and she participated in church settings in which a village raised a child and cared for the soul. For Reagon, there is no time that God has not been a part of her life; God has been with her just like the breath that she breathes.[30] Her breathing and singing helped her to become one of the Refining Fires of the Albany Movement.

Reagon experiences song and stories as life giving, as breath. She learned song could transform, make one feel good, and instill an ability to fight; she also heard stories about slavery, Black heritage, and Black music during her childhood. A contralto soloist in high school, Reagon majored in biology because she preferred doing music by ear as opposed to reading music and being constrained by a written score. She knew about lynchings in Mississippi, the Montgomery Bus Boycott, the Little Rock Nine, and the Greensboro, North Carolina, sit-in at the Woolworth counter,[31] and she came of age in the Albany Movement.

That awareness prompted Reagon's commitment to the youth division of NAACP. The Albany Movement began with the work of two SNCC field secretaries, Cordell Reagon and Charles Sherrod. The regional NAACP leaders did not want SNCC involvement. The fight was not only against segregation per se, but against the visceral embodiment of racism by everybody in it; so much so that the Albany College Dean of Students went down to the bus station as students were leaving for Thanksgiving break to make sure that Albany students entered the bus station on the "colored side." SNCC leaders were not allowed on the Albany campus. Reagon marched and sat in with the people of Albany as they sang songs, using edited Spirituals and rhythm and blues tunes. The mass meeting singing moved the Movement and became so powerful that all knew those tunes.[32]

Movement music Refined and redefined the Fire of hope and was invigorating and empowering within a context of cultural power that gave the music a deeper meaning: making a collective, a community statement. These group songs were sung with a fervor that created a kind of arrogance in motion, centering a person to take his or her place in the Movement and on the planet. The music of song and prayer became graphic and real for Reagon, for the whole people.[33]

Songs helped keep educated, uneducated, poor and middle-class people together in the protest and sane in jail. The activism level and music helped people define leadership and transcend class differences. When Reagon, a native of Albany, attended Albany State College, a segregated Black college, sit-ins had begun and schools were encouraged to participate in the Movement by student activists. All sorts of people were chosen to lead based on how protesters sensed an individual's commitment, integrity, and ability to stay with the program. Reagon, too, wanted such participation, given the on-campus harassment by off-campus White men. After losing her job and being expelled from school because of fear of retaliation when her name made the paper, Reagon and the other forty-seven suspended students were offered enrollment in schools in Atlanta. Reagon continued to work with SNCC but did not get as involved in the Atlanta Movement, because it was student-, not community-based. Reagon worked with and sang for the Movement. Music had become closely aligned with the Movement in the Freedom Rides. By the time of the Albany Movement, "We Shall Overcome," redacted from "I'll

Overcome," was the theme song. The Movement became a fountain of free-flowing sound, a revelatory, refreshing rhetoric of righteousness.[34]

Reagon participated in the Movement with gusto and came into a new voice. While getting her voice, she learned that groups who ought to work together are often at loggerheads. Reagon opted to work with SNCC because they were taking action. Reagon took action and reworked her first Movement song. After marching in protest about the first student's arrest, she sang "Over My Head, I see Freedom in the air. . . . There must be a God somewhere." The protesters changed the songs so that the songs would speak for them. At times of stress, someone would ask Reagon to sing; singing did not let embodied differences destroy each other, and it created space in a jail cell that had no space. Reagon believes that to do Black singing, one must sing, live, and struggle his or her way through the relevant obstacles. Singing allowed space for Reagon to have a conversion experience, to be born again in Refining the Fires of song toward a life of freedom. Her life sings empowerment as she travels throughout the world protesting and singing freedom with others as an ensemble. Her first performances with a formal musical ensemble occurred when she traveled with the SNCC Freedom Singers. They traveled throughout the United States telling stories through song and fighting racism. They felt their fight against racism was worth dying for. In her travels, she met, heard, and sang with Fannie Lou Hamer many times; they were two women struggling through song for freedom.[35]

When Reagon became a wife and a mother of two, she shifted her focus and looked for new ways to Refine the Fires of freedom and empowerment. She continued as a community activist, worked on festivals, booked tours, returned to Spelman College and graduated, and moved from Georgia to Washington, D.C., to pursue and complete her Ph.D. in History. She continues doing activism through song. Reagon has experienced the panAfricanist, Black Nationalist, and many other liberation movements. The Civil Rights Movement was a Refining Fire that let Reagon know herself, with music as the language of clarification and courage. Reagon sang with Harambee Singers when she needed to shift from the civil rights integrationist posture to a separatist stance. Reagon founded and today serves as artistic director for the dynamic all-women a capella singing group, Sweet Honey in the Rock.[36] A MacArthur "genius" prize winner, Reagon recently retired from serving as a curator for the Smithsonian Museum of American History and now serves as professor at American University, working on expanding her Wade in the Water Series.

For Reagon, the Movement altered her vision of herself and of her worldview. The Movement transformed lives as people confronted their demons— the things that frightened them. For Reagon, Albany was not about Police

Chief Pritchett or about the failure or success of Martin Luther King Jr. The Movement gave her the ability to challenge anything, any limiting boundaries. She learned that when anything or anyone puts you down, you have to fight back. One needs to be a refining fire or be open to being Refined by the Fires of justice, freedom, empowerment, transformation, and conversion. The Movement changed Albany and changed the country because the Movement exposed the depths of systemic oppression. While the Movement brought about only limited changes in power relations, given the number of elected officials, there remains the gifts of possibility and change.[37] During the Movement, Reagon changed and evolved into an awesome spirit, civil rights activist, researcher, curator, writer, historian, musician—a majestic matriarch who once defined herself as a "performer, teacher, researcher, and historian with a strong social, political, and economic consciousness." She works to provide new spaces for people to live and act in new ways; she nurtures, sifts, and invites us to help in this preparatory process for what can be new in time.[38]

Jo Ann Robinson

A fellow Georgian who helped prepare the way for others was Jo Ann Gibson Robinson (born 1912). She was the twelfth and youngest child of Owen and Dottie Gibson, prosperous African American landowners and farmers. After her father died when Robinson was six, her mother sold the farm and moved to Macon. Robinson graduated as class valedictorian and received her bachelor's at Fort Valley State College. While teaching in the public schools of Macon, Robinson married. After their child died in infancy, Robinson left Macon for Atlanta to pursue her master's degree in English from Atlanta University. Following a stint teaching in Texas, Robinson accepted a teaching position at Alabama State and joined the Dexter Avenue Baptist Church. After being humiliated by a bus driver for sitting in the "White section" of the bus, Robinson thought the Women's Political Council (WPC) should Refine the Fires of protest by taking on the segregated buses as a project. The WPC, founded by Alabama State professor Mary Fair Burks, focused on inspiring Blacks to empower themselves, think critically, rise above mediocrity, fight adult and juvenile delinquency, register and vote, and increase their group status. This collective women's power unit organized to fight all social injustice against African Americans.[39]

On May 21, 1954, Robinson wrote a letter to Montgomery Mayor, W. A. Gayle, on behalf of the WPC that called for improved conditions for Black passengers on the Montgomery city buses. Her letter threatened to boycott if changes were not made. Black women Refined the Fires of instigation and activism, making them a major factor in the Montgomery bus boycott, not just the personages of Rosa Parks, Martin Luther King Jr., other ministers, or E. D. Nixon. Robinson wrote her letter a year and a half before the actual Montgomery bus boycott began. Robinson and WPC members did a great deal of preparatory work enabling the Montgomery bus boycott to happen.[40] In response to the wretchedness and humiliation meted out daily to African Americans, the oppressed of Montgomery boycotted bus transportation for thirteen months, until the Supreme Court ruled that buses must not segregate.

Robinson participated in another civic organization that affected the Movement, the Montgomery Improvement Association (MIA). Robinson served on the executive board of MIA, edited the monthly newsletter, and served on all the major committees at King's request. Many Black citizens had been hurt. One man was murdered for simply riding the bus. The WPC discovered that the intense stress related to bus riding resulted in family disturbances from juvenile delinquency, violence, theft, and intoxication to spousal and child abuse. There were several probable test cases, but the WPC under Robinson's presidency decided to Refine the Fires of discontent and called for a boycott when Rosa Parks was arrested for not giving up her seat. Though Mary Burks takes exception to the idea that the boycott was Robinson's idea, as Robinson claimed, Burks also counters by stating that the fact that the boycott happened is a crucial element.[41]

Several citizens, including Robinson, had tried to negotiate the plight of Black citizens but to no avail. Once the boycott started, WPC joined with MIA. Many women raised funds, and MIA organized "taxi" services. Despite arrests, the growing White Citizen's Council, the bombings, and inclement weather, protesters remained faithful and Refined the Fires of steadfast witness. Robinson worked closely with King in MIA, providing clerical support and organizational strategies, and speaks only with admiration for him in her memoirs.

After the boycott, Robinson, like other professors from Alabama State, resigned rather than face possible recriminations for their participation. Once news of the resignations surfaced, all of these professors were offered other posts. Robinson taught in Texas, Alabama, Louisiana, and California, before retiring in 1976. Since then, Robinson has continued to volunteer with the Los Angeles city government and with many women's organizations dedicated to community uplift. She continued Refining the Fires of responsible citizenship by her voter registration work, senior citizens' assistance efforts, and community work at a child care center, until her health declined in 1987.[42]

Coretta Scott King

Robinson's legacy paved the way for one whose light has increased with time, Coretta Scott King (born 1927). Coretta Scott was on scholarship at New

England Conservatory of Music when she met Martin King Jr. Born in Alabama, she came from hard-working, land-owning parents who wanted her to get a good education. She had had a scholarship to Antioch college and wanted to pursue a career. The question remained: How would marriage to King, a minister, affect her career? After King proposed and Coretta realized she wanted him as well, she changed her program from a four-year performance course to a three-year public music course. After marriage and graduation, the Kings moved to Montgomery, where Coretta did several concerts in the area, until her first pregnancy. She continued to pursue a part-time singing career during the time of the Montgomery bus boycott, Refining the Fires of creativity at the Manhattan Center in New York along with Harry Belafonte and Duke Ellington. She did other concerts during the early pregnancy of her second child. After Martin recovered from the 1958 stabbing incident in Harlem, he and Coretta traveled to India. In 1962, while Martin continued to press the Movement, Coretta began Refining the Fires of nonviolent protest by speaking about Christian love and on behalf of peace. In 1963 she did Freedom Concerts, a nine-day concert tour of song and story that benefited the Civil Rights Movement.[43]

Coretta King supported her husband during his protest ministry. Her biography of King is a running commentary of his pursuits, and she speaks of him only in admirable terms. She traveled throughout the world with Martin and took care of their four children—from Europe to Ghana, India to Oslo, Norway, where King received the Nobel Peace Prize in 1964. She spoke with Malcolm X days before his assassination, and prior to 1968, she often fulfilled engagements that her husband could not fill. After his death, Coretta King devoted herself to her husband's protest ministry. She Refined the Fires of social justice ministry as she led the demonstration at Memphis, days after King's burial. She founded the Martin Luther King Jr. Center for Nonviolent Social Change in Atlanta, Georgia, to preserve and expand his legacy. She received the Presidential Medal of Freedom, awarded posthumously for her husband in 1977. She worked to secure the surrounding neighborhood of twenty-three acres of King's birthplace, which was declared a national historic site in 1980. During the 1980s, she opposed apartheid, helped establish Martin Luther King Day as a national holiday, and has spoken at London's St. Paul's Cathedral and Harvard University's Class Day exercises, the first woman to do so.[44]

Coretta King notes that she and Martin believed that freedom, peace, and justice must go hand in hand. She finds that peace is impossible amid massive oppression and repression. Since all people desire peace, freedom, justice, work, love, and community, we must work to make that happen, and we must shift our focus from arms to peace, to replicate Martin King's inclusive dream that all come together to create the beloved community.[45]

In reading Coretta King's writings, one wonders about what she does not divulge. In a recent interview, a Civil Rights activist had this observation:

> This strange, mystical woman tends to be a suspicious diva; her entourage moves twenty to thirty feet away from her. She has a feminist status reading of herself [that is, she views herself as a feminist]: is this the lie? . . . Perhaps hers is a politics of survival and place; a set of images being played—who controls, who is the authoritative keeper of the shrine? She loves the international aspect. Theologically and politically, she is not a diplomat . . . responsible for the legacy [during a] peculiar moment in history: no legacy; no memory.[46]

Part of her lot may have been like that of Jacqueline Kennedy, who stood by John F. Kennedy despite his shortcomings and chose to keep her personal considerations private. What is the alternative for a woman who agrees to "stand by her man" for her enhanced sense of place, when the limelight intensifies his persona and he has to prove to himself with various escapades that he is as good as his press? What are her options when others excuse his behavior, particularly if others perceive him and he perceives himself as on a divine mission?

Like the songs, the women within and without Refined the Fires of inspiration that moved the Movement. With a song in our hearts, we owe them all a debt of gratitude.

5. Ballads, Not Bullets:
The Nonviolent Protest Ministry of Martin Luther King Jr.

Particles of Justice,
Crushed beneath the pain
Of many thousands gone,
Midst repression, hate, ignorance.
The empowered will not
Give freedom to the impoverished:
A gift?
Compromise?
A choice? A gift?
A drum major prances
To the March of Freedom,
To the beat of Faith,
With instruments for the masses,
Orchestrated by God;
Faithful, loving;
Them made sacred
Them broken, forgotten, discounted
Them without the shoes
Of opulence, of status.
Of gods:
Of whiteness, power, status,
Of privilege, tradition, manifest destiny,
Of greed.
A drum major marches
To the music
Of Spirituals, blues, R & B,
Of gospel, hymns, Old 100s,
Of America,
Of moans, prayers,
In bas-relief,
Of hope unfulfilled.
Can I get a witness?
Is there no rest for the weary?
Will I be free at last,
Oh Lord,
Free at Last?

Freedom Songs: African America's Spirituals Redacted

Singing moved the Movement. Without the singing of Freedom Songs—
redacted African America's Spirituals, traditional hymns, new lyrics to popular tunes, and original songs by Freedom Fighters—the 1960s Civil Rights
Movement would not have had the same impact. These Freedom Songs
Refined the Fires of empowerment, as internal bolsters of strength and as
weapons against White racist, supremacist, hegemonic tyranny. Women and
men sang these songs. Although some misogynistic males, as cited earlier,
thought that the only place for women in the Movement was flat on their
backs, hundreds of grassroots women and men marched, rallied, and died for
freedom. They were the Movement's foot troopers led by such prophetic
voices as Martin Luther King Jr. This chapter juxtaposes the Refiner's Fire of
vitality amid the power of song and the religio-political, nonviolent direct
action protest ministry of Martin Luther King Jr.: Fires Refined to affect
social justice in the midst of blatant oppression. After reviewing the socio-
historical and religious climate of the 1960s Movement, I will explore the
impact of the music and review King's protest ministry.

Wade in the Water: The Turbulent 1960s

From 1945 to 1950, America "Waded in the Water" of blossoming religious
renewal in the aftermath of World War II, amid collapsed social structures
and the horrors of war. This religious upsurge was antithetical to the other
nations in the world and to the United States of America's past. By 1960, 69
percent of the population of the United States belonged to an organized
church, and they contributed substantially to church building funds. During
the Cold War, Russia represented atheistic communism that needed conversion, while America symbolized the religious ideal. Traditional fundamental-
ists like Billy Graham used mass media to gain new followers. In this postwar
revivalism, fundamentalist religion overcame the stigma from the 1924 Scopes
Evolution Trial. Religion became the tool that enabled many leaders to convey
their messages. In the late 1940s a religion of National Manifest Destiny
replaced the national religion of Social Justice where working-class folk pro-
tested their poor working conditions. By the 1950s the United States consisted
of three religious identities: sects of self-improvement, sects of national destiny,
and sects of fundamentalism, with significant overlapping. As politicians used
references to God to affect unity, America's civil religion blossomed.[1]

America's Civil Religion

America's civil religion constitutes those American cultural experiences and
institutions that people prescribe as religious entities: America's civil religion
is a religio-nationalist system that parallels other established religious bodies

in the United States. These entities have their gods, prophets, martyrs, sacred events and places, myths, rituals, and symbols, and they regulate power. America's civil religion espouses the gods of the presidency, political parties, the Supreme Court, the prophets of socio-cultural, journalistic, and economic forecasters, and activists and martyrs for justice and global wars; champions the sacred events of oaths to office and legislative sessions; consecrates sacred places of national monuments, libraries, museums, socio-cultural, historical and frontier myths, and patriotic rituals and symbols; and regulates power through local, county/parish, state, and federal laws and governing bodies. A public religion evokes a public morality. Public morality tends to compromise individual, internal religious experiences, in which people often identify emotionally with fundamentalism, but in which their theology locates them with the cheerleading of Norman Vincent Peale or his secular equal, Dale Carnegie. In a world where the new consumer capitalism shattered meaningful ties to family, race, and community, "a religion of upward mobility encouraged adjustment, amicability, optimism, and conformity."[2] Church and state separation in the realm of America's civil religion is more wishful thinking than fact.

African Americans have always known the blurred, paradoxical lines between church and state, which foster assimilation. Blacks have noted the progressive slants in Protestantism as an alliance for recalling America back to a notion of democratic, constitutional covenant. Many live out Wilson Moses's notion of America's civil religion—that all citizens worship the same God in the context of a special, covenantal relationship in which God will lead this country toward a superior prosperity, with the citizens living a life devoted to justice and liberty for everyone. This God is for the oppressed and for those with worldly success, for the poor and the privileged.[3]

Many Black activists have supported America's civil religion as an underlying morality that could and should influence social, political, and economic progress for African Americans. Some Black nationalists saw the hypocrisy in this religion of alleged equality that actually assumed God never planned for Blacks to share full American citizenship. King spanned the distinct and blurred lines of church and state with revivalistic qualities in Civil Rights efforts. King saw Blacks as missionaries called as divine "humanizing agents" for social justice and reform first to America and then to the world. The Movement's use of nonviolence and mass media worked. Unfortunately, the Movement could not overcome the socio-economic, political community problems and pathologies from the remnants of slavery and systemic, institutionalized racial discrimination. Many activists and organizations assumed that the answer to segregation and discrimination was to pattern the lives of Black folk upon that of upper-middle-class White America, with the federal government as arbiter of social gospel programs: wading in the water like

White chocolate. This modus operandi was already behind the progressive reform attitude of that day. The belief in the inevitability of progress, that race relations would ultimately improve, has not panned out. Black religion must also see that Black civil religion, rooted in a notion of divine righteousness and purpose as the basis for changing public policy and enlisting governmental and White liberal support to carry this out has not resulted in change for the masses of Black and/or poor folk, particularly since liaisons among the Black church, Civil Rights reform, and the puritan, ascetic sense of abolitionism and social gospel no longer exist in 2000.[4]

Many who were parents in the 1960s lived through World War II, when they could legally kill White foreign enemies and receive the blessings of the church via military chaplains: civil religion at its best providing African Americans with praises from the state (Caesar) and from the church (God). Those Black soldiers had proven themselves on the "stage" of war and returned to the United States, where they were not allowed "standing room." These veterans' children heard their parents' rage, cynicism, and despair and, like King, wrestled with civil and political life. They sought to respond through protest for equality and social justice and not march to a drumbeat of a deferred dream. The Movement, from King's perspective, was a response to immoral White supremacist uncivilized behavior toward Blacks. He sought to deconstruct White Southern segregation, to Refine the Fires of empowerment for Black Americans through *agape* (unconditional, sacrificial love), to exorcise the "incubus of segregation," to reconstruct America's society, and to effect the salvation of all humanity.[5]

Nurtured on salvific themes of divine love, justice, liberation, hope, and righteousness, Civil Rights groups fought against injustice. Black preachers in Black Churches taught a righteousness that co-suffers with and liberates the oppressed. To fight racism and segregation, the NAACP, the National Urban League (UL), the Congress for Racial Equality (CORE) and, later, SNCC relied on these themes and on church folk and used church property as meeting spaces.[6]

The Ethics and Theology of Martin Luther King Jr.

King's ethics and theology celebrated and Refined the Fires of populism, civil religion, religious fundamentalism, and the creed of self-improvement. Who was the Jesus worshipped by many conservative Christians, if not an heir of a carpenter, a populist prophet who sided with the poor? In King's sermon, "The Drum Major Instinct,"[7] the need to be acknowledged as unique and special links these threads of King's thought. King noted that perverting this instinct in the United States meant U.S. involvement in war crimes, especially in Vietnam. King argued that revisioning this success ethic ought to focus on social and community success and service to others, against poverty, war, racism, and exploitation. In himself, this drum major instinct for peace and justice worked because American society was obsessed with being unique and successful but failed because poor peoples' lives did not change. The Movement did not defy the systemic problems underlying racism and war but demonized its opposition without grasping the complexities behind social problems.[8] This time of change included the quest for democracy in Africa and the slave diaspora to the United States. At the onset of the 1960s protest, drum majors and grassroots protesters walked to a beat towards justice.

Christian African Americans adapted their faith to their socio-cultural and individual life experiences, as they adapted a transcendent God concept and assumed that American society was accountable to this God and to moral law. 1960s Civil Rights grassroots protesters came from this contextualized faith to participate in the Movement. These people called King to lead them, and he connected his Christian idea of love, from the Sermon on the Mount, to Gandhi's teachings on nonviolence and the promises of the Declaration of Independence for freedom and equality, to connect with other developing countries of color in overcoming White supremacy and racism. King became aware of the interconnectedness of global liberation struggles when he attended the ceremonies marking Ghana's becoming an independent nation state, ritualizing a universal quest for morality and justice.[9] Just who was this drum major who Refined the Fires of equality?

Precious Lord, Take My Hand: The Preacher-King

Born in the bowels of the American South, African American King had Irish blood paternally, and Indian blood maternally. His maternal grandfather built Ebenezer Church, which King later co-pastored. His paternal grandfather was a poor, illiterate, violent alcoholic. In 1916, King's father, a Morehouse College alumnus, moved to Atlanta, where Martin was born in 1929, in a comfortable middle-class setting.[10] Called to preach, King learned success from his father and wisdom from his mother. He had a steady, peaceful temperament and was suited to use ministry as a way to channel that love.[11]

King, a genuinely likable person with a fondness for personal grandeur, fondly and ironically called "De Lawd" by his closest friends, was anchored in a soulful spirituality. Unencumbered by repulsive piety, he was short, sturdily built, and vulnerable, with a sense of humor. The church was the place where he led mass meetings, the place he loved, the place that gave Black folk authority and emotional power. As King accepted leadership of the Movement, Blacks in Montgomery shared a joy known by people who found their prayers for a leader answered, affording them the choice of participating in their own change.[12]

King chose to answer his call to the Christian ministry. Gifted and involved as social activist and ethicist, theologian, charismatic, political leader, personalistic philosopher, and orator, King's roots were in the Black Baptist Church. The revolutionary prospects of the Gospel and the deliverance and liberation motifs of the Hebrew Bible shaped his use of Black cultural artifacts like the Spirituals, Black southern mores, morality, and faith. For King, his call to ministry was key to healing the United States. Being a preacher personified the spiritual and political wisdom the Black Church required of its leaders. His public oratory was preaching, his sermons were civil religious addresses. This preacher, prophet, poet, and social reformer placed his theology in his sermons: the arena of cultic performance, his intimate thoughts and feelings, and his brilliant use of metaphor to couch local injustices amid ultimate truths, amid biblical texts. He championed a priestly covenant of inclusion toward freedom. In the last years of his ministry, he Refined the Fires of inclusion toward deconstruction. King spoke less of redemptive suffering and sacrifice and became filled with anger, tempered by his practice of nonviolence. He became militant, exercised prophetic rage, and gave authority only to God. King Refined the Fires of America's dream of liberty, justice, and the common good for all in his own faith, writing, teaching, and preaching.[13]

King's ability to inspire engendered people's support, love, and loyalty. He had conviction and was not one to seek personal aggrandizement. In the spring of 1968, he changed his strategy, goals, and philosophy for two reasons. First, Blacks were tired of being beaten and jailed for trying to exercise their constitutional rights. Second, the Civil Rights victories did not trickle down to the Black masses. His ministry shifted from Refining the Fires of nonviolent direct action in the Southern pulpit to the Northern pool room. He moved to Chicago, drank beer, and played pool with hustlers. When his children became hostile and warped by the ghetto malaise of despair and hopelessness, he sent them to live with their grandparents in the South. Having read Franz Fanon, a Black psychiatrist, and from his experience with Black Power advocates, King knew that when hope dwindles, hate usually turns most harshly on those who first fostered hope. Now King was up against the combined forces of exploitative merchants, corrupt politicians, amoral gangsters, and Black politicians strongly immersed in the White power structure. Aware that his strategy had not addressed the socio-economic problems, King returned to Atlanta to address race and class.[14]

King and the SCLC

King developed a hermeneutic of protest to address issues of race with the SCLC as a base. He responded to and initiated a patterned activist Movement ministry. King, with a local minister who usually had just been released from jail on bond, preached a number of revivalistic Civil Rights sermons. These sermons used phrases from Spirituals—Keep Your Eyes on the Prize, Ain't

Going to let Nobody Turn Me 'Round—and biblical calls for justice and equality (such as Amos 5:14). Second, King locked arm in arm with a local leader and would lead the congregation in a nonviolent march and protest to face danger for the cause of constitutionally guaranteed freedom. These techniques worked, and the issue was resolved through local negotiation and federal executive or legislative action. Often local judges, in violation of the First Amendment's right of peaceable assembly, ordered Civil Rights workers not to gather or march, which Refined the Fires of protest and was an indictment against segregation and hate.[15] King "inspired Blacks and pricked the consciences of Whites . . . [as he created] a coalition of conscience" among all, to change America from a country of White people to a nation for all.[16]

Consciousness-raising involved the class issue of economic injustice. Initially King saw economic injustice problems but did not address classism or see U.S. political economy as germane to Black oppression. Most activists argued that the socio-political and economic systems in the United States were good and that the only problem was the exclusion of people of color from the benefits of this good. When he did confront poverty in the United States and the war in Vietnam, King's prophetic journey moved from the locus of power to the periphery. He obsessed about a big Movement triumph and his own death, given the fifty FBI-investigated assassination plots and his daily hate mail. His radical prophetic voice merged with the Black church to form an "interpretative partnership," in which they embraced and Amened the Bible in celebrating the "Sacred Light" of Freedom.[17] Deemed a subversive early on, King was later seen by many to be a moderate, compared to those who cried Black Power in 1966. King, the moderate, a practitioner of nonviolence, came to support Black Power. He saw injustice as theological, where one offended God, and saw himself as a revolutionary who used Black Power tactics, without the slogan, to garner power.[18]

King and Nonviolence

Nonviolence, King's personal and social ethics strategy that put one in harmony with God, influenced his work for Civil Rights and human rights and economic justice. King had a teleological ethic of responsibility. The limits of his moralistic Christian nonviolent ethic occurred while dealing with a non-Christian constituency, when it lacked certain psychological needs of the oppressed. Many saw nonviolence as a tactic, not an ideal, while King saw nonviolence as the absolute modus operandi and rejected violence as either a tool or ethic for social change. When King's nonviolence became more militant, it remained tempered by his middle-class status and his evangelical liberalistic social gospel message. King enhanced his ethic by using his theology of a personal God, amid a faith of justice, love, and power, which supported his belief in nonviolence and aimed toward preserving human life and redeeming human personality. Yet violence played a part in King's nonviolent strategy as his main triumphs happened when protesters experienced violent reactions, which generated public support. Ironically, the strategy often failed when the threat of violence was not apparent. In studying the means and ends of an ethic such as nonviolence, one must build in enough flexibility when putting it into practice. One must acknowledge when universalizing a particular ethic that many gray areas exist.[19]

King used Gandhi's nonviolence strategy, shaped and molded by Black church tradition, to build his justice model: he mixed democratic freedom with the Exodus and biblical justice and liberation, blended with the New Testament view of suffering and love, revealed in the Cross, and Refined to create a theology that could call all Americans toward the beloved community. King moved toward the work of Paul Tillich, Henry N. Wieman, and Reinhold Niebuhr as a product of the theology of that period, combined with the Baptist Hebrew Bible prophetic based on Black church traditions and Black folklore of Atlanta. Like most Blacks, King's theology arose from the songs, sermons, prayers, testimonies, and stories about oppression and slavery. King's theology, steeped in freedom and hope, was apparent in his life and preaching, his vocal movement and rhythm, and the content of his message.[20] King did not think of himself as a leader but as one divinely destined to serve in the Movement: a genuinely shy person thrust into leadership in the conservative, passive city of Montgomery. There King developed a theology and hermeneutic of freedom and justice amid nonviolence and New Testament reconciliation. He met the threat of death with a sense of humor, which allowed those close to him to recognize the constant presence of death and continue with their work. They realized that for King, the effort to change American society required people to be willing to be suffering servants, for Jesus himself died a violent death.

Seeing that change demanded a social crucifixion and a resurrection, King carefully thought through new challenges and weighed the costs, for King and the majority of the Movement participants believed God was on their side.[21] Free of preoccupation with self-importance, King loved people and had no inner need to hate White racist segregationists. In Montgomery, he began to hew his political theology into a hermeneutics which also included justice, America's civil religion that relied on the cross and resurrection, the remission of sin with the shedding of innocent blood, and African American heritage.[22] His genealogical legacy and his education forged his perspective in a profound manner.

King and the Black Church

Though a youthful King had problems with the emotionalism and simple piety of the Black Church, he returned to that institution as his venue for

Black socio-economic empowerment. King used the philosophical and meta-physical ideas of a personal God of his graduate education, along with the Black Church's personal God, to articulate a prophetic vision of freedom, justice, and equality. Relying on Howard Thurman's interrelatedness of love, forgiveness, and reconciliation, King created his own vision of the beloved community with Black people as redemptive participants in a vision of Black messianic hope. He felt Blacks had the unique historical, spiritual place in Western civilization to help transform the world because of their power based on love, good will, understanding, and nonviolence. King's vision of messianic hope involved the Black commitment to Christianity, the biblical notion of a messianic people and nation, a heritage of other Black thinkers who have posited Black messianism. King was the only one to tie love and violence closely to this ideal. He knew the shortcomings of Black people and the Black Church, yet he believed Blacks were uniquely suited, morally and spiritually, to help lead a Movement to affect a new humanity.[23] He used the Black traditional device of call and response to engage himself and the listening community in a hope and dream for freedom now.

The West African tradition of "call and response," which signifies the African sense of unity and harmony among all of the universe and within the community, is a part of the music and sermon rhetoric of Black America. This strong sense of community, steeped in orality, resonates in African American Spirituals. As the invisible institution became the visible Black church, call and response continued to bring a cohesiveness to the worshipping community. Call and response infused the music and became a major tool in the communication between preacher and congregants. The minister states a subject, the "call," and the congregation "responds" with many answers: "Amen"; "Go 'head"; "Fix it, preacher"; "Take your time"; "'Sho nuff"; "I hear ya"; "Watch yo'self." Such Afrocentric idioms of *nommo,* or word power, tempered by Black America, helped mold King's oratorical power.

Nommo (in singing, preaching, rapping, and signifying) is a principle that rebels and resists; is the vital life force uniting the Spiritual and the physical; and names, hears, and calls as it gives, embraces, penetrates, and causes all life.[24] King's *nommo* helped communicate his faith, located in his beliefs, his fasting in jail, and mass meetings.[25] King's implied Christology relied heavily on Western christological forms, mixed with his Black Southern Baptist tradition that signifies Jesus' humanity, Jesus as one who came to point the way. King used Jesus Christ's trailblazing instinct in ministry at the cross and the resurrection's liberating message as motivation and Gandhi's nonviolence as his method.[26] In sum, King's theology meshed with his philosophy and ethic of love, integration, and nonviolence, steeped in his eschatological hope in the resurrected Jesus, symbolized and revealed in messages of exodus-liberation and cross-love. Holding to his grandparents' ideas of divine righteousness, King answered "There Is a Balm in Gilead" to the prophet Jeremiah's question.[27]

The Only Way to Freedom

King saw nonviolence as the only way to freedom and as the basis for developing human relationships. He tied redemptive suffering to nonviolent direct action, and his "no pain, no gain" was "no suffering, no true liberation." One must be prepared to suffer, even die, for social justice, but one must not retaliate by using suffering against others.[28] King knew it would be difficult to teach people to think and live in nonviolent terms when they had been taught to meet violence with violence, but Christian fulfillment meant stressing neighborly love and existence, or nonviolent protest. Nonviolence would allow one to exercise the virtues of altruism, civic spirit, and friendliness, which required that one first be open to such a message or have a conversion experience that would create an environment where grace, divine loving activity, and love manifested among humanity might occur. King redefined nonviolence to make nonviolence amenable to facing and shattering evil structures, yet maintain harmony with biblical tradition. He challenged the Black church's dualism, in which it was pacifist in domestic matters and militaristic on global matters,[29] as he called his followers to Refine the Fires of beloved community and justice.

A beloved environment where people can overcome the reasons for hate and injustice—fear, pride, prejudice, and irrationality—needs to be in place before the fruit of nonviolence, of beloved community, can be realized. Such a community would exercise altruism, the expression of neighborly, sacrificial love among strangers, empowered by divine agency; civic spirit, an obligation toward a cohesive, shared socio-political community life; and friendliness, an impetus to meet and be with former enemies or those with whom one had shared misunderstandings or difficulty. King's protest ministry was a Christian ministry in which church and state together provided a world where the beloved community could thrive, allowing the fulfillment of life as individual and community. For King, the purpose of the Movement was to transform America's socio-political structure, in which America's citizens desire change for all, America's traditions of public protest demand freedom for all, and America can be faithful to her creed of democracy for all, affirming her dogma that this is a land of freedom and liberty for all.[30]

The Movement Since 1955

The Movement since 1955 has been a saga of "successes and shames." When the foot soldiers marched they took an oath to nonviolence that gave accent to a set of Ten Commandments to:

1) Meditate daily on the life and teachings of Jesus.
2) Remember always that the nonviolent movement seeks justice and reconciliation—not victory.
3) Walk and talk in the manner of love—for God is love.
4) Pray daily to be used by God in order that all men [*sic*] might be free.
5) Sacrifice personal wishes in order that all men [*sic*] might be free.
6) Observe with both friend and foe the ordinary rules of courtesy.
7) Seek to perform regular service for others and for the world.
8) Refrain from violence of fist, tongue, or heart.
9) Strive to be in good spiritual and bodily health.
10) Follow the directions of the movement and of the captain on a demonstration.[31]

King soon realized that he had erred in thinking that Southern White ministers would support the Movement once they were challenged. As White churches got involved, confrontation tactics became diluted, notably in the March on Washington, in August, 1963, when the marchers were diverse but did not confront the injustice.[32] King's nonviolence theory does not deal with such dilution nor the maldistribution of power that undergirds racism, making his ethics problematic.

William R. Jones and the Problematic King

William R. Jones notes that he finds King problematic: (1) many White Americans dubbed him the Black Messiah and gauged other Black leaders based on how they measured up against King; (2) King's nonviolence was deemed the only approach to bring social change, which often skews presumptions about ultimate reality, institutional change, and ethical decision making; and (3) King tried to import Gandhian two-pronged nonviolence to a different context. Gandhi's nonviolence theory stated: first the resister tries to transform the oppressor by penetrating their conscience and reason; second, if this does not work, then one tries to force the oppressor to see that they cannot maintain repression and injustice, or deal with their immorality: a test about power. Gandhi's nonviolence program worked because the Indians were the majority and the English were the minority; in the United States, African Americans were the minority and had to rely on Whites for support. Jones notes that both King and Gandhi erred in thinking that the suffering of some would convince the oppressor to stop; Jones believes that this theory could lead to self-initiated genocide. Further, if one person considers another person/group as less-than-human, the suffering or death of the latter does not change the oppressor.

According to Jones, King's analysis of violence fails to analyze racism as a will to power and fails to define violence in a concrete rather than contextual manner, which results in too much ambiguity to be helpful for doing ethical analysis. Second, King's theory makes it difficult to see how a Christian ought to respond to institutionalized oppressive structures created and maintained by violence; for example, will nonviolence deter a Klan-led lynch mob or a militia terroristic bombing? If his agapic unconditional love for the neighbor is a love that comes from an exalted position, as Jesus the Christ is God, emptied, become human, and later exalted (Phil. 2:6-11), then only one who has preexisting power can love. When King came out against Vietnam, Whites no longer exalted his nonviolence, and King became persona non grata to the militarists who saw international communism as a greater evil and threat to America than institutional racism.[33] At heart, this preacher-king Refined the Fires of justice as a minister, not a politician or civil leader.

King as Prophet

King did not intend to lead the national Civil Rights Movement. Yet he was catapulted into the Movement with less than a half-hour to prepare the speech that helped start the bus boycott, which lasted three hundred and eighty-one days.[34] His conversations grew out of a worldview of Black social gospel and Black religion that merged from Old Testament slave theology that signified freedom, Black homiletic traditions that created self-worth, and a sense of sacred time in which one can go beyond secular and sacred considerations to make sense out of paradoxes. To this matrix he adds themes like "I've Been to the Mountain Top" and "Free at Last" to read Western history into the Black preaching tradition. Some of King's speeches, like "I Have a Dream" involve a performed unity that pressed toward the beloved community via covenant. Covenant symbolized the connectedness between sacred and secular, religion and politics, that let King be faithful to Christianity. Beloved community is the metaphor for his dream that envisions all people in a great "world house" where all people of all faiths must learn how to live together in peace.[35] King was a dreamer, pied piper, preacher-king, and prophet.

The dreamer had dreams about what America could be. The dream changed and evolved with new needs and oppositions, and helped birth other dreams and movements. The original dream focused on integration, Civil Rights, and racial justice, toward freedom, to be accomplished through "creative suffering." The new dream shifted to include economic justice for the poor, as an international push against colonialism. The dream expanded to include housing, employment, and foreign policy.[36] In the "I Have A Dream," speech, King does theological proclamation based on the idea of "realized eschatology," where God's just kingdom has already begun and continues to be fulfilled. This speech exists today as a clarion call for the ideas of equality and justice. In his early ministry, King believed in the dream, the possibility of personal and social change.[37]

King Refined the Fires of change as a totally radical Christian who developed a teleological ethics and theology of nonviolence and a personal God that has being and value and consciously guides and directs the world and lovingly hears prayers. God creates persons who are sacred beings who must be respected and must oppose all oppression like racist and economic injustice and war. King saw the connection between racist segregation and economic injustice. His philosophy of nonviolence used the work of the American Friends Service Committee, the Fellowship of Reconciliation, and Gandhi, tempered by the eighth-century Hebrew prophets and Jesus.[38] For King, the mature Christian's geometrically queued life involved the length (individual interests), the breadth (interests or welfare of others as neighbor love), and the height (one's relationship with God). Within the beloved community, King saw these three aspects as critical to attaining morality and social justice (vital to human fulfillment) and to acknowledging the sacredness of human life.[39] King used philosophers and theologians to explain his thoughts or actions and to shape his theology through the Black church's message of liberation and black people's experience of oppression. He could lead Black people because he symbolized, embraced, and lived Black church's faith.[40]

The son and the grandson of Baptist preachers, King became a preacher himself while at Morehouse, studied at Crozer Theological Seminary, and received a Ph.D. from Boston University. His unpublished sermons reveal that the Black church tradition was his training ground and his constant, theological stabilizing force. The oppression of Black folk and the liberating message of the Black church formed the rubric that moved him to develop a theology that took seriously Christianity and African American's socio-political needs. When thwarted by despair or contradictions, King Refined the Fires of embodied piety. He turned to prayer as conversation with the biblical God of the Black religious faith. This faith tradition helped King be militantly and aggressively nonviolent, Refining Fires beneath an unjust social order, and initially be optimistic about White liberal support, as the Black church remained open to fellowship with the White community. He developed his theology and ethics based on the language of freedom and hope in his preaching and writing: theological style and content, using the people's language. When talking to White audiences, he used White philosophy and theology; when talking to Black audiences, he used his Black faith preaching tradition. He preached freedom and a present, realized, Black eschatological hope that allowed him to stand in solidarity with "the least of these."[41] King relied on the God of Black experiential faith with a love ethic of beloved community that stands firmly connected to liberty and justice for all, hopeful of

God's imminent caring presence.[42] This God is present in King's sermonic rhetoric and discourse, which enhanced his importance as a moral, public, and spiritual leader. He established a range of possibilities that informed their order of values and enacted a shared vision of a union between audience and speakers that depicted moral living as a beloved community, a flexible, powerful image of the ideals inherent to America's constitutional commitment to liberty and equality, within civil and social rituals of oppression.[43]

King's Beloved Community

For Black Americans, King's beloved community provided a vision of a world where Christian love handled the tensions between racial equality and liberty and bolstered their self-esteem and pride. For White Americans, beloved community pressed them to rethink the nation's revolutionary roots as a usable past, aware that justice revolutions could be bloodless. The beloved community rhetoric could bind diverse elements of King's fragmented audience into a unified whole by identifying core communal values; hierarchically structuring them (a transcendent liberal-Christian existentialism that sought to manage the tension between individual rights and communal duty rather than to sacrifice either); and publicly performing the beloved community's transitory existence (displaying the collective power of love, justice, liberty, and equality via nonviolent resistance). King's metaphor helped the nation see the "moral crises" and enact some of the most far reaching Civil Rights laws since the Civil War.[44]

The Albany Movement

One of the communities in which King faced criticism and conflict was the Movement in Albany, Georgia. The Albany Movement showed the complexity and strains of leading the Movement and had a far reaching impact through song to uplift protesters and to end oppression and segregation. After Albany's NAACP Youth Council elected to integrate local bus facilities, SNCC began a freedom ride campaign to Albany. SCLC sponsored and financed SNCC, which put the local NAACP and SCLC in conflict. To avoid clashes, they formed the Albany Movement, led by G. T. Anderson, a local leader and medical doctor. Anderson and King said they would remain in jail until things changed. When things had not changed and King accepted bond and left jail, he met with tremendous criticism. King left because a local Black leader became delusional and would not leave jail as long as King stayed. King and his colleagues all agreed that a worse case scenario would be for the White jailer to learn and publicly state that a key local Black leader was insane. After the discovery of this leader's mental illness, King accepted bail the next day.[45]

Many SNCC members criticized nonviolence and the adults in the Movement. Some could see nonviolence as a tactic, but not as a way of life. They thought King could have done more for the South, questioned SCLC funding, and had mixed reactions when told that King's image, worth $250,000, helped to bankroll SCLC. SNCC did not want King in Albany. They had helped create a people's movement without being dominant, and they felt King was a distraction. Serious tension developed between SCLC and SNCC over Albany, and many sensed King was insensitive to the terrible jail conditions in Birmingham.[46]

King's Dream

The miracle is that King's "dream" tactics actually worked, for history shows that those who attain freedom are those who have the power to take freedom. King knew this but saw power as redemptive love and suffering. His dream pressed him to deal with global injustice, for he saw the parallels between global racism, poverty, and war. King's resolve to do a Poor People's March on Washington caused him to lose support by his best peers and allies. Notably, his attack against the Vietnam War cost him the support of the Johnson Administration; most of his victories occurred through federal government legislation.[47] King's model required a reworking of American economic, socio-political value systems—a call for international justice and equality.[48]

Toward the end of his life, King began to see the need for Black power in the Black community to build individual and community self-esteem and erase self-hatred. Black power and antiwar movements, along with American materialism and dehumanization practices shaped King's dream. The absence of dignity and self-respect meant Blacks could not effectively participate in forming a beloved community with others. In shifting toward Black power and the horrid plight of poor people, despite the Civil Rights Act (1964), the Voting Rights Act (1965), and President Johnson's War on Poverty, King saw his earlier dream fade to become a nightmare. He saw Johnson's Vietnam War fail and the U.S. Treasury debts rising from a no-win war. Without pride in personal and communal heritage and socio-economic power, one could not share or negotiate with mutuality and an ability to contribute. King found this discrepancy so critical that he began to think Blacks might need to temporarily separate and not immediately integrate in order to achieve a beloved community.[49] Part of King's nightmare was realizing America's duplicity in violence. He spoke about this violence with a prophetic judgment, claiming that God would break the United States if this country did not care for the poor or for effecting peace.[50]

King, as agent and advocate of change, won the 1964 Nobel Peace Prize. This prophet shared concerns with the NAACP, such as biracial, primarily

Black, middle-class membership, and used moral and legal tactics to affect change. He and the NAACP had close ties to the Black church. Their shared goals included a commitment to end racism and discrimination, valued the Constitution, and relied on the White American liberal conscious to help America offer all citizens life, liberty, and the pursuit of happiness. Both used the legal system and believed in integration: "We're black and white together." Their differences concerned ideals and tactics. King used confrontational situations like sit-ins to effect change; he relied on coalitions and the courts. The NAACP relied solely on the courts, and some members saw King as an extremist and only partially supported his work. The hardest NAACP reprimand to King came after his Riverside Church sermon, which denounced the Vietnam War. King's edict forged a crisis moment for segregationists and the Black Establishment as he merged the old Black religious experience with new radical thinking: this appealed to Black youth, but scandalized many in the NAACP. Despite this divergence, King and the NAACP retained mutual respect:[51] "Martin's greatest strength was the NAACP's greatest weakness: he had a new, aggressive approach and mass appeal. Likewise the NAACP's greatest strength was King's greatest weakness: the NAACP had superior organizational development and administrative know-how gained from years of experience."[52]

King, a twentieth-century Pied Piper, was about the task of exposing and ridding the Hamelin town of America of its plague of rats—oppression and violence. Colonialism, an oppressive evil, concerns one powerful group being economically dominant over a weaker group. Racism, another evil, accords superiority to one group over others based on biological features and cultural heritage. These rats attacked, obstructed, exploited, and denied Blacks and the poor of their livelihood and brought them sickness and death.[53] Between 1965 and 1968, King realized that his messages had not moved Whites to change but did move Blacks to action. His inability to effect freedom in the present moved him to take an eschatological approach: if not now, then soon, somehow.[54] King had begun to address issues of class by targeting poverty and moving to help the poor help themselves. He had challenged violence but had not yet dealt with sexism.[55]

A Legacy to American Culture

On the eve of his death, King used the repetition of "If I Had Sneezed" to signify what he would have missed and not experienced in the 1960s Movement. Had he sneezed after a deranged woman stabbed him at a book signing in New York City several years earlier, he would have died.[56] He did not die in New York but later in Memphis, fighting for garbage collectors. But he left a legacy to American culture. He Refined the Fire of America's vision of "equality" as an essential and basic commitment of and for the national community.

For King, two people attain equality when both are indistinguishable from and interchangeable with the other, within his beloved community where one experiences complete assimilation and integration of all races and creeds. Using biblical imagery, he calls a universalized audience to *agape,* where people love because God loves them.[57] King provided the Movement's political and philosophical logic of racial equality.

> He inspired poor blacks to risk their lives for freedom and shamed many whites into supporting them. . . . prick[ed] the conscience of both white and black Christians and thereby enlist[ed] them into a mass movement against racism in the churches and the society. . . . He . . . communicated the Christian message of freedom more effectively, prophetically, and creatively than any one in the U.S. before or after him.[58]

How Music Moved the Movement

The Civil Rights protest songs included hymns, redacted Spirituals, and the 1960s Freedom Songs that focused on the theme "Freedom Now!" These revised versions of traditional Spirituals had an intense relevancy for the 1960s and for King because they named contemporary people, places, and events and used concurrent singing styles. Thus, "Over My Head, I Hear Music in the Air" became in the 1960s "Over My Head, I Hear Freedom in the Air." Singers Refined the Fires of justice as they named enemies like Governor Wallace, Sheriff Pritchett, and Bull Connor; they named places like Albany, Birmingham, Alabama, and Mississippi; they named events like voting, Freedom Rides, and sit-ins; and they used three major performance styles: (1) mass meeting or congregational style; (2) ensembles like the SNCC Freedom Singers, a quartet; and (3) solo song leaders. The Spirituals, part of Black oral traditions, celebrated remembrances, traditions, and expressions of identity and community and are keys to deciphering the riddle of the African American experience.[59] The Spirituals, as buffers against subjugation, marginalization, and hatred, depict a synthesis of an African holistic, religious-musical tradition and the European church, biblical, and hymnal traditions. Spirituals embody theological, historical, anthropological, socio-political, and literary outlooks and the musical textures central to both the African and European experiences.

The Spirituals dared the American conscience to reexamine the places of God, humanity, evil, and freedom. These metaphors for King's own vision and faith let him view the dialectics of good and evil, optimism and pessimism, hope and apathy, and affirmation and pain. King's search for his beloved community led him toward the question of theodicy as he claimed that God limits divine power to allow human freedom and human responsibility. King posited that God permits evil to support human freedom. He used the Spirituals to reflect on the place of God, the oppressed and the oppressor regarding societal responsibility for evil and suffering, toward complete liberation. The Spirituals provide symbols of personal vision, faith, and the dialectical nature of the spiritual, physical, and ethical life for King. Before King, mystic theologian Howard Thurman saw that the Spirituals record the suffering and Jesus' gift of liberation. Black theologian James Cone, who places King and Malcolm X in dialogue, views the Spirituals as documents of confession, resistance, and theology to address human salvation as power.

Freedom Songs

Some of those powerful Spirituals sung during sit-ins, freedom rides, voter registration campaigns, and at 1960 sit-ins include: "We Shall Overcome," "We Shall Not Be Moved," "This Little Light of Mine," "If You Miss Me from the Back of the Bus," "Ain't Gonna Let Nobody Turn Me Round," "Oh Freedom," "Woke Up This Morning With My Mind on Freedom," "Keep Your Eyes On the Prize," "Get On Board, Little Children," and "I Been in the Storm so Long."[60] Other Freedom Songs include traditional Black gospel or hymnody, protest movement songs, where the words and music were written by Civil Rights activists, and edited secular songs.

Traditional Black Gospel

Traditional Black gospel or hymnody served as staples for Movement singing, largely because mass meetings were held in churches. Singing songs like "We Are Soldiers in the Army" helped protestors gather for mass meetings during the evenings, looking from outside, listening for testimonies and hope. And they sang, often with their whole bodies.[61] The singing experience raised questions, solidified issues, and provided a forum where Black students could transform and redefine themselves—who they were and their role in society.[62] Hymns and familiar hymn tunes Refined the Fires of protest and righteous indignation. People sang with conviction that kept them walking and not taking the bus, as change occurred while singing. Initially the protesters sang the hymns as printed. As the struggle continued to change the quality of their lives, the songs often changed. The singers changed their words when they needed to restate their convictions and commitments to face death. Other times they changed their words when they reached the sanctuary of their meeting place, after having confronted the segregationist system. King himself offered a new hymn to the old tune of "Old Time Religion": "We are moving on to victory, with hope and dignity, we will all stand together, until we all are free."[63] In Montgomery and Nashville, the songs created a power based on rich Black harmony and improvised choral singing combined with the crises of institutionalized Jim Crow racism and the daily possibility of death. Freedom Fighters sang "Amen," a traditional one-word Black sacred chant popularized in the 1960s movie, "Lilies of the Field," repeatedly with a call by a leader. That same song became "Freedom" in Nashville.[64] Other hymns or gospel tunes that fueled the Movement included songs from: "Come and Go with Me to That Land" and "I'm on My Way to the Freedom Land" to "I'll Be Alright,"[65] with favorites like "What a Fellowship," "What a Friend We Have in Jesus," and "Sing Till the Power of the Lord Comes Down." Other songs based on the protesters' musical appetites included original songs by activists and edited secular songs.

Other Movement Songs

Activists used their personal experiences under segregation and Jim Crow to write new music, particularly as they sat behind bars. James Bevel and Bernard Lafayette wrote the words and music to "Dog, Dog." This song sings about the irony of Black and White children living next door to each other, not allowed to play together, but their dogs would.[66] Other songs were adapted from the militant labor songs of the '20s and '30s of the Movement, e.g., "Which Side Are You On?", "Birmingham Sunday," and "Demonstrating GI."[67]

They edited popular songs from rock and roll and rhythm and blues tunes popular during the 1950s and 1960s. Bevel and LaFayette parodied the rock and roll tune, "You Better Leave My Kitten Alone," recorded by Willie John, to create "You'd Better Leave Segregation Alone."[68] Other redacted popular songs include "Moving On" by Hank Snow, which becomes "Segregation's been here from time to time, but we just ain't gonna pay it no mind, Well, it's movin' on, well, it's movin' on. . . ." "The Banana Boat Song" by Erik Darlin, Bob Carney, and Alan Arkin, popularized by Harry Belafonte, becomes "Freedom's Comin' and It Won't Be Long." "Hit the Road, Jack" by Percy Field becomes "Get Your Rights, Jack, and Don't Be a Tom No More."[69] Song leaders led songs, ensembles traveled the country singing, and people sang together in mass meetings, all with a common message: singers, lyrics, and music championed the Movement with religious sentiment. The styles included fast and slow, spirited, blues, rock and roll, rhythm and blues, and gospel. Using popular songs focused on personal situations and experiences, they dealt with relationships between "actors and objects of action" as they sang with an earthy, rich, textured vocal quality, later known as soul.[70]

The Highlander Folk School in Monteagle, Tennessee, gave the ethos and space for protest song development. Highlander workshops involved adult education and student development as they discussed race and politics. They talked, sang, and focused on creating the tools and the environment for sociopolitical change. Building on local cultural traditions to bring together Blacks and Whites, college students and rural citizens, Highlander helped forge a sound and a sense of the Movement that produced powerful singing leaders.[71]

King and the Role of Women

Many of the powerful singers trained by the Folk School were women, who confronted not only triple oppression from the dominant culture but also gender oppression within the Movement from the "drum major" himself. King understood the power of song, but like most 1960s men living in a patriarchal society that sanctioned women's subordination, he did not see sexism as an evil related to racism. The cultural mores of the day do not justify or excuse King's sexism or his adultery. He expected all wives to stay at home, presuming they were physically and aesthetically suited. In her book *My Life with Martin Luther King Jr.,* Coretta Scott King notes that her husband thought women were equal to men in intelligence and capabilities yet saw his wife only as homemaker and mother to his children. Several mindsets kept sexism out of the agenda: (1) a strong focus on Black male assertiveness; (2) the belief that racism was the culprit of oppression and that Black men needed to lead the programs working for change; and (3) the reality that most Black women either kept silent and/or supported the male agenda. Further, gratitude or commendation for the women in the Movement by King was unwritten and unspoken. He failed to commend grassroots women for their work: Jo Ann Robinson, Mary Fair Burks, and the Women's Political Council for the Montgomery Project; Fannie Lou Hamer for her work in Mississippi; Ella Baker for her dream of a youth protest organization with group-centered leadership (SNCC); or Dorothy Cotton and Septima Clark for their work with the Citizenship Education Program. His sexism softened somewhat eventually, but not to the extent of his historical ancestors who supported women's rights—Frederick Douglass and W. E. B. DuBois.[72] King and SCLC assumed the "Men Led, [and failed to note] Women Organized."[73]

The Strong Black Man

The Movement occurred amid a focus on the strong Black man, which led to angry, articulate, courageous, socially conscious, macho behavior. This behavior led many leaders to discount the presence, concerns, and values of Black women to the point of becoming sexist and chauvinist. Concerning this macho syndrome in Southern Movement leaders and Northern gang culture, King suggested that Black males should move beyond those constructs to a stance of self-sacrifice for the greater good. Many Black men rejected King's leadership and his vision of self-fulfillment because of their own lived realities. King felt men should honor the rights of women since women liberated and transformed the home. He suggested that mothers and wives be responsible individuals without giving up traditional female roles; that fathers and husbands share responsibility and authority with women-folk; that children experience and thereby be taught trust, humanity, and love with their parents; and that family behavior manifest neighborly love, "breadth of life," practicing acceptance, forgiveness, tolerance. Thus marriage ought to build on an ethic of cooperation, respect, mutuality in the daily practical and moral issues of living as community.[74] We take note, however, that King's own lack of personal morality took a back seat to his public ministry.

King's Personal Morality

While we can discern King's theology in his oratory, his sermons did not tell about his adultery or any other sins. They focused on the fragmented nature of life. He categorized sins as intentions and destructive habits and claimed bad habits would destroy self and embarrass society and family as he spoke of sexual impunity in his sermon, "Is the Universe Friendly?" Many sources allege that King's sexual misdeeds threatened to compromise the Civil Rights campaign and his own effectiveness, so much so that aides participated in cover-ups and had difficulty in dealing with the contradiction between King's public and private persona. (King himself chose to obscure the homosexual liaisons and Communist background of his confidant and brilliant tactician, Bayard Rustin.) King was more concerned about exposure than his immorality. These conflicts ultimately led to King's depression and despair. When he preached about despair, he did so without personal conviction and/or confession.[75]

> Like the union of the believer and Christ in medieval mysticism, the spirituality of the sermon's final celebration is often couched in sexual imagery. It is a climax. Its purpose is "rousements." It is intensely pleasurable, and it cannot be faked. . . . Although in his use of the climax King maintains extraordinary facial and bodily composure . . . he too participated in a culture of preaching that understood women as [passive] receptacles of the Word [semen] who are aroused by the eloquence of the speaker. The Movement preachers around him were known to brag about their ability to move "the sisters" to shed their sexual inhibitions [and achieve orgasm,] and King himself occasionally evoked highly sensual congregational response in the [sexual] climax[es] of his sermons.[76]

J. Edgar Hoover, head of the FBI, regarded King as a sexually obsessed reprobate who slept with Black and White women, and he had his minions tape these trysts. An intensely human King could revel in his preacher jokes, tease others, and yet be sensitive and hurt. Troubled by external and internal conflicts, King felt he had not earned the right to lead. He felt guilty, was troubled and angry. The power of his anger was also the power of his love. He cared for Coretta King, but only spent about 10 percent of his time at home. His troubled soul pressed him toward passion, intimacy, and reassurance from other women. King noted that he was not a messiah, nor did his close circle judge him as such. For King, the gospel of love involved *agape* and the erotic admiration of countless numbers of desiring women. He felt guilty about his indiscretions and bemoaned the evils of sensuality, but in times of weakness, King gave in to his personal demons.[77] By 1967, he had major difficulties. The FBI had taped damaging information about his personal life. There were many personality conflicts, arrogance that hurt local relations, and turmoil within SCLC, particularly over "Black Power." Because SCLC hesitated to support him, King kept quiet about creating a peace army and of condemning Vietnam, until 1967.[78] Fortunately, not all Black men are sexist or oppressive in light of America's history of injustice.

Several Black scholars and leaders, like Alexander Crummel, Martin Delany, and Frederick Douglass, have advocated women's liberation. Douglass told the horrors of slavery, was a key advocate of women's rights, never supported Black male misogynism, and was one of three vice presidents of the Americans Equal Rights Association (ERA) in 1866. W. E. B. DuBois supported women's voting rights, connected racism with classism, and said that along with problems of peace and the color line was the uplift of women as socio-political and theological issues. DuBois publicly challenged Black male misogynism, yet he and other nineteenth-century intellectuals still managed to form the American Negro Academy for the Promotion of Literature, Science, and Art and limited membership to males. One of the first in the twentieth century to take public notice against sexism was not Martin King, but theologian James Cone.[79]

Despite his lofty goals and moral ideals for America, King had many adulterous relationships and he plagiarized major portions of his doctoral thesis. While his plagiarism met with tremendous uproar, his philandering is still dismissed because his protest ministry championed a great cause; because society tends to have lower expectations of Blacks; or some think usual ministerial mores should not apply to Black clergy. In January 2000, the American Catholic Bishops submitted the names of King and Oscar Romero to Rome to be listed as "Twentieth Century Christian Martyrs." Ultimately, we eulogize his name for Refining his fiery dream and that "he was the chosen instrument to dance a morally imperative change in our common life," not for his personal virtue; nevertheless, we cannot afford to discount the import of personal morality.[80]

> Drum major, preacher king,
> Refining the Fires of justice and hope—
> Noble one, with dented sword and shield
> From the battering of your own soul against the tide;
> And blessed love of Jesus
> Who says to you,
> Come unto me, you laboring ones; I'll give you rest:
> Your magnificence
> Your foibles, Yourself.

6. Soul Sisters: Girls in Gangs and Sororities

Women, girls, those divas,
Takin' care of bizness,
Building families,
Surrogates, homies, line buddies,
Manifesting community,
Refining the Fires of Friendship.
Secrets, symbols,
Special colors, distinct dress,
Identifying, bonding,
Nobility of one for all.
All for one.
Cliques, groups, peers,
Stepping to their own beats,
Middle class sprawl, ghetto slum
White Flight, Black Night.
Worlds apart and yet the same.

For some, Jesus wore the wrong colors, ate with the wrong people, talked with the wrong women, and crowded the turf of the Pharisee and Saduccee "gangs." Jesus was crucified by the Romans for his trouble. Juliet and Romeo, caught between the Montague and Capulet gangs, were part of a deception that went awry: two lovely teens met unlovely, senseless deaths. In "West Side Story," Maria and Tony, caught between two cultures and two New York youth gangs, the Sharks and the Jets, die young. The expense of untimely deaths Refines the Fires of pain and destruction and collapses social realities and politics. People, social beings who need community and family, will go to great lengths to create groups that provide structure, authority, affirmation, and belonging. Some of these groups are gender specific.

Many females attending public and private high schools and colleges Refine the Fires of engagement as they become members of sororities and get involved in imitative or mimetic acts of socialization and decision making about values, as they follow in the footsteps of mothers, sisters, mentors, and friends. Sororities bond, label, differentiate, mythologize, perform rituals of initiation and behavior, revere symbols, have kindred organizations—auxiliaries and alumnae chapters, and so forth. Sorority women engage in imitative intimacy and rivalry and create a "socially acceptable" surrogate family. Sistah Gang (girl gang) members engage in parallel activities in less visible societal forums. Youth join gangs to fill a social need, a need that may create a family structure, and because they desire protection, power, and recognition and seek a sense of belonging, commitment, and responsibility. Young men and women join groups that afford activity, excitement, training, friendship or companionship, stability, discipline, and love.[1] In addition, sorority and gang sisters have an ethos of secrecy that may or may not intimate sacrality and violence.

This chapter explores the dynamics of soror and sistah imitative or mimetic societies and the levels of internal and external apathy and responsibility, Fires left unrefined by society or family in loving, meaningful ways. After relating their paradigms of meaning and socio-cultural structures, I explore the functions of desire and scapegoating mechanisms; analyze internal and external onus of these two parallel societies; and critique society's response and expectations of sororities and sistah gang members. Only a limited literature deals with sororities; even more scarce and sometimes suspect literature exists on female gangs because of the usual male interpretative stance. Much work remains to be done, hopefully and notably by female interpreters: ". . . Women are more than capable of speaking about and interpreting their own experiences."[2] This chapter explores sororities and sistah gang members in general with a focus on African American sororities, especially Delta Sigma Theta Sorority, Inc., and African American gang sistahs, especially the Five Percent Nation.

African American Sororities

African American sororities include: Alpha Kappa Alpha, Delta Sigma Theta Sorority, Gamma Phi Delta, Sigma Gamma Rho Sorority, and Zeta Phi Beta Sorority. The strong tradition of Black women's clubs (their ethos is discussed in chapter 4) is beyond our purview here but remains important in studying African American women's history of advocacy, protest, education, and empowerment; historically significant organizations include the National Association of Colored Women's Clubs and National Association of Negro Business and Professional Women. When the term *national* is part of a group's name, while another group with a similar affinity uses the term *American* (such as the National Medical Association versus American Medical Association), usually *national* connotes a predominantly Black group while an *American* group is predominantly White. In addition to sorors, sistahs, and Black women's groups, there are less formal associations such as the Five Percent Nation, which sees itself as a cultural and religious movement geared toward teaching young African Americans the correct ways of Islamic life.

Despite this stated purpose, the New York City Police Department catego-
rizes the Five Percent Nation as a street gang.[3]

Society often dismisses, denigrates, and demonizes women. Professional,
socio-cultural, academic, and religious organizations tend to reflect these attitudes by marginalizing women's issues and contributions. When topics shift
from theory to praxis, women's experiences are sublimated or subsumed within
a male-dominant context. Religious institutions often ignore the created mutuality in Genesis 1 and the reconciling litany of Galatians 3, which transcend the
need for negative imitative desire and envy related to race/sex/class. They listen
instead to the singular voice of Genesis 3, in which the expulsion, not a Fall
from Eden, states men are to rule over women. Genesis 1 invites hopefulness,
reciprocity, and new possibilities. For some interpreters, Genesis 3 authenti-
cates, validates, and celebrates the inferior assessment and treatment of women.
Many strive to confine female participation to menial jobs or sentence women to
"hard time" in the home, without a spiritual, psycho-socio-economic appreciation for the rigors of being "just" a housewife. Despite these constraints, women
Refine the Fires of self-actualization, camaraderie, and the joy of wholeness, particularly in shared group support systems, like sororities and sistah gangs.

Gangs Defined: Then and Now

Gangs, from lawless American frontier kinship bands and 1920s organized
criminal racketeering clubs with female gun molls to modern industrial,
inner-city counter-culture cliques, involve "secret" groups of persons geared
toward ongoing criminal activity. A gang is a group of individuals, collective
identities, or personalities who willingly use deadly force to seize territory,
assault rival gangs, steal or exhort money, and engage in group orchestrated
crime; it names itself and is perceived as a deadly or dangerous presence. The
gang generates violence; violence defines the situation, in relation to gang
diversity, situationality, functionality, and fluidity.

Risk factors that often coalesce as a catalyst for a person adopting a gang
lifestyle include experiencing a dysfunctional community and family; lacking
strong educational background and training; lacking conflict resolution techniques; facing racism in a nonsupportive environment without networking;
and being influenced by the media. The presence of graffiti that mark turf
may push some individuals to identify with that particular gang.[4] Yet some
talented youth from loving, secure settings may choose a gang lifestyle after
catastrophic events, from parental death and loss of attention to the confus-
ing experiences of adolescence, which often fosters angry rebellion.[5] Consider
Patricia Hearst's affiliation with a terrorist gang, which led to bank robbery
and the murder of a grandmother at the bank. This vast spectrum demon-
strates the complexity of gangs and gang membership.

Gangs and Sororities: Catalysts of Culture

Gangs, refiners of identity and power, are both a result and a symptom of the moral, spiritual, economic, and structural crises we face, evident in the gang members' blatant disregard for others' lives and property. Social greed, obtrusive consumerism, social injustice, and idolatrous practices have manifested in disintegrated community, spiritual degradation, and violence.[6] The gang problem is not only "their" problem, but also our problem. Structurally, gangs differentiate along age, gender, and class lines and often have multiple, informal leadership styles.[7] Gangs have permanent features that transcend gang generations and individual gang friends and are pliable, dynamic, and kaleidoscopic. Steeped in a culture grounded by specific connotations, talk, meaning, context, and social structure, in which distinct values develop, gang culture emerges within the social location of violence, patterns of violence, and the gang's own internal logic.[8] The Manson gang with its David Koresh/Jonestown charismatic leader is not atypical.

Sorority culture serves as a catalyst for campus socio-political life. Sororities are honorary, professional, or social "secret" organizations (similar to Skull and Bones) comprised of female college or university students. Social sororities Refine the Fires of love and hospitality as they provide a home away from home, a sense of belonging and empowerment, and a construct for development and maturation. Sororities create sisterhoods that share themselves and college life, giving their members an immediate set of friends and a national network of sisters. This sisterhood involves lifetime membership, shared goals and rituals, and an institutional milieu created by women and for women that promotes love, commitment to societal good, friendship, and womanhood. Sororities provide a forum in which women can develop and learn how to live with and in support of others. This society within a society, like girl gangs, is complex and involves responsibility and perseverance.[9]

Dual Dimensions of Love and Power

The sisterhoods of sororities and girl gangs have paradigms of meaning and socio-cultural, hierarchical, relational structures that concern purpose, perceptions, and power constructs. Dual dimensions of love and power, affiliation and dominance, warmth and control undergird these structures and shape the orientations of people and their tasks.[10] While men tend toward power constructs, women are said to look for love and intimacy. Love and intimacy create purpose, which empowers women as they engage in diverse social intercourse. Society commonly sees a sorority as an elite, partying, and service group whose values and public persona make membership desirable. Sororities symbolize success, professional clout, and upwardly mobile class consciousness. For society, girl gangs epitomize the undesirable, the extreme other, the predator—the antithesis of the supposed "virtuous womanhood"

(Proverbs 31). An individual's perception of sororities and sistah gangs reflects his or her social location and historical knowledge.

Female or Sistah Gangs

Although males comprise the majority of gang memberships, females are often auxiliary members of male-dominated gangs or belong to all-women gangs. Males outnumber female gang members 20 to 1 due to psychological or geographical area, gang activities, gang recruitment efforts, and police pressures; females tend to join gangs later and leave earlier than males. Females commit about 5 percent or less of the crimes committed by gangs.[11] Sistahs engage in power struggles and violence in large urban settings like New York, Chicago, Los Angeles, Detroit, and Philadelphia; criminologists are unclear as to why some cities have girl gangs and others do not. Girl gangs form around the common denominators of race, neighborhood/city, residential proximity, language, social class, and so forth.[12]

The male-dominated literature tends to view sistah gang members, who are typically in their early teens to early twenties, as sex objects who flaunt their sexuality to gain male attention or tomboys who deny their "feminini-ty" by donning male attire and sporting more aggressive street names, mov-ing to succeed in male terms. Joyce Carol Oates's novel, *Foxfire: Confessions of a Girl Gang,* about an adolescent girl gang during the 1950s and 1960s, por-trays her lead character in a masculine, sometimes androgynous guise. This novel poignantly reflects concern over memory and ontological oppression: "What is memory but the repository of things doomed to be forgotten, so you must have history. . . . First comes fear, then respect . . . the oppressed of the Earth, rising, taking their own law."[13] Male gang researchers tend to focus on sexuality as a means of reform, a rejection of social values, or a management issue. Because gender, race, and poverty or class shape self-identity,[14] sistah gang members, stigmatized by these markers, may reject female subordina-tion and identify with and join both male and all-girl gangs to secure protec-tion and security for themselves and their children. Girl or sistah gang mem-bers rationalize violence as a method or tool out of a need for what violence can accomplish for them or as a denial of responsibility. In sum, sistah gangs Refine the Fires of self-actualization and status by engaging in criminal activ-ity, while varying in sophistication, motives, intent, economic assets, and social location.

Structurally, sistah gangs form groupings that range from street, social, or corporate-type organizations to religio-cultural societies. The makeup of sis-tah gangs may vary, as in male-dominated gangs, with community conser-vatism or tolerance; societal (police and citizen) input; socio-political, eco-nomic, and ethical climate and place; multilayered cultural traditions and customs.[15] While viewed as law-breaking youth groups, sistah gangs provide a sense of home away from home and belonging, empowerment, and a means for development and maturation.

Sororities and Sistah Gangs: A Socio-Historical Review
Sororities

Sororities evolved seventy-five years after the beginning of Phi Beta Kappa, the first social fraternity or male secret society to use Greek letters, established December 1776 at the College of William and Mary. The first sorority, the Adelphean, later named Alpha Delta Pi, began in 1851. The first African American sororities, Alpha Kappa Alpha and Delta Sigma Theta, began at Howard University in the 1912–1913 school year. These Black women Refined the Fire of sisterhood as they embraced the scholarly, inspirational, and fraternal Greek ideals to support social freedom from racist and sexist oppression amid academic excellence, community service, and social uplift.[16] Deltas initiated a familial context of friendship, in which other sorors pursued scholastic excellence in nontraditional areas; suffrage to delete disenfranchisement; and social activism—including anti-lynching advocacy—while providing social, political, emotional, and practical support. A sorority house, for example, provided necessary, affordable housing and quiet study areas. On White campuses, dormitory housing was off-limits to minority and non-Gentile students; at historically Black campuses, housing was often limited and off-campus residential lodgings too costly.[17] To enhance collegiality, African American sororities stressed high student GPAs, bolstered morale and social health, and gained national status.

Some campuses welcomed a Greek presence, but some feared the imitative desire galvanized by the process of "rushing"; the campaign for increased membership and the accompanying financial, moral, and academic costs for enhanced social life would be prohibitive. Some campuses saw the Greek presence as good mimesis, leading to relational love. From their founding to the present, Black sororities focus on a mimesis that Refines the Fire of uplift in academics, social life, community service, and socio-political protest. Their organizational structure accommodates a national service agenda and sisterhood[18] that sustains their visions and goals. (This national sisterhood structurally includes national and regional offices, campus and alumnae chapters, high school and adult non-college women auxiliaries.)

Sorority membership cannot erase the reality of an individual's Blackness nor her femaleness, factors that for some are a license to abuse or exclude, often on the basis of lighter or darker skin hues. Are Black sororities perpetrators of what they abhor, exclusivity instead of inclusion? Black sororities may be exclusive in membership, but not always exclusive in vision. My limited survey of a few sorority members revealed that midst their many secret rituals, oaths, colors, symbols, and membership process, Black sororities have a basic desire to form lifelong social bonds with like-minded students and to serve the public. Many resulting friendships between women would otherwise not occur because of the diverse scholastic majors, hometowns, and campus sizes. These sisters Refine the Fires of self-development and group unity as they garner identity, pride, diversity, and character, while championing a sisterhood called to community service, stability, and empowerment.[19]

Additional preliminary conversations with members from three different Black sororities in April 1995 substantiated these findings. These respondents attended both historically Black institutions and historically White campuses. Some were charter members of their Black sorority chapters; others joined long-established chapters. Most respondents joined out of a commitment to community service. Other factors included being invited, family traditions, supportive environments, and stability. Most respondents viewed organizational ritual and history as critical and found sorority structure to be meaningful, supportive, and constructive. Pledge or initiation periods and the response to the hazing question varied. Hazing implies ridicule, derision, censure, mockery, mimicry, disrespect, and indignity, when initiates are harassed with meaningless, difficult, or humiliating tasks in order to join a sorority or fraternity. Some interviewees did experience hazing. Some saw hazing but did not equate it with acts of violence. Some did not see or experience hazing at all. The question of hazing became one of definition. Since the purpose of the pledge period is to effect team building in a short period of time, exercises in dressing alike, studying together, walking in formation, and so forth were a source of pride, of being chosen, of proclaiming to the outside world that they were part of the elect and select.

Most respondents viewed the pledge period as a time of growth: value systems expanded, and they uncovered strengths and weaknesses, developed individual strengths, worked as a team, enhanced leadership skills, and became less selfish and more giving. During the pledge period some respondents improved academically, while some stayed the same; for others, grades deteriorated as social skills were enhanced. Most respondents were satisfied with their sorority's level of political activity. The most memorable events were positive experiences that created an extended family, provided support during an emotional crisis, and celebrated the evening they "went over," that is, became a full-fledged sorority member.

Most respondents stated that the tensions within an established sorority are the same found in any group in which people have different opinions and experiences. Some experienced intense competition instead of collaboration. The majority did not cite a devastating experience. One exception was the death of a soror a year after graduation. All respondents would join the sorority again to experience the joys of service to others and the bonding and organizational support for Black women available through sororities—an undying sisterhood.

Sistah Gangs

Sistah gang members also have a power structure and seek sisterhood—that is, a sense of belonging forged by a desire to be included. Sistah gang members emerged with the first male gangs in the mid-nineteenth century. Gangs began during the immigration process, with the development and expansion of this country. Intense immigration produced local social clubs in large urban centers with male and female members. These clubs, run by middle-class professionals, Refined the Fires of building community and creating economic strategies, as they provided acculturation techniques and encouraged immigrants to speak English. Some youth resented this activity and saw the process as an invalidation of their culture; this view is understandable, since America has never been a "melting pot" but an assimilation process dominated by the White-male perspective.

Gangs spring from a childhood quest for excitement in the midst of poverty, minimal parental supervision, and failed acculturation, and influenced by organized crime, desired success and affluence, and a lack of resources and skills to attain the "American mimetic dream,"[20] a dream deferred for sistah gang members. Sometimes the dream metamorphoses into a nightmare—when teens assume gang behavioral traits. Contemporary gang practices include drug and alcohol use, violence, coded behavior, and symbolic events that Refine the Fires of imagination and making do by coping with urban life while in search of stability and identity.[21] Their front (dress, talk, gestures), street rituals (initiation, gang warfare), and symbols (tattoos, colors, graffiti) comprise a major politic of identity for vulnerable youth. A complex, multilayered atmosphere gives birth to and maintains gangs with street pressures and group identification methods and processes located in mainly urban settings.[22]

Despite American culture, which prescribes double standards as key to male and female identity and action, women can be and often are as violent as men in a gang-related social milieu. Strong, capable sistah gang members, like their male counterparts, live by a code of materialism, violence, and illegal drugs.[23] Shattered, deferred, forgotten dreams meld with imitation, angst, violence, support, and affirmation, often shaped by their race.

African American gangs coexist with Mexican American gangs on the same territory, especially in California. Territory is the space in which gang members deal in illegal goods and services and where they "hang out." Members have strong emotional ties to their gangs—their "homies"—and great animosity toward their rivals; their main focus is making money. Taking drugs results in sanctions in Black gangs because the practice inhibits one's ability to sell drugs for profit.

Black gangs may have no set structure or may have a vertical/hierarchical model with a board and cliques or branches or an influential horizontal/commission model. The catalyst for organizational structure may be the solidarity with their neighborhood or a charismatic leader. In sum, Black gangs tend to have large groupings, sell drugs, have a territorial imperative, be business oriented, be attached to homeboys and their set, and have a fluid organizational structure.[24] They are transfamilial social organizations that may include female roles, which are not always grasped and appreciated by male gang members, who often want girls to remain in subservient positions.[25]

Barrio (Hispanic, Latina, or Mexican) sistah gang culture differs slightly from Black sistah gang culture. In Barrio culture, young girls have always stayed around male gang members or street boys, as the boys often drink, get high, and fight. Sometimes both boys and girls participate in social or car clubs; in the last two decades, more girls have joined street gangs.

Cholo, the word used by some Latin American Indians who have Hispanic-based elite cultural roots, refers to a Latina gang and pertains to Mexican American cultural shifting situations in the southwestern United States. Usually barrio youths with troubled lives and in-depth street experience join gangs. Although early on female barrio gang membership was not considered respectable, today "the dialectic of multiple marginality applies to why females conduct their own gang-banging actions against rival barrio female members."[26] That is, a contemporary female gang-affiliated member is similar to an active male gang member in the 1940s. *Cholas,* or Hispanic/Latino/Mexican sistah gang members, are part of a cohesive, intricate, important though subordinate infrastructure of male barrio gangs. Wherever a male barrio gang member goes, his female counterpart is with him. Like with other gang participants, a cohesiveness emerges from the external negative forces, not from an internal positive ambiance. Joining a *cholo* is a process of acculturation, of participating as part of the whole community and assuming its ethics and politics. Barrio gang sistahs live within a value system that Refines the Fire of violence.[27]

Black Women in Sistah Gangs

Black sistah gang members are our children: our daughters, nieces, girlfriends, mothers of our children, the guardians and keepers of our future. Why has gang membership become attractive to many young Black girls? Gang activity appeals because these females feel neglected, lost, and abandoned by society. The gang lifestyle is the only way they feel they can Refine the Fires of achievement. The contemporary focus on materialism and individualism has fostered exclusion, fear, anxiety, hopelessness, and a lack of vision for the future. In African American culture and in society in general, the focus on the endangered Black male has left Black females distressed, ignored, and in dysfunctional environments. Such young Black females often find sistah gang life attractive. Young Black females sense abandonment from general society and Black leaders when they become victims of psychological and emotional abuse, incest, domestic violence, and rape.[28]

The plight of these young Black women, a scenario of silent suffering and pain, often results in therapeutic pregnancies; that is, they seek healing, love, and comfort through having a baby. Too often the lack of support and cognizance of their realities causes these young women, isolated by pregnancy, age, poverty, race, and gender, to be hostile and wounded within their own psyche and self-esteem. The fruit of their predicament emerges in the contemporary crack epidemic and violence. Addictions to crack cocaine and heroin, prostitution, AIDS, and the phenomenon of "babies raising babies" reflect the hurt, hopelessness, and broken hearts of these young Black females. They have adopted the hip-hop culture with pride and defiance. Hip-hop has afforded them a more public persona. Consequently, they have begun to mark their territory of men and space, to get into the drug trade, and to carry weapons, especially in the inner cities.[29] The context and depth of these experiences become clear when reviewing various experiential profiles.

The family life profile[30] of many girl gang members typically involves a large family with siblings who are also gang members; experiencing poverty, teen pregnancy, public assistance, and gang activity is normal. Sistahs rely on boyfriends, who are often gang members, for additional monetary help, and they rely on extended family until the next paycheck arrives. Sistahs pay close attention to personal hygiene and appearance for themselves and their children.

Sistah gang members tend to have behavioral or discipline problems at school, including suspensions, reprimands, and detentions. They tend to fail academically and do not attend college because of substance abuse and their dating profiles. Sistahs frequently use illegal drugs and drink alcohol, but they distinguish between recreational drug usage and addiction. The gang disapproves of habitual substance abuse and demands that gang members reform by getting clean. Most sistahs date boys who do drugs and often physically abuse them, and they usually marry gang members of their own race. Multiracial gangs, male and female, are almost nonexistent. In the Five Percent Nation, sistahs are "earth," support equality, and seek to have babies by the male members, their boyfriends, the "gods." The Five Percent Nation has an orchestrated catechism that relays members' duties and responsibilities via Islamic history of physical and symbolic facts about the universe, especially the expected behavior of a good Muslim woman. This quasi-religious relational structure does not alter their focus on materialism, toughness, and violence.[31]

Two Girl Gangs

Two girl gangs from New York vary in their numbers, purpose, and level of violence. The Deceptanets, a fifty-member group based outside of Crown Heights, New York, emerged from Graphic Arts High School in 1985. They wear jeans and Reebok tennis shoes and pull their hair back. These vicious gang sistahs carry mace, needles, and razors as weapons in their activities of robbing girls and victimizing subway commuters. They may stick a needle in the victim while they take his or her wallet. The Deceptanets, like the Brownsville Girls, recruit new members from schools.

The Brownsville Girls, begun in 1991 in and near Crown Heights, have roughly twenty-five members who dress with a neat and conservative flair, wearing blouses, slacks, and Timberland boots. These sistahs emerged out of need for defense—to protect themselves from other girl gangs. Their weapons of choice are razors. They do not instigate violence, but they will hurt others as their mode of defense. These girls do not go to school.[32] Other profile patterns of sistah gang members include violent socialization, combative personality, and mimetic motivation and maturation.

Sistah Gangs and Crime

Sistah gang members sometimes carry weapons, have previously been involved in fights, participate in gang violence, have shot a gun, and most often have a permanent tattoo. They do not see victimless offenses as wrong even if they are illegal, for criminals are either crazy or offenders. For example, Carla did not define a drive-by as immoral, even if that drive-by resulted in a person's death:

> "You don't see what happens. You just pull up, blam, blam, blam, and you're gone. Maybe you hit someone, maybe not. It's not like you aim at someone in particular. . . ."
>
> "But if someone gets shot in the heart, they're just as dead as if you did it looking them in the eye, aren't they?"
>
> "It's not murder," Carla insists. "I can't believe you don't understand this. If you don't see it happen, how can it be murder? . . . But let me tell you this. If my brother did get shot, I'd have to go out looking for who did it. I'd have to get revenge. . . . And I know that wouldn't be murder."
>
> . . . "If it wasn't murder, Carla, what would it be?"
>
> Carla smiles. "Justice."[33]

Violence and a Sistah's Personality

Refining the Fire of violence underlies a sistah's personality. She usually knows the label of deviance from others and does not trust other people. She will not back down from a fight and thinks she can stand her own against a beating like any male. She may sense a need to break things, to fight first and talk later. Talk and language usage are weapons. Sistah gang members, like academicians, lawyers, and others have learned that language cuts to the quick, humiliates, and destroys (see chapter 8). Imitative behavior shapes a sistah's attraction to this lifestyle because the gang provides action, excitement, popularity, family, and friends. The gang secures her activities and territory, confrontation of other gangs, a home, marijuana, protection, and conversation. In this environment, a sistah goes from being a "young girl" to "street-wise" to an experienced "old head." Membership accords respect, a reputation, and proficiency, often in deadly violence. Joining a gang is usually easy and may or may not require an initiation. The new sistah gang member must prove that she can uphold the gang's philosophy and heighten their reputation.[34]

Sex and Sistah Gangs

A sistah's maturation includes a sex behavioral profile, signifying image and activity. Sex is only one interaction of sistahs with male gang members. Male members may impose concepts of "sex object" or "tomboy." With some Puerto Rican sistah gang members in New York, a healthy identity includes being a responsible mother, practicing serial monogamy, and rejecting marianismo (female subordination).[35] Certain sistahs take the role of "sex object," some only have sex with boyfriends, and others totally abstain. Gang members carefully scrutinize and shun sexual promiscuity; most support serial monogamy in which girls are expected to sleep with their steady partners. Both males and females reject "loose" girls or "ho's." Female levels of participation in coed gangs shape the level of sexual activity. Some male gangs have no female members. Some gangs are solely female, like the "Holly Ho's" (whores) of Philadelphia.[36] Some females who identify with such groups call themselves crews.

Crews and posses

Crews or posses are self-identified groups of loosely linked youth without real hierarchies, defined turfs, or loyalties. Women belong to coed and female-only crews. Female crew members avoid picking names, although they "tag," tease, and intimidate others to gain control and live life to its capacity, and they fight men and women to protect themselves, although they tend not to initiate violence. Crews as family do not want to see their sisters hurt, and they guarantee a sister respect. Without respect on the street, a sister is a target for harassment and victimization. While some crew formation is not inherently violent, a crew protects itself and has control and territory. Crews, unlike gangs, usually do not fight over colors but will fight over territory. Violence, a means for acquiring respect, assures personal safety on the street and economic stability when legitimate channels fail.[37]

Gang violence includes rituals against other gangs (drive-bys, gangbangs) and violence against non-gang members (robberies by threat or actual force; extortion of school children and businesses, assaults, and rape). Rarely are rapes by gang members reported by the victims.[38] Subjecting another to violence becomes a means of reducing the frustration from anything that encumbers—rejection, authority figures' attitudes, and the abyss that occurs when other symbols fail to work.

> My answer to all of the frustration is to do what I do [violence]. And I feel good, I can't deny it. I wish I could change it, 'cause I know it's bad . . . 'cause I was brought up by my grandmother. She brought me up strictly Catholic, through the Church, and I say, God, please help me, but he [*sic*] can't. There's no other way for me to relieve the frustration. Or no other way suitable for me.[39]

Crews may form themselves as a group as early as third grade. The crew consists of people deemed trustworthy who will react when accosted. If a crew member fails the trustworthy test by not helping another crew member, she will get jumped, often through name calling. Drugs provide a sense of being in control midst countless problems: sex, lack of understanding, or a desire for everything. Many crew members believe contemporary teenagers have more problems than older people, especially since they want things they cannot have and have problems with family and boyfriends. Appearance is essential, and boyfriends may provide little things for them by selling drugs. While the crew may appear to be a support system with a positive direction, the girl crew sees no contradiction in the fact that their boyfriends sell drugs, because these accessible guys do not addictively use drugs. Sometimes the girls hold drugs or weapons for the guys because male police tend not to conduct body searches on female gang members.[40]

Crew members are honest about their activity and have a tough persona, though often weak regarding boyfriend-girlfriend relationships. Crew members want to be loved by someone other than their parents and friends; they want a sexual partner. These girls are tough with their peer group and "trust the crew more than [they] trust any guy."[41] While they wonder about life and death and have friends who have died violently, they get tired of living a threatened existence. Conversely, many of them would not think twice about doing violence. They are stressed and depressed about Refining the Fire of violence, but do not see that their acts of violence are "bad." Many lack self-esteem and know hate. Girl crews use deadly weapons and conversation to intimidate and to communicate; they have a sense of family and know how to be calm and look out for each other.

The God Question for Gang Members

Many gang and crew members experience a great deal of anger, and part of that anger is directed at God. For example, since God put people on earth, why would God allow babies to die so young?[42] The God question comes up for female and male gang members in a variety of ways:

> "God made me so that I could learn how to commit crimes," he fin-ishes. "What's some judge or some probation officer gonna do?"
>
> I see he is looking directly at me now with those dark eyes, an old man's eyes in a sixteen-year-old's face. . . . There is nothing more sad than the sight of hopelessness in one so young. It is a look . . . reflected in every boy's face in the room.
>
> "God made me so I could do terrible things," Elias says. "Why couldn't God help me learn how to be a father?"[43]

That boys ages fourteen through sixteen in the juvenile justice system ask such questions is not surprising. Elias never changed. He loathed the system, missed school, did drugs, and was in and out of county-run boot camps. His best friend died in his arms; his grandmother was murdered; an uncle went to jail. Elias finally desired a future, accompanied with normality and responsi-bility: he was arrested as an accomplice to murder three days before he became a father.[44] Violence had become as unconscious and normal as breath-ing. Adults do not understand these young people's world. Everyone has guns, and guns bring loyalty, honor, and an ethos bigger than themselves.[45] For male gang members, sistah gang members, and crew members, violence is critical, but so is bonding. Females Refine the Fires of affirmation and a sys-tem of domination, an ethos, a spirituality, a religious obligation unto death, wherein might makes right.[46]

Imitative Activity of Sororities, Gangs, and Crews

The worlds of sororities, gangs, and crews are rife with desire and scapegoat-ing—imitative activity. Many African American college women desire mem-bership in an organization that helps others and empowers them. Many gang sistahs and crew members desire membership in an organization that accords them protection and respect. The desire is imitative in that a soror or gang sistah has a desire that imitates the desire of another—that is, to have the rights and privileges of membership. Since the closer people become, the greater the mimetic desire becomes, the questions arise: Does increased desire in these two settings lead to intense rivalry and violence?[47] Does desire for this membership result in conflict over a scarce resource or in loss of identity? Does the desire collapse, with the desire shifting focus from being like the other to being the other? Does the desire intensify to a point that violence or intentional harm and intrusion on another's dignity occur, thus creating an environment of love-hate relationships or destruction? Does that violence threaten human survival, toward a violence of differentiation that causes alienation and separation, or forced conformity?[48]

Mimetic Intimacy

In my research and conversations with sorority members, African American sorors seem to move toward Thee Smith's notion of mimetic intimacy, which gratifies desire, embraces the other, and experiences mimetic transformation.[49] Mimetic desire becomes creative as a good mimesis[50] takes the form of community and channels human behavior and desire to benefit self and others. The desire for sorority membership does not result in conflict, unless the selection process of who does or does not get accepted for the pledge class creates a sense of scarcity. The respondents note that shared desire enhanced their self-esteem and ability to be team players without a loss of identity. Conversely, those instances where hazing becomes ridicule that seeks to censure, mock, impose indignity, or harass are bad imitation and collapse a relational mimetic format and process of subject, model, and object to an intense rivalry between members and pledges, Refining the Fires of pain, humiliation, and objectification. Such imitation violates the pledge's personhood, eradicating difference by forcing ultra conformity, where power becomes absolute, corrupting member and pledge. In public service efforts, sororities unmask the bad mimesis incurred through oppression and sometimes expose the scapegoat mechanism, in which African Americans have been oppressed due to race, class, and gender.

African American sororities also participate in public education and empowerment. Their interests include the empowerment of Black women, affirmative action, and civil and human rights. Individual and community well-being issues are related to employment training, socio-economic equity and development, poverty, teenage pregnancy, child care, domestic violence, families, comprehensive health care, AIDS awareness, community service, leadership development, and voter education. Historically, sororities have also worked on Black college development, career planning, counseling, grants, mentoring, international affairs, the arts, youth training and higher education, affordable housing, women in business, leadership development, advocacy, and strengthening families.[51] The questions remain: Do the public service activities of sororities and other like-minded groups allow our society to continue to scapegoat the "other" via racism, classism, and sexism? When will "they" become "we"?[52] Can good imitation or mimesis transcend an apparent social need to be cruel, to control, to scapegoat?

In my sistah gang research, personal interviews have not yet been possible. In response to my initial queries in the Research Triangle of North Carolina, state, county, and city officials claimed girl gangs were nonexistent, although evidence seemed to be emerging to the contrary. Research from such interviews, however, shows that the lines of demarcation between good and bad imitative behavior blurs.

Sistah gangs operate out of imitative desire and generative violence: they want to be like those with privilege. Their complex existence in a world that denies their reality often subsumes much of how the myth of redemptive violence occurs in television cartoons, comic books, the vigilantism of class Westerns, and the seduction, lying, stealing, illegality, and murder of spy thrillers.[53] Violence is the means to attaining the ends of physical and socio-economic security. Losing security and personal priorities make some gang activity more temporary than others. Increased desire may arise within the group; other times desire between gangs leads to rivalry and violence. Desire for sistah gang membership often results in conflict over the level of respect one receives and over the scarcity of money and power to have what one wants. Sistahs have to deal with frustrations, with anger that comes from living in the ghetto and seeing no options. Shared desire that creates enhanced communal identity may or may not collapse into the double-bind where the desire shifts from being like the other to being the other. The desire intensifies to the point that violence or intentional harm and intrusion on a crime victim occur. Sometimes realizing her powerlessness overwhelms a gang member, increasing the anger and appetites for destruction, which threaten the perpetrator's survival and that of all of society.[54]

> By the time boys are twenty-one, most will be disabled, in prison, or dead. We need to learn new skills for the future—have our own meetings and operations, defend our own neighborhood. Home girls pack weapons. . . . Women don't use weapons to prove a point. Women use weapons for love.[55]

Internal and External Onus: Society's Response and Expectations

Sororities and sistah gang members see themselves as viable entities with a sense of identity and mission and an inherent allegiance to their sisters. Both use words that express solidarity, care, and respect. Sorors, during the pledge period and afterwards, continue to have a bond. Some graduates join alumnae chapters and remain active. Others become inactive but will automatically identify with members of their sorority. Ideally, campus chapters enhance the student's academic and social career and instill a sense of responsibility for the entire Black community's empowerment. Those chapters that act irresponsibly have violated persons and caused damage. Some sorors appear to be elitist, excluding those outside academic or community life and politics. Some in the community disregard sorors' positive contributions or place them on a pedestal and do not take them seriously. Sorority members may become a scapegoat for those with an anti-intellectual spirit, as they deny and ridicule the members' hard work and contributions by projecting the anti-intellectual's failure back onto the sorority. Generally, the Black community applauds accomplishments of Black sororities. Those college students that remain independent often do so because of time constraints, a need for independence, and perceptions (real or imagined) of hazing, financial investment, and different personal values and goals.

Sistah gang members often provide a haven for females who experience a sense of rootlessness. The gang provides respect, goals, and responsibilities. With a male-dominated interpretation, society often scapegoats female and male gang members and makes them "other" as it denigrates and blames gangs for societal ills. Sometimes females also receive the blame for the dissension within predominantly male gangs.

My goal is not to romanticize female gang activity, but to call others to take seriously sistah gang reality when dealing with the issues of crime, welfare reform, and the reclamation of inner cities. Often society views sistah gang members as a homogenized criminal element, making it easy to buy up ghetto areas and buy into gentrification: bulldoze property and build condos that almost no middle-income person and certainly no low-income person can afford. The American public's ability to slough off the deaths and degradation that amass from drug usage emphasizes the demonizing of illicit drug use, ignoring the reality of suburban clientele's involvement in the drug trade and the equal opportunity, tax-free drug economy. Drug selling in decayed, depressed neighborhoods results from the isolated apartheid of the inner city, of the silent majority, of the mothers, daughters, sisters that remain nameless and faceless. This dangerous, ignored underworld grows and provides employment for those who daily live in and around this culture. Does the vile reality that guns give females a security blanket in a hazardous environment make them criminals or deviants?[56]

Such environments challenge the morality and spirituality of this country towards a transformative, liberative invitation to embrace each other as neighbor. Our problems are complex, and real solutions can only come from understanding a connectedness between structural destruction and self-destruction. Respect must outweigh consumerism; the politics of community must embody conversion and transformative justice to override the politics of meaning. Using Mohandas K. Gandhi's seven social sins—politics without principle, wealth without work, commerce without morality, pleasure without conscience, education without character, science without humanity, and worship without sacrifice—we can begin to see the relationship between our public lives and our ethics.[57]

Gang Summits

This connection between public life and personal ethics had a role to play in the events of the 1993 gang summits in Los Angeles and Kansas City. When gang members first came together to talk truce, the air was ripe with suspicion, tempered by cautious hope. Many of these youth, who had plundered and murdered, looked young and enigmatically vulnerable. Female and male gang members spoke of the need to come together to stop fighting and, using the metaphor of slavery to make their point, they discussed their lack of trust in the dominant culture that continues to degrade them. They spoke of the familial relationships of gangs simultaneously with their sense of betrayal by the system that continuously told them if they did well, stayed in school, got a job, they could be successful. Some had tried, and they could find no legitimate work. Many gang members abhor being reduced to selling drugs; they do not import drugs, but they do need to support their families.[58] To date no public policy has confronted the reality that for many inner-city communities, dealing drugs is the only equal opportunity employer. In a spirit of good will and hope, gang leaders began to network toward the fruition of the National Urban Peace and Justice Summit, April 29 through May 2, 1993.

The summit session, closed to the media, Refined the Fires of conversion and spirituality. The media was banned because participants felt they were hostile, and the participants did not want cameras and lights present during serious proceedings. Gangbangers, preachers, and politicians met in a milieu of "strategy session, prayer meeting, and family reunion all in one."[59] In a call for counterrevolution and love, a Crip and a Blood, from Los Angeles's most hostile and violent gangs, came to the pulpit, confessed their year-long attempts to murder each other, dropped their colors, and embraced each other amid tears. Barrio and ghetto gang members lamented the failure of religious and secular systems to provide meaningful assistance. On the anniversary of the first Rodney King verdict, 126 former and current gang members of our nation's most powerful gangs and 53 observers from 26 states met on a platform to stop the killing. The diversity of geographic origin and social place merged in the commonality of pain.

The platform called for Refining the Fire of just equality via a reduction in the many kinds of violence: gang-related, underfunded schools, degrading media portrayal of minorities, and the media's lack of positive images of those deemed other. The summit was "not about just ending gang-related violence so white people in the suburbs could feel safer. It was about stopping the senseless killing, so people could get on with rebuilding their own communities."[60] Many present decried the simplicity of the "just say no" policy, when youthful drug dealers can support an extended family of thirty people with their earnings, while they otherwise would have to take a menial job in fast foods. The conference involved priests, prophets, and rulers from the Christian, Muslim, and Native American communities; the daily opening and closing prayers called for respect and community and repeated the mantras of self-control, self-esteem, self-respect.[61]

A most profound, unexpected gift was the female presence, almost one-third of the attendees, particularly in a moment of potential impasse. The Sisters of the Summit, who brought hopeful stories of change, were not involved in the planning of the summit. Most males expected them to sit quietly. In a dramatic, liberating moment, all the women walked out of the room to meet together—a ritual of feminist empowerment triggering global new beginnings. They returned with a statement, prepared to take responsibility alongside—not behind—their brothers.[62] The sistahs read a statement that named their roles, called for equality, denounced any possibility of them being silenced, named their experiences of violence, insisted on being part of advisory boards, and celebrated their strength, intelligence, and love. Their call for a unifying effort changed the summit. The women told stories of their street experiences, of carrying guns, of seeing people die. They recounted their experiences in the women's caucus where they cried and shared their pain—the pain of what was happening to their brothers and their hurt that their brothers have no similar way to deal with their pain. They asked that the brothers apologize for the pain and suffering they had meted out to the women. The bonding and sharing between older and younger women flowed out to their brothers, and their experience became a loving politics of empowerment.[63] The outcome of the summit would have been different if sistahs had not been present and had not participated. As long as we deny the presence of sistahs and the potential for Refining the Fire of transformation, society will scapegoat them and call for the building of more, bigger, better jails.

The Value of Girls and Women

Sorority and sistahs participate in imitation, good and bad. But each girl and woman has value, is priceless, and cannot be replaced. Many sistahs are not fearful, because their plight has already been so painful, so deadly, in neighborhoods rife with drive-bys, crack houses, open drug markets, poverty, pestilence, disproportionate child mortality, joblessness, and crime. Women become silenced, incognito, incommunicado:

> All that wacked out shit 'bout "just say no" is tricks. Welfare is for silly ho's; I make my own way. Later for welfare checks and case workers. Out here it's way you make it, girls got to understand that it's up to you. One thang is for certain, nobody gives a shit 'bout me; nobody cares. Education is what I got from all the teachers, case workers, all the niggahs coming out of the joint begging. . . . Begging out gets ya nuthing. I got mines, it's the dope, it's the only bank that lets a girl get straight.[64]

Such destruction does not have to be the reality. Carla learned she had options. She served her time in juvenile facilities and made the transition from the gang lifestyle. She learned how to get over, she learned to utter parroted responses, but she also reflected that the Carlas of the world, with time and opportunity, tools and support, can Refine the Fire of personal uplift by making choices to lead more constructive lives than that of the gang.[65]

As a society, if we listen and no longer deny their realities, contributions, and concerns, we may experience some beautiful truths and realize we no longer have to scapegoat someone else for what we are afraid to admit that we do. Whether we become a community with sorors or sistah gangs remains our choice; we desire to Refine the Fires of justice and community. Whatever we do, there are some startling statistics recorded by the Children's Defense Fund that tell us that we as a society better make a move and better move soon.

> Every 9 seconds of the school day, a high school student drops out.
> Every 17 seconds a child is arrested.
> Every 37 seconds a baby is born to a mother who is not a high school graduate.
> Every 56 seconds a baby is born into poverty.
> Every minute a baby is born to a teen mother.
> Every 4 minutes a baby is born to a mother who had late or no prenatal care.
> Every 4 minutes a child is arrested for drug abuse.
> Every 7 minutes a child is arrested for a violent crime.
> Every 19 minutes a baby dies.
> Every 2 hours a child or youth under 20 is a homicide victim.
> Every 4 hours a child or youth under 20 commits suicide.[66]

7. Build Up, Break Down: Language as Empowerment and Annihilation

In the beginning
God spoke.
There was nothing,
Until there was chaos.
There was, there is,
Love manifested;
There was, there is,
Language.
Language—
Signs and symbols?
Language signifying:
Body, spoken, sign, sound?
Refining Fires of much, signifying nothing,
Words, inflections, meaning?
Listening? Communicating?
Cacophony, harmony, Dissonance!!
Language:
Creates accessible power,
Invokes love, hate,
Builds up, breaks down,
Woos, kills.
Sentiments, weapons,
Endearments, empowerments,
In praise of widows and orphans: embodying God.
Pursuing anything, everything, nothing.
With Words we make joyful noises:
Adore, admire,
Burden, bother,
Cherish, caress,
Delight, deny.
In the beginning:
Language
What do we do,
When we have done

So much
To deny the other
Refining the Fires of indifference?
Evoking an invitation to dance
A ballet of words
That say
God spoke truth when speaking
The creation of the world and of human
As good.

Language: An Accessible Life-Giving and Death-Causing Mechanism

We use language to dance and to defy reality. We use language to communicate and compensate, to love, and to kill. We use language to Refine our Fires of interaction. Language, a series of signs and symbols, conveys information, creates and destroys—a simple, yet profound human deliberation. God spoke a word, and a world came into being; people speak on a continuum from the beautiful to the base. Body, sign, sound, and spoken languages Refine our Fires to give us freedom from isolation and freedom of expression in prescriptive and descriptive dimensions. The socio-cultural, historical, economic, religious, political, and aesthetic dimensions of a given society and our human conditions place limits on the power of language. The way we use language and our understanding of that use give language meaning. Language evolves within culture, a mechanism that provides meaning; supports human value and self-esteem; symbolically and literally denies death.[1] Mimetic rivalry[2] and the notion of scapegoat theory are ways of thinking about violence and the underside of the sacred in terms of the ways societies and cultures form and sustain themselves. Both paradigms concern human conflict, scapegoat mechanisms, the dynamics of culture, and the relevance of violence.

This chapter examines the implications for the power of language, as a Refining Fire of communication. After presenting related background materials of culture as the framework for language, I explore the dynamics of language and violence. Then I explore language as a tool that inflames and ignites hidden violence via verbal abuse and exclusive use. Here, language maintains the status quo as a means of control and as a way to quell violence, as we press toward transformation by exploring a theology and ethics of aesthetics and empowerment.

The Locus of Language Is Culture

Cultural anthropology pushes us toward exploring human behavior. We can understand ourselves broadly and focus on why we cannot peacefully coexist, why we engage in brutality and commit atrocities, and why we act out of aggression. Why are most average individuals so miserable, despite having physical ability, access to technology and comfort, and generally a solid lifestyle? Why are many human beings so unhappy, wretched, and miserable, despite physical and material plenty? We can begin to answer these questions by asking what differentiates humans from other living creatures: intelligence. None of us are alive because of our physical prowess, size, speed, or good senses. We exist by our cognitive complexities, are aware that we exist, and are self-conscious beings. That awareness of existence engenders a Kierkegaardian sense of fear, trembling, and dread: an awareness of our own mortality, our own death.[3]

Fear of Death

Ernest Becker posits that fear of death is a universal experience. Human beings, a union of opposites, self-consciousness, and physicality are conscious of the terror of their own death and decay as the Refining Fires of living exact a toll. One reading of the Garden of Eden myth is that death is humanity's peculiar and greatest anxiety. Awareness of death is the basic human repression, the catalyst for culture, a repression only experienced by human beings as self-conscious animals.[4] Our fascination with youth, age-defying cosmetics and related surgery, genetic engineering, and fetal and stem cell research legitimate the notion that humanity has a natural and inevitable urge to deny mortality and achieve a heroic self-image. People want to survive and consume but are conscious of the inevitability of their death. Is this fear not one of the root causes of human evil?

In the face of death, people often embody the language of denial. The basic fear is that of insignificance. Imagination, cosmetic facades, and self-transcendence through symbols create a fantasy that we can live indefinitely within culture. Such a fantasy does not help us deal with death. The anxiety about death and reality leads humankind to bring more evil into the world through hopes and desires.[5] The result of the vulnerability to death produces a struggle: first, to obtain power, and, second, to locate dangers and life-threatening forces where they can be placated and controlled.[6]

Human beings want to Refine the Fires of survival, flourishing, and acquisitive immortality by denying and repressing their mortality. Denying one's mortality initiates a psychological setting in which one uses projection to classify a particular person or persons as a scapegoat. Killing the scapegoat helps separate the self from death and gives one control, power, immortality. Becker's scapegoating mechanism allows one to deal with his or her Jungian "shadow side": the part of the self that is other, inferior, culpable, and thus projected outside of the self.

Scapegoats and Violence

One discharges the negative forces of the psyche and guilt, projecting that sense of inferiority onto the scapegoat, and then symbolically destroys him or her.[7] One gets to make up all kinds of language games to create an allusion of eternity—a mix between "let's pretend" and "wannabeism" in which no one dare speak the truth that the emperor and empress wear no clothes. We create scapegoats and do violence from the purviews of fear and frustration along with joy, plenty, and love; for we kill out of "the joy of heroic triumph over evil"—the evil of our own death.

If scapegoating is the process of discharging the negative forces of guilt and the psyche, most of us—young and old, rich and poor, amateurs and intellectuals—need scapegoats. The scapegoat mechanism, as the tool for immortality, is the revolution. Such a revolution, built on lies, embodies a champion and/or martyr system that pledges and often covenants victory over evil and death. The human desire for "righteous self-expansion and perpetuation" pushes us to develop social and personal lies, the paradox that undergirds the human condition: in seeking our own good, we do evil.[8] We fabricate, we lie, with language and deeds. We fashion scapegoats to have someone to blame, particularly for those things we cannot or do not understand.

We hunt for scapegoats because we need to be special. When we can degrade, humiliate, or attack, we raise ourselves to a superior place. We Refine the Fires of facades and innuendo, with spoken half-truths. We then make a sacrifice of these scapegoats. One can see sacrifice as a gift to the gods that is directed toward the current of power, a current that keeps the life force moving when previously it was blocked by sin. People use this sacrifice to feed the gods and give the gods more power so that humanity may have more. Such sacrifice involves an effort to conciliate hostilities found in a profound sense of insignificance and helplessness amid a terrifying universe. All violence, personal or national, then depicts people's need to accrue an "immortality account." The American sense of manifest destiny Refines the Fires of chosenness and declares that all those like us are the immortal chosen; the different, the evil other, the enemy are damned, excluded from eternity.[9] For Becker, the language of violence is the language that denies death and that mesmerizes us into thinking that we just might not die, as a part of cultural reality.

Culture Provides Answers to Human Questions

As human beings, we confront the physical problem of death, symbolically using our intellect and culture. We share sets of beliefs with groups of individuals that help us reduce the anxiety surrounded by our knowledge of the awareness of our death, mortality and animality, unconsciously developed over time. Culture reduces anxiety by using language to Refine the Fires of meaning—to provide us with answers to universal, cosmological definitions about the nature of life. We search for meaning that suggests the world we live in is stable, orderly, and important. Cultures are different, but all cultures provide answers to questions all human beings have: "Where do we come from?" "What am I to do?" and "What happens to me when I die?"

The first thing that culture provides us is meaning. Along with perceiving ourselves as meaningful, we experience ourselves as valuable or significant. Second, culture provides a sense of self-esteem, the most critical psychological factor for our well-being. All human beings have a need to feel good about themselves. Although this need is universal, the way one achieves and keeps self-esteem is culturally relevant. The third gift of culture is that it may deny death in two ways: symbolically and literally. In some faith traditions, if we live life right, then we enjoy eternal life.

While cultures provide the languages of meaning, self-esteem, and denial of death to help us cope, human beings still do not get along. Why do people have trouble coexisting? Some argue that human conflict results because reality is offensive and death-denying. People who are different from us undermine our own cosmology or worldview: a destabilization of all we deem normative and true. When we encounter differences, rather than see the experience as a challenge or opportunity, we usually feel anxious. Either we stand with confidence, assimilate, accommodate, and adapt, or we annihilate and minimize those who are different. Such activity arises out of our need to place someone we deem "other" in a position of inferiority, so we can feel better about ourselves and our own perceived inadequacies.

The Scapegoating Mechanism

One can use the language of violence and scapegoat mechanisms in biblical and secular literature not to deny death but to talk about the origins and survival of culture. A Girardian reading declares that the Hebraic themes of land and chosenness hide the violent scapegoating mechanism. Such scapegoating is a product of mimetic or imitative desire. Desire is mimetic in that it copies the other's wants or desires and not the outward expression of the other's actions. Within human relations desire produces vengeance and scapegoating, which can lead to Refining the Fire of resentment. This mimetic desire moves from acquisition to conflict by producing violence that destroys cultural difference. This breakdown and disorder creates a "crisis of differentiation," a mimetic or sacrificial crisis. To restore this collapse or breakdown of cultural differences requires a process, a psychosocial activity that causes or generates the mimetic or imitative scapegoating. This mechanism creates or originates all of culture through imitation and substitution to reproduce the differentiation that reciprocal or mutual violence is apt to eradicate. Scapegoating helps to relieve frustration by lashing out at some innocent person or blaming someone to avoid being responsible. The mimetic crisis ends when the group joins together and figuratively or actually kills the victim.[10]

If the language of the Gospels is the language of nonsacrificial redemption, sacrificial violence belongs to human beings, for Jesus gives his life to a nonvengeful God. If indeed the Gospels make scapegoating explicit, then they are not structured by a generative mimetic scapegoating mechanism. The mechanism concerns desire and its socio-cultural context.[11] Mimesis is the adversary of differentiation, or the division of society into proper categories and individualities. Modern society does not see that indifferentiation is violence and violence is indifferentiation. Consequently, all human institutions engage a type of violence.

Violent Patterns in Human Behavior

We find violence in actual human behavioral patterns and in the same patterns within art, music, and literature. When human societal institutions begin as violence—a primal murder by a whole group against some innocent, random victim—this founding murder, a vehicle of the community's hostility, unites the community. The victim becomes the hero or heroine, the bringer of peace, reconciliation, and unity—the source and foundation of all society and its institutions. The ritualization and repetition of the murder is the beginning of language itself. This sacral or religious violence leaves people unaware of what actually happened. One of the functions of religion is to mask generative violence. Primal violence exists in ritual and in myths. People feel hostilities that result in shared violence, which becomes hidden within police, prison, and judiciary systems. The source of hostility is the origin of human society.

The hostility that precipitates the violence is mimetic desire, our desire: we only want what others want.[12] Violence, a synonym for sacrifice, makes the victim a savior. The end of the spiral of violence is the refusal to sacrifice and is a system of giving of self and not taking of another self. Jesus refuses involvement in the spiral of violence concretized in his act of forgiving love. For some atonement theorists and Girard, this refusal, an anti-sacrificial move, is a free gift arranged between the Parent (God) and Jesus, with human violence ultimately being inconsequential. Yet Jesus' redemptive lifework shows love and a ministerial vision—a shift in one's experience and the traditional writings on atonement.[13]

The scapegoat, a victim of collective persecutions and acts of unjust violence or discrimination, provides a category for studying and unmasking racism and other kinds of oppression. Collective or widespread persecutions are a common form of violence that can be legalized and aroused by intense public opinion. Scapegoating is a consequence not only of mimetic imitative or representative desire but of collective violence. Racism, sexism, homophobia, classism, ageism, and other categorical types of oppression are not always recognized by the particular perpetrators or others as a form of sociopathology. A society may participate in repressive, subversive, systemic, insurrectional, open, or hidden violence, because some members of the society want to define themselves over against another person or other groups. As such, violence, an artistic midwife, reduces order to chaos.[14]

Collective Persecutions of Scapegoats

Collective or widespread persecutions of scapegoats are a common type of violence that can be legalized, especially when aroused or supported by public opinion. Societies produce such objects of persecution because individuals and groups need to define themselves over against one another.[15] The dominant groups can define themselves and find cohesion with one another by identifying a vulnerable group as "outside" and "other." The "other" group (distinguished by, for example, race, class, gender, sexual orientation, age, religious practice) must be visible and vulnerable. Otherwise retaliation and escalating violence follows. (Retaliatory violence is a type of mimesis that generates ever increasing violence.) These warring or monstrous doubles involve the process of creating differences, or the differences themselves create a definite kind of social order.[16]

Within culture, then, human beings imitate one another's desire, because when they come together on the same object, they use one another as models and begin to resemble one another. The result of the increasing similarities can be societal confusion and ultimately violence, if individuals and groups struggle to define themselves over against one another, to be different—particularly if people come from an "either us or them" perspective, as opposed to engaging in respectful dialogue around difference. Their struggles often result in their looking and acting more and more like one another. If some person or group within a group that has not defined itself looks different, acts different, and is vulnerable, that person(s) can be the target of a consolidated effort to define themselves and the other group by turning their own quest for power against those who cannot retaliate. A group establishes itself by psychologically or physically expelling the ones who are different. Refining the Fires of differentiation by lynching (or stoning to death in the ancient world) is the classic act of collective violence.[17] This ritual or execution by group sanction presumes the guilt of the victim and offers the opportunity to kill without guilt to group members. Everyone participates, and the lynching takes on a festive air.

Many individuals of the liberal persuasion and those most conservative think that lynching could not have been all that bad and that it is "passé." Many assume that lynchings only occurred in the South. The 1999 atrocious deaths of Matthew Shepard in Wyoming and James Byrd in Texas reminds us that violence by committee, a form of lynching, still occurs. *Without Sanctuary: Lynching Photography in America* documents that lynching did indeed occur and that it occurred not just in the South, but in California, Oklahoma, Kansas, Florida, Texas, Minnesota, Montana, Nebraska, Kentucky, Missouri, Illinois, Tennessee, Illinois, West Virginia, Wyoming, and Arkansas. These heinous acts were documented and disseminated throughout the United States on postcards. James Allen, a collector since childhood, searched through hundreds of flea markets and personal collections to assemble the collection of postcards and photographs that document

> the ritual torture or souvenir grabbing—creating a sort of two-dimensional biblical swine, a receptacle for a collective sinful self. Lust propelled the commercial reproduction and distribution of the images, facilitating the endless replay of anguish. Even dead, the victims were without sanctuary.[18]

To help diminish the denial that such lynching was not public sport, of the likes of our national pastimes of baseball, football, and now soccer, listen for the words that recount the essence of the demonic, reigning in the bowels of hell:

> On a Sunday afternoon, April 23, 1899, more than two thousand white Georgians, some of them arriving from Atlanta on a special excursion train, assembled near the town of Newman to witness the execution of Sam Hose, a black Georgian. Like so many lynchings, this one became a public spectacle. As in most lynchings, the guilt of the victim had not been proven in a court of law. As in most lynchings, no member of the crowd wore a mask, nor did anyone attempt to conceal the names of the perpetrators; indeed, newspaper reporters noted the active participation of some of the region's most prominent citizens. And as in most lynchings, the white press and public expressed its solidarity in the name of white supremacy and ignored any information that contradicted the people's verdict.
>
> . . . [Hose met a familiar death]. After stripping Hose of his clothes and chaining him to a tree, the self-appointed executioners stacked kerosene-soaked wood high around him. Before saturating Hose with oil and applying the torch, they cut off his ears, fingers, and genitals, and skinned his face. While some in the crowd plunged knives into the victim's flesh, others watched "with unfeigning satisfaction" (as one reporter noted) the contortions of Sam Hose's body as the flames rose, distorting his features, causing his eyes to bulge out of their sockets, and

rupturing his veins. The only sounds that came from the victim's lips, even as his blood sizzled in the Fire, were, "Oh, my God! Oh, Jesus." Before Hose's body had even cooled, his heart and liver were removed and cut into several pieces and his bones were crushed into small particles. The crowd fought over these souvenirs. Shortly after the lynching, one of the participants reportedly left for the state capitol, hoping to deliver a slice of Sam Hose's heart to the governor of Georgia, who would call Sam Hoses's deed "the most diabolical in the annals of crime."

The next morning, smoldering ashes and a blackened stake were all that remained.[19]

Group unity gives the impression of being on the "inside," of being "right." But this unity itself is a consequence of imitation. Everyone imitates everyone else's desire to kill. The murder discharges violence directed against someone who is powerless to resist. The victim is accused, charged, and executed based on random or nonexistent evidence. Evidence is beside the point. The strategy and hidden motivation of the lynch mob easily transfers to an institution when an entire culture yields to mimetic desire and its violent consequences.[20] During slavery, lynchings helped unify White supremacists, were a reaction to Nat Turner and Haitian slave insurrections, and incited fear in most Blacks. This violent act Refined the Fire of control, which caused most slaves to "stay in their place," creating a "peaceful" environment: cooperative labor and no slave revolts. Since killing the victim held a group together, the action is symbolically repeated to sustain internal peace. The symbolic repetition of the murder or maiming is ritual sacrifice. Rather than always lynching a person, the limbs may be broken or amputated: lynching cuts one off from life, amputations cut one off from easy mobility. These acts also make a statement to the community.

The Psychology of Imitative Behavior, or Mimetic Desire and Nondesire
In sum, we learn to desire by seeing what others desire, what others consider valuable. If all or most desire the same object, the value of the object increases. Conversely, if everybody devalues an object and considers it worthless or meaningless, the object, however worthy, has no value. Sometimes a persecuted, devalued group may buy into the majority opinion through mimetic desire and thus devalue themselves. This is true of any persecuted group, regardless of the reason for the persecution. The psychology of imitative behavior, or mimetic desire and nondesire, is contagious. The way a group values or devalues can lead to mass hysteria, or a group sickness. For example, World War II propaganda resulted in third- and fourth- generation Japanese in mainland United States, but not Hawaii, being imprisoned because of the popular belief by those in the United States that all mainland Japanese were monsters and would betray us. This same mass pathology creates the assumption that Jews

poisoned rivers to create plagues and a culture's assumption that persons of color are less than human, "diseased" or that women are inferior to men because they are physically smaller. Whether anti-Semitism, the carnage between the Rwanda Hutus and Tutsis, familial incest, the failure to ordain women, the demonization of the poor, or believing that a life of wealth assures no problems, oppression is mass pathology, an imperative to sin—to denigrate and deny the reality of holiness in human beings.

The Control of Violence

Religion can control violence: its myths, prohibitions, and taboos flow from a society's effort to sustain differences and to limit rivalry. In the beginning were violence and chaos. A group finds a victim in order to decrease internal rivalry and find cohesion. The collective effort to exclude, expel, or murder someone(s) marginal to the group helps the group to achieve peace, even though the murder occurred because of accusations that the victim was the cause of societal chaos. Murdering or destroying the victim conceals the truth of the situation: the real cause of the violence comes from those who instigate oppression. Yet for the model to work, violence must always be directed against those who cannot or will not fight back because the group will disintegrate into murderous rivalry: intense, destructive competition among themselves. For example, parents often punish or make greater demands of one child as a way to control the others. The system of ritual murder and expulsion is what Girard calls the *sacred*: "sacred" equals violence. Why? When a culture or a religion begins with a sacrifice, a killing, it begins with violence, the worst side of religion. Violence highlights the differences within society.[21]

How does this violence come about? When conflict begins, violence is repaid by violence in an imitative fashion. Rather than continuing to tear the group apart by fighting against themselves, they find others to vent their aggression against. After the assassination of Martin Luther King Jr., for example, rioting by Blacks in Black inner-city neighborhoods, often against store owners of other minority ethnic origins within the same inner-city neighborhoods, occurred across the country. In reaction to patriarchal and misogynist oppression, some feminists become patriarchal themselves. They patronize poor women or women of color by failing to consider these women's gifts and graces and talking down to these women who are deemed inferior, or who the patriarchal feminists sense need a "godmother"—support turned to control run amok. The heightened, retaliatory violence within a group generates a social crisis, which can be resolved by the group's deflecting their violence to someone near but outside the group. Thus a victim can actually stabilize a group, both the dominant and the vulnerable person or group.

Violence as dangerous play is destructive, antisocial, and degrading in its consequences; it is often deliberate and complex. One can view violence as the breakdown of social order or as the maintenance of a pattern of dominance. Violence in spoken language has power and creates a ripple or domino affect: an "energy" fashioned to hurt, harm, annihilate, or destroy. Violence in American literature Refines the Fires of mythic, ideological, or psychosexual vocabulary apart from the writing process, dealing with ideological and thematic processes or circumstances that surround or penetrate violence. One can examine language in an imaginative vein to note how the author develops the voices and characterizations in and around the language of violence.[22]

Language Connects Body, Mind, and Soul

Language—a body of sounds, then a practice—connects body, mind, and soul and affects peoples' attitudes. Words express people's thoughts, desires, and obsessions. No words are unessential or gratuitous. Language conveys and imposes a value system on a cultural, social, religious, and political level. For example, Communism imposed an authoritarian viewpoint through a language that allowed only one interpretation. Western society also manipulates language where words are used to promote a particular political, moral, social, or commercial agenda or product. Trendy phrases, sound bites, or jargon is used senselessly without precise meaning. Language as meaning concerns a singular, not a universal style or typical pattern in which singularity of language contradicts social order. Style is a characteristic of a collective arrangement. Within these arrangements, language embodies contradictions and struggles that make up social reality with persistent past contradictions and struggles, while anticipating future ones. "Language is both autonomous and not autonomous, governed by rules and unruly, arbitrary and motivated, stable, and corrupt."[23] Language is important in human relationships and plays a key role in the imposition of violence. Without language relations cannot exist—be it language through sign, word, or movement. Words are living, not static or neutral. Language changes and shapes our sense of reality, because the meanings of words change over time and affect the way we envision ourselves and our cosmology.[24]

Language, Power, and Knowledge

Language, a rule-breaking and rule-governed activity, is a place for variables rather than constants. Language speaks, follows its own rhythm, and has its own partial coherence. These sounds and symbols have an errant, redeeming, elusive, and effusive quality, as well as a generative principle with vices and virtues—an ethical strain. Language shifts from continuous responsibility to mere self-consciousness, which Refines the Fire of idolatry by creating a reactionary impasse to itself or becomes enmeshed in a self-interrogative, reflexive process that pretends to get behind the sources of oral or written thought.[25]

From the perspective of philosophy and linguistics, many thinkers have made claims about language and the dynamic impact it has in society and on individuals. Philosopher Ludwig Wittgenstein noted the ambiguity and dialectic of language, that it could poison, mislead, and bewitch or heal. As such, language games describe situations using words, extend the ideas of grammar and language, and depend on nonlinguistic features like human nature.[26] Postmodern theorist Michel Foucault made the connection between language, power, and knowledge. Foucault demonstrated how knowledge and power depend upon and actually extend each other, allowing social categories of deviance, such as racism, sexism, and imperialist practices. This power is not something we have or possess but is a strategic and resourceful narrative.[27] Noam Chomsky argues that the human brain has in itself an innate language ability, with a universal grammar; thus all children learn languages in similar ways. Chomsky equates language with humanity. As such, we comprehend and deal with reality and ascribe meaning through language, which has sound or phonetic representation and meaning or semantic representation and helps us to engage in social relations and self-expression.[28] The work of Wittgenstein, Foucault, and Chomsky affirms the aesthetics and ambiguity, the creativity and complexity, and the interrelatedness and centrality to human life of language, language games, and language systems.

Language is the root of communication, the elements or RNA/DNA that provide the tools that allow for law, science, doctrine, sermons, stories of love and life. Language invokes the vitality of song, the gems of rhetoric, the building blocks of stories, history, and literature. Literature mediates and shapes the way we see and how we experience our very beingness in the world, because stylistic customs, narrative conventions, and plot resolutions sanction and perpetuate cultural myths. These myths let writer and reader participate in a constructive rewriting of their social contexts. Literature can produce estrangement and exaggerate familiar scenarios that give readers a sense of recognition.[29] Prose and poetry function as play, communicate shared humanity or solidarity between author and reader, and have a provocative effect. Literature engenders ideas and helps revitalize and transform the world. Literature has an intellectual function that inquires about the value of life without dealing with external disruptions that make life unbearable. In sum, literature Refines the Fire of encounter with the experientially or intellectually new and demands we confront truths we would otherwise avoid through mimetic living: death and scapegoating, violence, and religion.[30]

Religion: The Arena of Ultimate Concern

Religion is the arena of ultimate concern, of deep commitment, where one Refines the Fires of the self, one's God, and one's neighbor. The language of the neighbor is the poetry and rhetoric of affirmation. But who is our neighbor, really? Is a neighbor also a friend, or one we befriend? Must we first truly love and celebrate ourselves before we can have a genuine relationship of being neighbor? Violence, an affront to the poetic and the rhetorical, is overt and covert, is physical and mental, and is an emotional and spiritual assault or injury by individuals or institutions that violate one's personhood and obliterate options of loving self or neighbor. Violence treats the "other" as an object not as a subject. Violent experiences fall under the larger cyclical pathologies of injustice, revolt, repression, disrespectfulness. Such oppressive languages are tools that inflame and ignite hidden violence through verbal abuse and exclusive use: a catalyst for generating scapegoats, denial, and lives.[31]

Language—words, gestures, and images—Refines the Fires of life-giving vitality and imagination, becoming a tool of inspiration, dissemination, and invocation. These same linguistic tools can Refine the Fires of social inequality: they segregate, harass, and humiliate. The impact and results of these divisive actions produce a "rhetoric of violence," and inflict deep wounds that go unhealed, festering and metastasizing until individuals and social groups are riddled with cancerous oppression, bad faith, and xenophobia. When the results are chaos creating, a rhetoric of violence itself implies that some order of language is at work. Once a connection exists between violence and rhetoric, the two terms ultimately become reversible within a system that exposes or names the violence. If violence is in language, both the rhetoric and concrete evidence of violence exist.

Violence and Rhetoric

The relationship between violence and rhetoric depends upon the representation of difference. The language of violence engages the trauma and terrors of abuse and pain kept in silence when seemingly there are no choices. The venues of no choice include the pictures of rape, the witness testimony that falls on deaf ears, the confession that one experienced abuse, only to be told that one imagined and wanted it or that "no" meant "yes." We must understand, then, that the notion she said "no" and meant "yes" is a smoke screen devised to blame and punish the victim, rather than punish the perpetrator of the violence. Relationships between those with and without power mean we, as individuals and collectively, may struggle physically, spiritually, and emotionally to overcome oppressive realities. We mentally struggle with the dynamics of intellectual persuasion at work. We risk the possibility that powerless, marginal, voiceless dissenters with ideas will never hear, will never be heard, and will be crushed by governmental or some hierarchical, maniacal power.[32] Violence and desire are found in language and in these linguistic practices. We fail miserably if we underestimate the power of language.

We teach children with a lie when we have the audacity to state that "sticks and stones may break my bones, but words can never hurt me." If words really were inert, we would not invest so much in their protection; it is a concept of expressive liberty predicated upon the innocuousness of its exercise. Words have power. If understood ironically, then "sticks and stones" makes a powerful adage. For murderous and destructive behaviors are grounded in the language of betrayal. People often betray others in a hallucinated sense of power. Many times the language of betrayal Refines the Fire of human destructive and murderous behavior: a dangerous form of pathology and concealment in which insanity lies, disguised behind the mask of poor mental health. Wearing a mask of serenity, Refining the Fire of delusion, and thus disguising a countenance of rage maintain the status quo as a means of control.[33] That mask cannot ultimately salvage the pseudo-liberalism nor hide the underlying violence.

The language of violence gets fueled by conformity to set values and forms. Success and self-esteem based on control and domination impair one's inner self and does not eliminate the related violence. Maintaining ongoing patterns of dominance creates a geography of pain, a mountain of destruction and tributary systems of themes, which makes people invisible. Words become acts, power dispensers, in which, for example, terms of female sexual organs become negative expletives. Words are so volatile and deadly because they are portable, accessible, and invisible, though the depths of carnage resulting from Refining the Fire of destruction are unfathomable. Such language of intimation, ridicule, and insult becomes inseparable from the injury. Such a reality makes the statement "love the sinner but hate the sin" an anathema, a lie, a deceptive and unfaithful practice. The injuries become concretized acts and experiences of inequality and discrimination, oppression, destruction, shaping everything we think and do, personally and in the various communities to which we belong.

Just as language shapes our social reality, society itself takes on a language, a living myth about the importance of human life, a creation of meaning toward a civil religion. The language of religion and violence in daily praxis concerns nuclear weapons, terrorism, the death penalty, sexual and racial violence, drugs, poverty, betrayal, war and colonialism, economic sanctions, homicide, suicide, and misinformation. These issues concern personal, political, and religious forces that may use violence for evil ends, such as the bombings of federal buildings, child care facilities, and abortion clinics in the last decade.[34]

Violence: The Language of Power

One might argue that despite the overwhelming evidence of violence, language does not fit into that category. Yet in daily life the language of power often juxtaposes one group over against other, creating hegemony and often embodying oppression, scapegoating, and control. The language of hegemony involves possessing the major cultural terms that categorize the "right" and "wrong" ways to exist as a human being. Such language of otherness creates polarization and dichotomies and sets up ill will and a cycle of oppression. Because violence exists in fact and in theory, theories of representation also maintain the oppression of particular subjects.[35] The words we use to represent the subjects and objects of violence are integral to the violent event. The expression of such hegemony actualizes languages like Jim Crow, our current phobias, the language of coercion, homelessness, exploitation, and the language of the media. How well we know the sensationalized feeding frenzies, the banquets and orgies on the likes of the Menendez brothers, O. J. Simpson, Jon Benet Ramsey, Michael Skalar, the Clinton and Lewinsky sagas, and the lives of the rich and famous.

The language of racism implants stereotypes and creates a rhetoric that demonizes Blacks and other people of color. This language assumes that children of color get a "good" education because of the melanin in their skin, disavowing the excellence that comes with grace and hard work. This language assumes Black women are hussies and Black men are studs. The language of racism makes common terms like *nigger, spick, hymie, honkey, chink,* and *wetback.* Few give a second thought to the connection between the demonization of people with Black skin and the situational negations that invoke language like black book, blackballed, and blacklisted.

The language of sexism implants gender inferiority and objectification that reduce women to someone to fetch and be subservient, the recipient of abuse and patronization evident in diminutive suffixes (waitress, deaconess) and terms like *the little wife, Jezebel,* and *dumb blonde.* The language of classism creates a dichotomy between the haves and the have nots, evidenced in notions like the "digital divide" to categorize folks too poor to own or gain access to computers. Such language makes the place of poverty undesirable, underclass, worthless, and lazy, when some of the hardest working people in the world are living in poverty.

Can we have less hegemony and less of the "isms" and have socially constructed equity within an inequity of discourse? The history of race relations says no, given that our justice system is perpetuated by a language of oppression and inequality. The language of male–female relationships maintains a rubric of love, honor, and obey. Men have used language to control women and to Refine the Fire of isolation, thwarting them from their sense of *imago dei* and from their bodies by robbing them of the language to talk about such things and to envision and implement such realities. Women and criminals tend to share the same silence. They tend not to have the required education to control the language of power: "no money, no instruction, no education, no family, no love, no health; no words or vocabulary to express or defend themselves."[36]

The language of sexual violence intimidates, destroys, isolates women and men who are similarly stalked, abused, and raped. The language of nothingness, insecurity, and rage dehumanizes those who end up in prison. Children experience the language of unimportance, betrayal, and abuse when they sense that their parents no longer care about them, splitting their psychic structure. Some children have never known love, and they become wounded adults. The language of violence against children becomes more political, especially when adults deny this abuse because it contradicts their need to believe that everything is all right.[37] The language of violence amid an ideology of power Refines the Fires of rupture and displacement as it fractures society and the self. Violence creates feelings of indignation, guilt, and shame that produces bodily violence.

Denying Death

Some of "those others" engage the scapegoat mechanism where they try to gain the most favorable position.[38] Some cowards and bullies seek to control through a violence of innuendo, insinuation, and threat. A deluge of such taunts can lead to self-hatred. Self-hatred, rooted in the basic lie that hides in silence, becomes one's own submission. Hatred relinquishes balance and tears at the fabric of wholeness and sanity. Denying death, the reality of difference causes wars, oppression, and dependence on a scapegoat, is a process that exacts a need to make someone else other and hinders the possibilities for transformation. Denying death simultaneously denies life and Refines the Fires of delusion, desolation, and defiance—a loss of true being.

Transformation

Transformation requires a reassessment of the language of invisibility and silence and desires a shift toward responsible use of all language and the acknowledgment of others and their language use. Celebrating one's presence means that a person will have options other than consenting to being silenced or scapegoated. An integrative, balanced reality and sense of self and others invites both a consciousness and a chance to change. Transformation calls for significant changes from using the language of existential compartmentalization where mind and reason are good, soul is wholly other, and body, sex, and emotions are dirty and bad.

Transformation calls for us to release the language of betrayal, negative "isms," diminution and gender identity in which we employ suffixes to define actresses and deaconesses. We can forsake the language of violence for the language of intimacy and the language of disembodiedness for the language of physical grounding. Transformation requires that we Refine the Fire of language as gift, an entrée to communication about that which is holy. Newness and wholeness also embrace the language of introduction. Often we hide from others, and we hide from ourselves. We are afraid to let others know us, the real us. Consequently, we introduce ourselves by giving information: occupation, hobbies, and memberships. Who we are is not the same as what we do.

Transformation is the process of quelling violence and Refining the Fires of new aesthetic possibilities of empowerment. Possibilities begin when we use nouns to name with respect, joy, and dignity. Possibilities begin when we use verbs to encourage conversations for action and justice, tempered with mercy and humor. Possibilities begin when we use adverbs and adjectives that are descriptors of nobility and anticipation. Possibilities begin when we use conjunctions as links to bring us together in harmony. Possibilities begin when we use prepositions that invite us into partnerships and community. Possibilities begin when we use interjections that help us embrace the option for love with joy and participles that allow us to embrace the ambiguity of active description, honoring all objects as we embrace all creation.

The Miracle at B. F. Franklin School

A most powerful example of language that Refines the Fires of transformation is the miracle at B. F. Franklin Day School in Seattle, Washington.[39] In the spring of 1988, Carol Williams began to turn things around at the B. F. Franklin Day School by seeking to give the students a language of identity. The physical plant was dilapidated and deteriorated and needed to be condemned. The faculty, staff, and students knew the language of rage and frustration, as all experienced a malaise of an academically and psychologically dying school. The school also housed two separate, unequal programs: the Orca accelerated program for the "gifted" students and teachers and the at-risk program for emotionally, socially, and spiritually needy children. The accepted modus operandi was to Refine the Fires of rage, altercation, and frustration.

Williams began to use the language of advocacy, collaboration, and empowerment. Of the children with behavioral problems, many were homeless, hungry, with personal and family problems, low-income, and at risk for failure and were being monitored for abuse and neglect. Some were suicidal. Williams initiated a change in language, which created an environment for action. Williams gave teachers permission to use the language "I need help." She empowered the school to use the language of family, which created a moral bond between teacher, parents, and social service personnel. Williams assisted Black and White teachers with interpreting the language of home-lessness, impoverishment, and ghetto life. She did not evoke a false sense of change and reconciliation or pretend that the problem did not exist.

The school developed the language of KOOL-IS (Kids Organized on Learning in School). KOOL-IS created success by providing basic needs and put a specific face with a specific need. The language of namelessness is vio-lence and makes cooperation difficult. Using cooperation and volunteers from the community, churches, university, and corporations, the changes were marked by the language that brought together work and friendship and that produced intimacy among all students, regardless of gender, color, or eco-nomic status. KOOL-IS created a language of social support, not social dis-tance. In settings that we know we can learn a lot from the language of healthy personification and advocacy: out with avoidance, in with acknowl-edgment; out with language as avoidance, in with acceptance; out with edu-cation as indoctrination, in with education as stewardship, freedom, and gift. Williams saw the possibility for an aesthetics of life and joy in the bodies of her charges racked with pain. When will we look? What do we see?

A Theology and Ethics of Aesthetics and Empowerment
The prophet tells us the context available to us if we really want to affect change and quell violence: do justice, love kindness, walk humbly with your God (Micah 6:8). A theology and ethics of aesthetics and empowerment are an invitation for us to change, to dance. With God and humanity together in dialogue and solidarity, we can Refine the Fires of a language of advocacy, lan-guage of romance, language of sensory and sensual perception, language of wholeness and health, the language of inspiration, peace, and joy.

8. Daughters of Zelophehad: A Constructive Analysis of Violence

Daddy's gone: dead!
We're unmarried, and alone.
Awesome characters of ancient times
Come to tell the world:
Give us our share!
Don't profane our Daddy's name!
We're women, we're Daughters,
We're somebody.
Not who you choose,
Not who tell you, who you think we are;
Not disposable property,
Not belonging nowhere.
Refining Fires of hope:
Honor the sacrality of women and men,
Of girls and boys,
In community.
Waiting to exhale the putrid garbage
That stilled the lives and vitality of too many.
Too many gone, too soon.
Is it too late?
Never too late to see your holiness;
Never too late to celebrate your sacredness;
Never too late:
Now is the time.

Today, if a group of sisters, newly grieving the death of their dad, were told that because of their gender they could not inherit their father's land, the information given to the daughters of Zelophehad after his death (Numbers 26–27, 36), surely they would protest. Legally, only the sons of Zelophehad could inherit land, and the daughters were not male. The land had belonged to their father. Ergo, the land ought to be theirs. In thinking about the many injustices that occur today because of societal and religious phobias and "isms," I remember these daughters. These daughters' dilemma and their quest for reparations were a scenario of injustice, a state of affairs involving sexism (being not male); a state of affairs involving class (their father owned land; their family was wealthy and not enslaved to anyone); and a state of affairs involving race (land had been promised to the Hebrews). Thus the "daughters of Zelophehad" is a provocative metaphor for grounding my Womanist analysis. This chapter uses the metaphor of the daughters of Zelophehad to engage a Womanist constructive theological and ethical analysis of violence, towards Refining the Fires of transformation. After recounting the story of the daughters of Zelophehad and engaging in a critical commentary on the relevant pericopes, this chapter explores the nature of divine and human violence. I question the necessity of divine and human-initiated violence in human society and propose a constructive theology and ethics of violence, with the Refiner's Fire as a catalyst for analytical conclusions.

The Story of the Daughters of Zelophehad

The biblical story of the daughters of Zelophehad (Numbers 26–27, 36) is unique in its concern for the right of women, of daughters, to inherit land from their father. Numbers, which gives key religious teachings and guidance for ancient Israel, focuses on communal faithfulness, inheritance and land distribution, community leadership, family, purity, and worship. For the most part, women are invisible in this text, other than Miriam's challenge to Moses' leadership. While the rituals surrounding purity apply to women and men, women are at the periphery in Numbers, with a strong exception being the daughters of Zelophehad. Like Miriam, the daughters of Zelophehad had also challenged Moses' authority, particularly in claiming that the inadequate divine decree needs revision. The text indicates that the father's name was at stake and the daughters were not opportunistic or desperate for land. While one could interpret this story to be about the daughters left destitute without the land, the key is the father's name: an issue for those men who have not sired male heirs. The lack of a male heir meant the loss of the father's name from one's clan. The other *patres familias* (male heads of household) in Joseph's tribe were concerned that their daughters would marry outside of the tribe, meaning the tribe would lose its land. Moses counters that the daughters should marry within their tribe to avoid possible loss or transfer of land, exemplifying the second generation's faithfulness. The boldness of the daughters' request and their landownership is short lived, for once they marry, landownership passes to their husbands. The daughters' story stands within the tension of limited freedom and shifts from a focus on their father's name (Numbers 27) to property rights and acquisitions (Numbers 36).[1]

These texts name the daughters of Zelophehad: Mahlah, Noah, Hoglah, Milcah, and Tirzah. These are great, great, great, great granddaughters of

Joseph, of the clan of Manasseh, of the clan of Machir, of the clan of Gilead, and of Hepher and are named twice within the texts when they take their case before Moses, Eleazar the priest, the leaders, and the entire congregation. Having no brothers, the daughters of Zelophehad argue that they should inherit their father's land, for their father died only for his own sins. Moses brings their case before Yahweh, and Yahweh says the daughters of Zelophehad are right. The usual order of inheritance is the son; if there are no sons, then the daughters are to inherit; if no daughters, then the man's brothers; if the father has no brothers, then his father's brothers or their uncles; if there are no uncles, then the nearest kin inherits.

A Change in Post-Exilic Familial Structures of Inheritance and Leadership
The listing of the clan structure that splits Manasseh from Ephraim under Joseph's house and the reversal of Ephraim over Manasseh, which makes Manasseh the seventh tribe, is important for priestly history. That Manasseh's clan involves seven generations, noted as the daughters of Zelophehad, makes the structure unique. The genealogy indicates that the daughters of Zelophehad, who previously could only inherit through levirate law of the clans, can now inherit independently. This shift is a change in post-exilic familial structures of inheritance and leadership.[2] Kinship groupings are integral to the makeup of genealogies. Ancient Israel's socio-cultural categories have four tiers: (1) family, (2) clan, (3) tribe, and (4) nation.

(1) The family, the father's household, includes husband, wife, all children, servants and their families, and any single relatives or wanderers who visit. The father has supreme authority and responsibility for every family member. The child owes its life to the father, for the mother is an incubator.

(2) The clan, a group of related families ruled by heads of families called elders, can defend itself and comprise a unit of worship. Here the *go'el*, redeemer par excellence, is responsible for members indebtedness. God is also known as the *go'el*, the one who protects the worshipper from outrage, oppression, disease, or death.

(3) The tribe contains a group of clans with a common ancestor. They assume blood relationships within the tribe, led by a chief or sheik, who has final authority after consulting heads of clans. Responsibility passes to the family, the tribe, the next generation. After the settlement, the tribes increasingly give way to the nation.

(4) The nation, with a king as ruler, is the final unit. Politically, Israel was a united nation for only two reigns: David and Solomon. Israel is more a religious community than a nation state in the Hebrew Bible. With a religio-patriotism, the king is chosen by God, even though the king may come to the throne by heredity. The king leads the people in worship. In

Samuel, the covenant God reminds the prophet that it is not you, the prophet, whom the people reject, but the people reject Yahweh when they reject the true king. Thus, God is on the side of Zelophehad's daughters.

Genesis 12:1-3 and the Priestly, Everlasting Covenant

A larger frame for reading the Hebrew Bible and the Numbers text, in particular, is Genesis 12:1-3, restated in the Abrahamic covenant (Gen. 15:7-21), and as the priestly, everlasting covenant (Gen. 17:1-27). God promises Abram land and an heir by whom Abram will become a numerous people, and God will make Abram's name great, building a relationship with God that benefits all people. With heirs tied to land inheritance, it becomes important for a man to marry the right wife, to give birth to the right son who inherits the land, even when the inheritance is stolen or taken away and given to the second born twin, as in the case of Esau and Jacob. Given the inheritance of Zelophehad's daughters, understanding the socio-location of ancient women is an imperative. In raising questions about egalitarianism, one must reckon with the abyss between contemporary life and ancient biblical reality. For example, while the Hebrew Bible mentions 1,315 male names and only 111 female names, the Bible focuses on public and communal life, a life dominated by men.

Life in Ancient Israel

Life in ancient Israel was rooted in farming with intergenerational, extended families as the norm. In these families, women grew grains, olives, grapes, and other garden crops. They kept the animals and produced and refined grain-based produce and dairy foods. Women's work involved skilled, intricate operations. Women were also held responsible for producing large families to support the farming enterprise. The implied favoring of male heirs relates to the patrilineal transfer and inheritance of land. Though childbirth was fraught with peril and no panacea, remaining childless was an even less desirable option. Economically and maternally, women had strong roles in family life.

Despite some popular assumptions, there are no explicit statements in the Hebrew Bible that dictate male supremacy over females. Even with Genesis 3:16, often read as a text of dominance, one can see that we might better understand it in its context, in which sexuality concerns increasing the birthrate, not an increase in male social dominance. Since for most of the women in the text, relational and occupational interests were germane, the category of "woman" had little significance. Households were related to female sexuality; only when separated from the household would the category "woman" surface as a relevant issue regarding Genesis 3:16 women's identity.[3] Further, the goals of most women are not identifiable as feminine.

> The Western dichotomizing categories of female submissiveness or pas-
> sivity as opposed to male aggression or action simply do not apply to the
> Israelite concept of gender. . . . It is even possible to view legal materials
> that seem unfavorable to women as not concerned with women as such
> but rather with trying to promote family and territorial stability in a
> patrilineal context.[4]

Most Israelites were agrarian. When they moved to the city, then polarization
emerged. When women move to the city, households are not self-sufficient;
the households are smaller, nuclear, and the changes in economics were
accompanied by socio-economic stratification. Nevertheless, the focus on
family life remained.[5] Land inheritance remained a family matter.

The issue of daughters' inheritances, however, becomes a legal case because
Torah does not cover the matter of daughters inheriting. This is one of only
four cases in the Hebrew Bible in which an ambiguous legal matter warrants
special divine revelation as a remedy. While Zelophehad's participation in
Korah's rebellion (Num. 27:3-4) might have resulted in his daughters' losing
the land, that he "died for his own sins" indicates he was responsible for his
individual guilt and thus was not a reason to cause the family to lose its land.
Therefore the daughters claim that they have a right to inherit Zelophehad's
land, that they might perpetuate their father's clan name. God pronounces
the daughters' claim to be bonafide, with three theological bases: (1) divine
ownership of the land; (2) Israel as a tenant of the land; and (3) the inalien-
able right of Israel, here Zelophehad's daughters, to possess part of the
Promised Land. To insure that the land remains in the tribe of Manasseh,
Moses rules that any daughters inheriting land must marry within the
daughters' own tribe.[6]

When interpreting the meaning of the daughters of Zelophehad, the
question of intermarriage, solely related to land inheritance, emerges. In the
United States, most people avoid marrying their first cousins. One problem
of marrying within one's own gene pool is that such intermarriage can lead to
inherited physical and mental abnormalities. Katharine Sakenfeld sees the
business of conditional intermarriage to preserve tribal property through
three interpretive lens: (1) literary, (2) culturally cued reading, and (3) historical inquiry.

The literary approach sees these daughters of Zelophehad as bold, progressive, going where no woman has gone before; unlike Miriam, these daughters
of Zelophehad are rewarded for challenging Moses. The end result is that the
price of such freedom, surrounding their own initiative of securing their
future, results in restricting whom they can marry. This is a stroke of irony
and of deceptive freedom! The culturally cued reading uses an androcentric
lens to ponder the loss of family name. Though wrapped in ambiguity, the

story links the daughters' inheritance with preserving their father's name, followed by questions of tribal property holdings. Here the problem of intermarriage concerns economics for the Gileadite tribe. The daughters of Zelophehad story situates land inheritance not just as a tribal issue but as an issue for the clan that even further limits the daughters' choice of prospective husbands. A reading from historical inquiry helps us see that in limited, specific cases women could take their claims directly to a male authority without having a man to intercede on their behalf. Women could inherit and then own property, and daughters, inheriting in these situations, were limited in their choices of prospective husbands.

While not divulging much information about the institution of ancient marriage, the text does stipulate that a daughter can marry her father's brother's son, according to Levitical code. Sakenfeld argues that while the interpretations stand in tension and we cannot make definite claims on the daughters' motivation, the story was probably canonized as a means of preserving the father's name. Such a reading brought comfort to men who were unable to sire a son, meaning that the father's name could still be preserved through a daughter.[7] The daughters of Zelophehad Refined the Fires of boldness, family, and inheritance. As such they symbolize a metaphor for creating a radical shift in dealing with violence.

Divine and Human Violence

The God of the Hebrew Bible uses violence to create. That same God exacts and excuses violence in the name of restoring covenant relations and of exacting deliverance on behalf of the select, the Chosen. Sometimes the ambiguity and the silence around divine decision making, which utilizes human perpetrated violence, boggles the human mind. If we see violence as creative energy run amok, as things torn apart and reconfigured, then God has recreated original chaos, a kind of violence; out of that original chaos, God created an orderly world and humanity. The process of human birth can take on that same energy, as the mother's cervix may be torn when the infant is pulled from the birth canal.

That same God accepts Abel's offering of first-born flock and disregards Cain's grain offering. Cain kills Abel; Cain is cursed in his tilling and made a fugitive and wanderer—exiled from the land and perhaps from God. But anyone who dares to touch Cain will be the target of divine vengeance seven times over. Why the different divine treatment for the two brothers? How can a good God destroy what that good God has created as in the case of the Noah story?

God destroys all the people of the earth save Noah and his family. When the enslavement of Israel, foretold by God to Abram in a deep sleep (Gen.

15:13) occurs in Exodus, God plays the divine puppeteer and hardens Pharaoh's heart, even after Pharaoh agrees to release the children of Israel. Once Pharaoh releases the children of Israel from slavery in Egypt, following the killing of the first-born Egyptian infants by the Angel of Death, God then hardens the Egyptians' heart. The Egyptians pursue the Israelites and drown in the Red Sea. Many argue for the divine right to be in charge and contend that God tempers justice with mercy. Granted, this is often the case. Yet, all of the Egyptian families did not enslave the Israelites nor seek to return them to slavery. Is the God who created the Israelites not the same God who created the Egyptians?

On the one hand, we can see God's privilege of refusing to answer Job, for Job was not at the beginning of the world. Yet if Job was a just person, the only person labeled "righteous" in the entire Hebrew Bible, why must Job lose everything and become a pawn in a chess game between God and the Adversary, a heavenly attorney? What about the death of Job's family, his innocent children? Is this a way of saying there are no innocents? Or that finally, because God gives, God can also take away, regardless, and blessed be the name of the Lord? Or is it that divine authority allows God to make God's sun rise on both the evil and on the good, and sends rain on the just and on the unjust alike (Matt. 5:45)?

Violence: A Part of Legal Documentation

In the Deuteronomic Laws, we often see violence done as a part of legal documentation. The Deuteronomic text affirms a close relationship between Israel and Yahweh and affirms the human responsibility for faith, while relating the significance of social justice in context of covenant. Covenant is a contractual relationship between Yahweh and Israel, in which love is used as a political term. Love is an emotion of affection, yet it demands absolute faithfulness to the overlord, to no other. Jealousy is also a religious metaphor, specialized language of intimate relationship. Unlike love, jealousy is not found in ancient political treaties. Yahweh is a jealous God (Deut. 5:9). Clearly in Deuteronomy, God is One, a God of history. Yahweh chooses Israel. Israel is called to participate in absolute monotheism amid an ethos of retributive justice, of blessing (obedience) and cursing (disobedience). As liberating as this election of Israel by Yahweh is, the text still objectifies and therefore violates women in many instances. Women are objectified for marital and sexual purposes. Women can be acquired during war, like children (Deut. 20:14; 21:10-14).

The business, the contractual nature of a betrothal and marriage, becomes even clearer in reviewing the consequences if an apparent virgin is found to be damaged goods. If her hymen is already broken, and consequently there is no blood evidence on the wedding bed, she is dubbed a harlot, and the men of the city can stone her to death. Rape may exact a punishment of death or payment of fees, if the woman is not yet engaged (Deut. 22:21). Adultery is a capital offense, with a sentence of death by stoning. Violations of honor and vows result in violation by death. Interestingly, however, since adultery is a property offense, that is, since the wife is owned by her husband, when another man has sexual intercourse with her, he has stolen from the man by coveting his wifely property. The offense is against the husband, for men control women's sexuality. Women do not own their sexuality: a "husband who has extramarital sexual relations with an unmarried woman is not considered an adulterer: the very existence of prostitution implicitly tolerates nonexclusive sexual behavior by men."[8]

Violence and Patriarchy

Violence accompanies us daily and never takes a holiday. We see destruction and manipulation of power in war and colonialism, fueled by the desires to control land and natural resources and to dominate public policy and political alliances that apparently demand military campaigns. A deep hunger for power adds to seeing the role of conqueror as a kind of manifest destiny. One geographical, political, and sovereign power decides that its good is the higher good and it needs to control another sovereign, allegedly for the sake of human rights and global peace. In the realms of sexism, gender, and domestic violence, one's sexuality may put one at the position of lord and master or servant. Biology allegedly predicts that women are physically weaker, and therefore the lesser and delicate, powerless ones of the human species in every way. Historically, patriarchy and the accompanying systemic misogynist practices that have become so internalized, until many cannot see other options even today, dictate that women are deemed helpless and therefore treated as inferior. Inevitably, females become their husband's or partner's means of venting aggression. Women are denied education, fair pay, and other rights available to men. In some faith traditions, the same women who bring children into the world and are their first teachers of faith and religion cannot be ordained or officiate at religious, liturgical gatherings. A penile appendage qualifies or disqualifies, legitimates or denies a call by God.

Racism violates the beauty of creation, the marvelous palette of humanity. Thankfully, we do not all look alike. Again, the fear and ignorance surrounding diversity and difference are mind boggling. Why would anyone want or need everyone else to look, act, and think like them to get along? The millions who have died in pogroms, ethnic cleansings, lynchings, and military genocide of civilians indicate that God made a mistake. Obviously, God made a mistake in adding so many elements to the mix of human nature, since we seem to use difference as a marker to justify abuse, violence, and denial. If

God did not make a mistake, why do humans experience such trauma and drama around difference? Why do we assault with conversations and destroy our relationships?

Violence and *Imago Dei*

The violence that we engage wears so many faces, has so many masks. Violence, the use of physical, psychological, mental, emotional, spiritual, and economic force, does internal and external harm. Unintentional harm often produces the same result as premeditated violence. Violence is a misdirected, misunderstood creative energy that embraces dysfunctional pathologies. Violence can be ruthless, can involve scapegoating, and can be blaming. Violence involves individual, systemic, societal, and corporate misuse of power. This misuse of energy causes pain, dehumanization, domination, injury, and diminishes or separates the acknowledgment of a sense of *imago dei* within a person and the concept of aesthetics, of the beautiful in humanity and creation. No parameter of human life and culture is immune from violent thoughts, speech, and actions.

Men and women do violent acts. In chapter 2, we explored the women in the Bible who have participated in violent acts. Like their biblical counterparts, women like Lizzie Borden, Ma Barker, and Susan Smith have killed in modern times. Thus, although testosterone seems to ignite violence, those with heavy estrogen deposits are not immune. The increasing number of child abuse cases, the Munchausen by proxy syndrome,[9] and escalating numbers of children needing foster care placements substantiate that women as well as men engage in physical and emotional violence. While male physical dimensions usually allow for men abusing women, there are sufficient documented cases to show that women have used psychological abuse, passive/aggressive behavioral patterns, and physical violence to abuse men and children. Neither gender, poverty, race, wealth, good intentions, nor elitism ever gives one of us the right to perpetrate violence on another.

Is violence perhaps a global initiative, though the party line for the United States and for many other parts of the world is peace? In the twentieth century over 200 million persons died due to government action: war, economic sanctions, deliberate starvation, and nuclear/biochemical disasters. The collective global pain, from the Holocaust and the purges in Russia to systemic slavery and the genocide of Native Americans in this country, has exacted and continues to wreak havoc. This pain is visceral and systemic and will not go away until we begin to name, own, confess our complicity, and where possible make amends. How do we know the depths of this pathology?

Along with government-related murders and destruction that chip away at the human spirit and vitality, in the United States alone the most recent statistics available state that 2,314,245 persons died in 1997. The top ten causes of death were: heart disease, malignant neoplasms, cerebrovascular disease, chronic obstructive pulmonary disease, accidents (motor vehicle and others), pneumonia and influenza, diabetes mellitus, suicide, nephritis, and chronic liver disease and cirrhosis. For persons ages 1 to 44 the chief cause of death was accidents. For our teens the second and third causes of death were homicide and suicide. The pain and desperation in our society is so great that either we are dying due to internalized violence and stress, often arising from our ecological violation, or we are exacting violence externally on others.[10]

Human Pain: Physical, Emotional, and Spiritual

Often the level of personal physical, emotional, and spiritual pain dictates how certain persons respond. The depths of this pain, this woundedness, is so powerful that we end up with dysfunctional families and institutions: religious, corporate, and educational. I am indebted to my spiritual friend and sister, the Reverend Faye Morris, who has opened my eyes to the depths of chaos and the severe chronic nature of this woundedness. Years after much deep tissue work, analysis, and healing around this level of illness, individuals can still relapse. Others find themselves still living with the effects of their malaise. Some are in such pain that the only way they can possibly cope is tremendous "DENIAL": Don't Even Know [when] I Am Lying. The abuse and mistreatment of children is like the ever-ready battery that just keeps on going. To tell one who is suffering to "just get over it" merely reinjures, is disrespectful, adds insult to injury, and shows callous disregard for the well-being of the individual and his or her community. This woundedness is the symptom of cancerous thinking, being, seeing, and engagement of those we deem other, those we fear, those we really do not want to be responsible for, those we need to manipulate and control because of our own pathology.

Woundedness is the product of sin. Somewhere, somehow, we objectify a beautiful spirit, which then becomes fractured and torn. That fractured, wounded spirit, out of great pain and distress then learns to act out, to react by inflicting pain, to do an end run on the pain that others have and will probably continue to create. Given the violence of God and the staggering statistics that document human violence, is violence a necessary component of human existence?

Violence in Society: A Necessity?

When we study sacred texts, literature, music, film, and human history, it seems that violence is a necessary part of life. Refugees, criminals, and explorers from Europe came to these shores to flee persecution. Some were banned and unwanted in their own homelands; others came to conquer and trade. In the last three hundred years, the offspring of these pilgrims have lived out a manifest destiny that takes, commands, and consumes. In the name of progress, we have violated the land and become so mobile that maintaining a sense of neighborhood community has become a major challenge. Many of us have come to worship at the altar of consumerism, and we daily shortchange critical relationships. Somehow, with all of our alleged enlightenments (perhaps we need endarkenments), we still manage to subjugate some groups of people and privilege others. In the year 2000, the cost of property in some metropolitan areas is so exorbitant that it is vulgar. Violence runs rampant in arenas of family, work, and play and in our governmental, business, health, and educational systems. Yet, we fail to see the import of difference and equity and how we commit sacrilege when we profane and dishonor the godliness in creation. Are we to acquiesce and think present reality is irreparable, or can we work to trouble the waters and model a different way of being and doing? Is such a challenge too complex, ambiguous, or impossible?

The betrayal and denial of Jesus by Judas and Peter, the tragedies of Othello, King Lear, Macbeth, and Hamlet, the demises of heroines in Tosca, Madama Butterfly, or the Dialogues of the Carmelites document that one aspect of the human condition seems to be that we exact violence upon ourselves and others. In biblical, literary, and operatic accounts, and in our world historical record, people hurt other people. We manipulate, intimidate, and betray friends and foes alike. There seems to be a preponderance of violent acts committed in the name of progress and in the name of religion. Mimetic rivalry and acquisitive mimesis appear to be normative. Apparently, even when we desire to put forth our best efforts, to engage, to do the just thing, the need to be right, to be the best, to be somebody triggers a defense mechanism. Many times we react out of our own sense of unworthiness and incompetence. If we sense that we are not up to par in a certain matter, we project our own lack of self-worth on someone else, so that we can attempt to feel better about ourselves. In other instances, we punish ourselves for our perceived shortcomings. Sometimes our self-punishment lodges in the areas of sabotaging our body through compulsive, addictive behavior. Other times we sabotage our relationships; we reject and treat others with ill will, before they can do the same to us. We fear success and are terrified of being loved for who we are, not for what we can do. We remain suspect of persons who are generous. In our woundedness, some of us assume that persons who extend acts of kindness and generosity must have a hidden agenda.

On a systemic level, particularly in the United States, we tend to have this insatiable desire to be big brother and big sister, to fix everyone else's problem, out of some misguided sense of manifest destiny and messianic complex. Yet we have never atoned for the many acts of violence perpetrated on people living in our fifty states. We also lump everyone into a single category of United States citizen, seeking to deny the aesthetic diversity and ways of being among us by creating a cookie cutter model of what it means to be free in the United States of America. Our justice systems have become dualistic, where money and clout buy one a way out, poverty and lack of resources pay your way in—a gross simplification, absolutely, but in too many instances, horribly true. The Jon Benet Ramsey debacle is a case in point.

The irony of the O. J. Simpson case was that there was clear evidence of his guilt, yet the prosecuting attorneys overplayed their hands and assumed that women, including women of color, would see this instance as a time to "get back" at the brutality of the stereotypical Black male bully—the boyfriend, the deadbeat dad who makes babies and leaves. Instead, some of the women saw this as one more time the justice system was trying a Black man unjustly. Further, when Simpson tried on the gloves found at the scene, and they did not fit because he had latex gloves on, the jury had their excuse to acquit. The defense attorneys thought through their opponents' best strategies and played out those scenarios, played out the defense's best and worst case scenarios and then played a supreme game of chess; they won, reiterated in Johnny Cochran's infamous chant broadcast worldwide, "if the glove don't fit, you must acquit."

Violence and Social Identity Issues

That being said, it becomes clear that all of the money and prestige in the world do not remove one from violence. Violence is a class issue: the cases of Patty Hearst, the Menendez brothers, O. J. Simpson, Jon Benet Ramsey, and the Columbine murders have taught us that lesson. If you are poor, you are often thought to be lazy, you get poor representation, and you are deemed a statistic, an other. Violence is a gender and sexual issue: if you are female, you are often seen as a semen repository; you are often the victim of domestic violence, of date rape, and of the violence surrounding prostitution. If you are gay, lesbian, bisexual, or transgendered, you are often the victim of projected sexual identity rage by those in denial. Violence is an age issue: if you are young or old, you are often seen as vulnerable, an ideal punching bag, a nuisance, and a liability. Violence is an ethnic/race issue: if your skin hues are anything other than identified as Caucasian or White, then you are seen as inferior, suspect, of welfare mentality, as animalistic, as object.

Biblical and classical literature, opera, plays, and actual world history indicate that violence is inevitable, is necessary. Institutionally, politics, business, education, human services, medicine, professional sports, entertainment industry, the worlds of art, science, and religion have all been stained by violence.

In his analysis of literature, René Girard revealed mimetic rivalry, scapegoat theory, and mimetic desire, the desire to be like the other and ultimately be the other. This phenomenon is so powerful that Girard places the generative impetus behind culture and society in mimesis, particularly with the founding murder, real or symbolic, that allows societal formation. In our sociological configurations, it seems that when violence is not necessary, then it has become indispensable.

Sergio Cotta, a political and legal philosopher, argues that violence is pervasive in all sectors of society, in our language and communication, in personal and public moral sensibilities and that it is ancient and new. One difference in how we understand what is at stake in the analysis of violence, for example, between a Girard and a Cotta is in the way we perceive and evaluate violence. Cotta distinguishes between legitimate force, exacted by public authorities in the line of duty, and illegitimate violence, that exacted by private groups. Because only heinous violence makes the news, nonviolent, peaceful behavior is not exceptional and becomes irrelevant, not worthy of notice in the news. Today we use the language of violence broadly and without precise meaning, when we label every unjust act as violent. Historically, unless a crime was committed with brutality or a war was deemed unjustified or exceedingly cruel, these crimes and wars were not labeled violent.

By extending the concepts of violence to praxis and theory, in time and space, today we also blur the line between force and violence. Since the nineteenth century we have exalted violence. Such exaltation assumes that violence exists everywhere and in everything and leads either to resignation to the violence or to attempts to completely eliminate violence, an impossibility. In rejecting the second option, we would ameliorate the use of violence, rendering the use of violence constructive and hoping for neutralization and disappearance of violence.[11] Nevertheless, the use of violent acts against other violent acts requires a revolution. The ancient concept of revolution pertained to going back or returning to origins or beginnings. The modern notion of revolution is to forge a complete new beginning from a clean slate, "that is a supreme hope transformed into a concrete activity and aimed at the realization of the absolute values of" humanity.[12] Allowing such a legitimization and exaltation of violence that correlates with the notion of new beginnings and revolution, explains the prevalence of violence in the wake of Gandhian nonviolence. That is, "nonviolence converts itself from an expression of the revolution of love to a strategy. . . to create conflict and aggressiveness."[13]

Cotta argues that we cannot afford to exalt violence, for we cannot survive from a sense of unadulterated crisis of decline, a crisis of a reversal of values. At stake is the loss of the common good, which undergirds the structures of public life, as we have shifted to a Nietzschean notion of value dictated by power. Paradoxically, of course, whatever is common is often not seen as good. What emerges from the subsequent contradictions between love of self, love of neighbor, the confusion between public and private dictates, and the value of the individual human is the contemporary contraposition of values and

conflicts that will forever produce violence. In society, when the issues of freedom, authority, and respect are collapsed, we see that freedom exists only for
those with power. The one named "other" is objectified, and, mistakenly, violence evolves and represents itself as the implementation of freedom. Freedom embodies spatial, social, and subjective movement, relating liberatively
to things and time, persons, and self. The prevalence of violence suggests that
to effect change and transformation requires a synthesis of the eternal with
the development of the self as part of a collective and as an individual; otherwise we are left with destruction.[14]

In thinking through the being of the self and the divine Other, violence
seems to be part of the human condition, perhaps one human option. Violence is "an unregulated, nondialogic, and noncoexistential counteractivi-
ty."[15] Sometimes the metaphysics of subjectivity eliminates the structure of
violence to the point of concealing it beneath the cloak of liberation and freedom. Since violence generates more violence, ultimately the radical, revolutionary reversal of violence occurs in the superabundance of charity; the I
opening up to the divine Other, under the generosity of forgiveness.[16]

Refiner's Fire: A Constructive Theology and Ethics of Violence

Can violence ever be viewed as a good? What happens if we scrutinize both
violence as vice and violence as virtue? Violence, a nihilistic energy that
defames God, humanity, and creation, is that which exacts harm and often
derives from those who have been previously harmed themselves, the walking
wounded. To construct a theology and ethics of violence, from a Womanist
perspective, one can perceive violence as destructive. Conversely, we observe
that violence transformed is constructive. That is, we first recognize the *imago
dei* in all persons and the grace of God bound in nature. We also posit an
understanding of God that disavows God's capacity to exact violence on any
of creation because God is a God of love.

The redaction of the biblical texts that interpret the occurrence of divine
violence requires one to Refine the Fire of clarity and take a stand. One can
read divine violence in the biblical text as (1) an ancient hermeneutic to justify what transpired; (2) myth and allegory to teach lessons about what human
beings ought not do; or (3) the divine ego giving itself permission to exact violence by choice. Theologically, ethically, and hermeneutically, I opt for either
choice one or choice two. I find it incomprehensible and reprehensible that
God would intentionally destroy and hurt innocence. For the same reasons, I
find that the philosophical and theological arguments on theodicy, that is, why
a good God allows evil, incomplete and flawed. I am also suspicious of most
atonement theories and consequently find Delores Williams's focus on the
ministerial vision of Jesus quite intriguing and useful.[17] That being said, we

may take, as an underlying premise, that the energy that frames human violence, prior to and in the immediacy of the act, is that same violent impetus that when transformed becomes virtue. The destruction itself is not undone. But the energy that can potentially become destructive, can at any moment when operating from choice become virtuous and constructive out of *agape* and the acknowledgment of the sacrality of humanity.

Acts of violence are not only individual and communal but systemic and part of institutional cultures. Because institutional cultures exist, it is significant to understand that institutional culture allows for shifts only in little ways. The institutional culture is established with the founding of the particular organization. The strengths and weaknesses, the ambiguities visible in that structure, reflect some of the components and idiosyncrasies that are present at the inception of the institution. Unearthing the locations of systemic violence within institutional culture hinges on ontological and epistemological realities.

Collaborative, community thinking and action involve creating a way of being and knowing as a process of mutuality, respect, and ongoing dialogues. Collaboration employs cooperation and community building instead of violence, competition, and confrontation. Collaborative communities require commitment and passion in which friendships can develop and self-confidence is nurtured; they also provide opportunities for intergenerational interaction. Yet even in the best spirit of collaboration and camaraderie, violence may erupt, and voices may not be heard. When difficulty arises in collaborative or cooperating communities, the differences usually concern faulty communication skills, confusion related to sex, or desperation related to money. Communication, sexuality, and money often get scrambled with issues of power and authority.

Power and Authority

I define *power* as having control and influence, taking seriously the Greek terms *dynamis,* the ability to perform, and *exousia* with a modified definition. *Exousia* means power as the gift of freedom from any inward restraint in the exercise of that freedom. Using these concepts, I define *power* as having the gift of freedom to listen or not to listen to oneself, God, and/or others in making decisions and *authority* as the means to be invested with the privilege of decision making. Thus, power is the gift, the freedom of being in charge and in control, of having influence. Authority is the institutional investiture, sanction, and privilege of making decisions. The abuse of power or authority produces violent actions and tampers with the realized *imago dei* and sense of communal relationships. People given authority to exercise power need to be responsible and accountable.

When leaders walk into an office, a classroom, or a pulpit, they have a certain amount of power—the power of the office, the power of presence, the power given us by our institution. In saying yes to the call or the appointment, we automatically assume a certain level of responsibility. The institution and its constituents have expectations. We have expectations of them and of ourselves. Here we will construct a Womanist theology that Refines the Fire of responsible life amid the reality of destructive violence by examining the elements of dialogue, identity, sacrality, spirituality, and power.

To engage in dialogue, we must understand the power of words. Words once spoken cannot ever be totally retracted. Words can exalt and Refine the Fires of empowerment, love, and goodness towards grounded relationships. Words can Refine the Fire of hurt, igniting pain, deceit, desire, and desolation. If our framework for using words is intentionally orchestrated by a healthy understanding of God, then our starting point for conversation is one of respect, even when we desire to Refine the Fires of hurt, manipulation, and intimidation. In that moment, we can choose to change our minds and elevate the conversation to a level of decency. We can convey respect through a choice of vocabulary, vocal inflection, manner of greeting, and level of intimacy, as language systems have means for encoding ways of showing respect, particularly factoring in class, kinship relationships, age, gender, occupation, religious affiliation, and socio-cultural location.[18]

Just as the daughters of Zelophehad used words to register their existence, question tradition, and evoke divine disclosure, we too use words to Refine the Fire of change. To create change requires conversations for action. In addition to verbal exchange, our body language—our gestures and physical movement—also have meaning. If we are conscious of being in God's presence from moment to moment, we cannot Refine the Fires of deception, inappropriate touching, or any unwanted intrusion on the presence of another. Our cognizance and understanding of language in dialogue affect our ability to live a nonviolent life and our predisposition to engage in violent acts. Sometimes, like King Saul or Queen Jezebel, we literally self-destruct, because we are not clear about our ultimate identity, about who we are.

Double Naming of the Five Daughters of Zelophehad

Theologically, the identity question for an individual and community looms large. The biblical text twice names the five daughters of Zelophehad. This double naming is most unusual, given the many unnamed women in the Bible. Their naming twice signifies the identity of the five daughters of Zelophehad, and their clarity about who they are gives them the fortitude to object to and reject the contemporary legal precedent. The identity question does not ask what we have accomplished. The identity question does not concern itself with what our family sees in us or who they would like us to be.

Philosophically, the question of personal identity inquires about the facts that attest that an individual existing at one particular time is in fact the same person existing at another time; that is, we talk about a person's individuality over time. These questions of personal identity involve issues of epistemology: that is, how do we know, how do we experience memory, and how do we access our own past histories and the histories of others. The other questions of personal identity involve moral and evaluative concerns and moral responsibility for past actions, our own survival, and our future well-being.[19] When I ask the question "Who are you?" and you in turn ask of yourself "Who am I?", theologically we ask: "Who did God create you to be?" "How is it that you are called to Refine the Fires of love, justice, and relationship?" "What is the status of your physical, mental, emotional, spiritual health?" "Is it well with your soul?" "Do you even have an idea of what it would feel like to be well, or have the Fires of oppression, repression, and often the accompanying self-doubt and self-loathing so Refined your reality that you have no idea about what it means to feel good and to love yourself?"

Some of us live on the corner of Depression Avenue and Self-Loathing Road. Unlike the daughters of Zelophehad, "do we have unresolved issues with anyone or anything?" "Are we good stewards, realizing that stewardship is the gift of guardianship and responsibility?" "Subsequently, do we live a life of inclusion where we celebrate the Refining Fires of diversity, or do we utter lying words of solidarity and instead we are living the rubric of lies and hate?"

Multiculturalism

Juana Francis, a woman of faith and graduate of the Pacific School of Religion in Berkeley, California, celebrates life with a passion: "I love multiculturalism. Think about it: everything God created has color—the animals, plants, sky, water, people, everything and everyone has color. So why is it that people are afraid of diversity?" (my paraphrase). Like the daughters of Zelophehad, Francis asked a logical question. Many, then and now, would balk at this question of elegant simplicity and visceral authenticity. In the quest to Refine the Fires of a joyous life and an aesthetic appreciation for creation, as communities and individuals we must ask: "What are our biases, and how do we embody them?" "Are we racist, sexist, elitist, ageist, and homophobic?" "Do we acknowledge our level of privilege and accept our related responsibilities?" Before you answer "I am not prejudiced," ask yourself: "Who are my friends?" "Whom do I associate with?" "Whom do I tend to blame, be suspicious of, or ignore just by the way they look and move?"

To deny the existence of our own biases is to engage a pathology in which we actually escalate our behavioral prejudices, thus Refining the Fires of hurtfulness, mean-spiritedness, or disrespect for another. Ironically, what we fear most in others is what we do not like in ourselves.

What arrogance and audacity that we denigrate any category of people who were made by the hands of God. How sad that the depths of our hate for another reflects the heights of our own inadequacy, insecurity, and ignorance. We lose sight of the fact that even with six billion people on the planet Earth, each of us is a distinct individual. We have unique and distinct DNA configurations, personas, desires, and bodies—even those identical individuals who result from the splitting of a single zygote. Yet with all of these individualizing characteristics and the particularity of each person's emotional, psychological, and physical orientation, there is a sameness about us, because we are all human. The human condition, then, Refines the Fire of paradox: we are unique, yet we are one. Like the daughters of Zelophehad, we may belong to a particular family, clan, and tribe, but ultimately we all belong to one global nation, the city of God, which makes us sacred.

To Refine the Fire of radical revolutionary righteousness is to know that as children of God we are all sacred and that life is sacrament. For some this concept may be blasphemous; for others, beautiful. Is it not logical to say that if God, the quintessential embodiment of the sacred, created humanity, then humanity is sacred by definition? Individuals, nature, and things are sacred as they are consecrated through the artistry of a Refining birth by God or for the worship of the divine, of ultimacy evoking languages of emotion, aesthetics, liturgy, symbols, and acts. Individuals and artifacts are not idolatrous as objects of worship themselves. Individuals can worship God or individuals, and artifacts become elements used in the worship of God, thus sacred by definition of creation and function. The realm of the sacred as liturgy Refines the Fires of generosity and love, where life is gift, relational, and salvific. We can Refine the Fires of inspiration and gratitude, providing a basis for destructive violence to cease to be attractive and for it to become unacceptable to violate ourselves, other persons, or our universe.

Participation in worship as sacred transcends the need for being a self-righteous perpetrator or victim. Such a transition can be incredibly difficult for persons in the throes of oppression, depression, and addiction. One has to be willing to engage and stay the course, without needing to be rescued when reality sets in. In addition to the physical, psychological, and cultural predisposition of some as addicts, there is still the element of choice. Many find the option to choose sobriety one day at a time unattainable. The substance or activity has become a life jacket, without which some addicts cannot survive. Ultimately, their life is tortured and becomes that of the living dead. Such addicts are incapable of Refining the Fires of health and hope; they have never been able to grasp that they are sacred. The concept of being sacred is anathema to them. The blessed assurance that comes with knowing one is of God, sacred, and thus worthy of love is so intense as to be unreachable for some.

Others fear this kind of relationality. Some doubt that such energy exists. On some level, the daughters of Zelophehad understood themselves to be in relation with God, so that they could demand an audience with the religious leaders of their community and a new answer from God. To Refine the Fires of assurance and confidence attests that destructive violence is not an option. With this confidence as a framework, one can live a life of covenantal spirituality.

The Spiritual Life as Confessional Existence

Confession Refines the Fires by acknowledging the presence of God and the onus of personal and communal responsibility with a desire to become authentic. Womanist spirituality is authentic in that it affirms life and loving for all people and sees the global connections between humanity and the universe. Such a spirituality understands the domino effect—that each of our actions are important, that each of our actions can precipitate other actions that either affirm or negate, ending in hopeful life or a tragic situation. Our spirituality builds on the redemptive and salvific nature of God's grace, which makes available options for a healthy relational human life. Grace is a gift. Confessionally, grace helps us identify and give witness to the sacred within all humanity and the cosmos. This witnessing spirituality helps us to realize that there are other forces beyond us and that we wish to be well and in community. This spirituality urges us to speak in generous, loving ways and to integrate the various areas of our lives. Consequently, exercising and eating properly, getting ample sleep, reading to nurture our minds, being prayerful and at times quiet to nurture our spirits and total well-being become our way of life. We engage in these practices not simply to look better and lose weight or have more energy but because we are compelled by the reality of God in us, our *imago dei*. We then no longer can Refine the Fires of cruelty, of being vindictive, or of worshipping a violent God. We come to focus more on the gifts of faith, healing, and helping. In our helping, we learn to share power in joy as opposed to anxiety and greed.

Theologically, God has given us the power to choose to live, contribute, and excel. We can also choose to die. The ability to choose is to partake of power as a gift. This distinctive kind of power embraces the freedom of being in charge and in control, of having influence. This freedom energizes and does not need to control or oppress or be at the mercy of an environment, circumstance, or personality. To embrace such freedom is to Refine the Fires of sacred presence, to experience life fully in its most vital form; to take energies that could be channeled as destructive violence to become a catalyst for communion or eucharist, the most intimate connection between human and Divine. This connection resonates with all that is holy and embraces difference—race, gender, class, sexual orientation, age, intellect, and so forth, which become colors on the palette of life, not elements needing to be controlled or denied, but rather elements to be appreciated and celebrated. The height of inclusive freedom, then, Refines the Fires of holiness and that which is sacred throughout the cosmos. Just as God created chaos and created human beings out of chaos through grace, we can live within a heritage and propensity for chaos or violence and choose to Refine the Fires of justice and inclusion.

Aristotelian Poetic Plots

How we know these stories takes us to the arena of Bible and narrative, the language of prose and poetry. Aristotle envisions poetic imitation as complete and unified, for the poet's duty is to report what will probably happen, based on the rules of necessity or probability. The poet is responsible for crafting the simple or complex tragic plot. The simple plot is one in which the development is continuous and unified; the complex plot involves continuous action, where the action either shifts in an opposite direction, or the action shifts from ignorance to awareness and pathos and involves painful or destructive action. The characters in these Aristotelian plots must meet four qualifications: they must be good, appropriate, and consistent and champion human nature.[20] A transforming community engaged in emancipatory opportunities invites everyone to be a poet and to engage in the plots of shared knowledge, communication, and growth that embody the Aristotelian concepts cited above. These revolutionary poetics allow us to stand amid the tensions of diversity and improvisation, Refining the Fires of noble consciousness and respect. A starting point is creative generosity, when we sculpt our language of invitation and coexistence. Language is the crux of relationships. To live in peace and a creative violence that never erupts in harm is to speak and to listen from the context of authenticity and authority.

Lessons from the Daughters of Zelophehad

Authority in transforming, love-based communities is not just the institutional investiture of making decisions as relates to organizational governance. The authority embraced by the daughters of Zelophehad is a self-generating authority, an investiture of power given by God. Abuse, dismissal of person, and other forms of oppression undermine personal authority. Such violent actions damage and distort the *imago dei* within individual and communal relationships. God has endowed each of us with an authority by virtue of our existence. Our lives are eucharistic as they embody a sacredness that we often deny. Our liturgies proclaim that we are not worthy but do not teach the paradoxical reality, that though we may think we are not inherently worthy due to our human status, we are worthy by the investiture of God's love and grace, which call us to be responsible and accountable. We have sung the song of unworthiness so often that many of us have become fixated on our unworthiness and have to set out to prove just how unworthy we really are.

Like the daughters of Zelophehad, we are characters in the ongoing story of life: we "play" various roles, and we also have a particular character or persona with particular attributes or features that distinguish us as individuals. "All the world's a stage, and all the men and women merely players."[21] We are all players. Some of us write our own scripts, framed by our faith. Others assume the roles designed for them by family, convention, or society. Some of us Refine the Fires of imagination, beauty, and risk. Others Refine the Fires of hopelessness, victimhood, or boredom. In the global cast of human characters on the complex stage of life, there are six billion characters, with many, many plays being mounted simultaneously. Some stories receive kudos and global awards. Some plays never open or apparently fail on opening night. Some plays have long runs but are quickly forgotten. Other plays are not particularly successful in the way that we often measure success, but the lives on stage are productive, making a difference in their own communities. We are prestidigitators; we are powerful; we are impoverished yet wealthy in God's grace.

A closer examination of these plays and stories reveals that some of the critical sustaining factors are the rituals at home, in society, in faith communities, celebrating special days and moments. Rituals are the prescribed use of words, gestures, symbols, and colors, experienced within sacred or civil religious ceremonial action. "Rituals are often mimetic, a kind of acting out of the story. . . . The flow of the story can be influenced by the rite in which it is enacted."[22] Ritual evokes encounter with tradition, the sacred, and community. In ritual practices, we share our formal and informal belief systems. Rituals Refine the Fires of passion and commitment, whether a lynching or the eucharist. To couch these two concepts together is an act of defiance, not blasphemy, as both liturgical acts relate to murder, to generative violence. As the daughters of Zelophehad enjoined the authorities to hear their plea, that is, they opted for a peaceful solution, a desire for transformation presses us to choose rituals of compassion that give voice to those silenced and foster healthy, balanced relationships.

Nurturing such relationships requires violence reduction and education as the practice of freedom. This freedom that respects the *imago dei* in humanity calls for a distinctive, Refining Fire of rebellious intellectual action and related rigorous praxis. Miscommunication and marginalization arise out of domination. Instead of loving the whole people and dealing with the sacrality and preciousness of people's lives, we continue to practice dominance and cruelty. We help to create bifurcated modes of being that can be the catalysts for more dis-ease that precipitates and contributes to increased hypertension, migraines, depression, cancer, stress-related disorders, and premature deaths. Our understanding of how we talk about the nature of these relationships is the realm of ethics.

Ethics: The Value Factors

Ethics, the art and science of the systematic study of humanity's conduct or behavior, focuses on determining the value factors in a given culture or setting. Womanist ethics values the whole people, their health, and their empowerment. One can discern what a given group values by noting where they focus attention, time, energy, and human and financial resources. We cannot claim to value something or someone and never invest anything toward that person or thing. Valuing is not a process of objectification but of appreciation. To place value is to Refine the Fires of gratitude, awareness, and hope. To choose destructive violence is to Refine the Fires of hopelessness, indifference, and punishment. In the quantum moment at which the impulse to do violence arises and one chooses not to follow through with this urge, then the impulse toward violence has, creatively, become a good.

Destructive violence desecrates and kills off the good found within individuals and society, with inklings of slow or immediate suicide and homicide. Violence transformed provides an opportunity for symphonic listening, being, and doing—a modality that allows for many voices, many colors, many variations on a theme. A composite of information on the personalities and the process of transformation becomes clear when observing behavior patterns and determining who/what qualifies for visibility and who/what remains invisible.

Facets of Human Behavior

Numerous fields of thought study facets of human behavior. Theorists and practitioners study what, how, why, and when we do and what we do, look for patterns, and toil to configure ways to change our behavior. These facets of human behavior are studied from the perspectives of archeology, history, culture, psychology, sociology, and religion. Taken together, the stories of humanity, since time immemorial and in this very moment of history, demonstrate that we Refine the Fire of violence that prompts harm, hurt, and hate toward ourselves and others. Yet despite the staggering statistics of violence, there are countless persons who live their lives quietly, daily Refining the Fires of courage, compassion, and community. To help transform our world, these stories of courage, compassion, and community are the ones that need to become visible.

What a different world we would have if on a daily basis we honored and helped to make visible the care illustrated by the grandmothers who take care of the drug-addicted children of their children. What if the headlines, sound bites, and breaking news reports occasionally focused on random acts of kindness? What if we honored the *imago dei,* the sacredness in everyone, by having the courtesy of acknowledging people's presence when we walk into a room? What if we actually take the time to listen, not always concerned with "what's in it for us"? The Womanist paradigm is intentional about honoring the voices of "the least of these"—poor Black women, who represent those whom society often deems as other. The daughters of Zelophehad honored their own visibility and made their presence known to the rest of their community, their leaders, and God without apology. As we begin to really see, know, and then honor the sacred humanity, the magnificence in others and ourselves, we can Refine the Fires of love and respect. We can live authentically and function with integrity.

Integrity is one of those concepts that we banter around when discussing the dynamics of leadership and what we expect of genuine friendship. To have integrity is to be real, honest, and grounded in healthy love of self and our neighbor. When one has low self-esteem or lots of self-hate, it is difficult to have integrity because of the propensity to self-destruct and then to project the cause of this pathology on someone else. Self-destruction and self-hate afford jealousy, denial, and misinterpretation of reality. Integrity helps us Refine the Fires of honesty, unity, and completeness. To engage in violence is antithetical to integrity. One of the factors that can stop us from being caught up in the adrenaline rush that comes from violent acts is a commitment to integrity.

Theory and Praxis and the Escalation of Violence

Most of what we do has theory and praxis, the thoughts behind and the actions that implement. If we only pontificate and muse about theories of halting the escalation of violence and take no action, even to sensitize our own attitudes about the multiple levels of violence and our daily complicity, then we are frauds: theological and ethical charlatans, con artists, and impostors. To develop theories about Refining the Fires of violence, or anything else for that matter, and then fail to try them out is cheap arrogance. We need theories to give us insight, just as we need divine actions to ground our lives. And it is in being created sacred and living out of that holy context that we can begin to Refine the Fire of radical change, commensurate with bell hooks's notion of "killing rage."[23]

Killing rage is a Refining Fire, an electrifying tool for change, a catalyst viable for public and private sectors. Killing rage energizes and encourages; triggers but thwarts violence; instigates yet incriminates apathy, dominance, misery, and complicit behaviors, thoughts, and processes. Killing rage, as movement toward liberatory praxis, signals an alternative lifestyle and undergirds my understanding of Womanist theory and theological ethics as praxis. The work of educating for freedom and transforming culture is subversive activity. Not everyone has the stomach for it; not everyone wants to be healed. Some of us like the status quo. Sharing rage spawns communication and facilitates connections. Shutting down rage leads to assimilation or absorption and forgetfulness.[24] The historical Black church was the place where Refining the Fires of one's killing rage fueled opposing ways of thinking and being that enhanced people's ability to survive and thrive. The antithesis of killing rage is victimhood. To offset the rhetoric of victimhood, hooks encourages a dialogue of self-determination, as we work to end racist, sexist, classist, heterosexist domination.[25] Such dialogue begins at home and in our own context, as we examine our own stories.

Who Are We? Whose Are We? What Is Our Purpose?

The process of knowing what needs to change, what needs to stay the same, and how to be sensitive to timing and priorities begins with a heightened consciousness about the spaces in which we live: our physical, spiritual, mental, psychological, and socio-historical individual and institutional locations. Who are we? Whose are we? What is our purpose? We are complex beings, with roots in many places. We embody the replication of particular patterning from our DNA, and thus we stand amid a cloud of witnesses from our past and present. We express a Refining of all experiences up to this point, and we often soar or fail to thrive, even as adults, according to the depths of realized, eschatological, genuine, unconditional love that we have experienced. We are who we are, shaped by our troubles and the nature of our life's journey. We are oft amazed and astounded at some of the good, the bad, the ugly, and all between that has occurred. Our lives follow the patterns that support our comfort or risk levels.

In sharing our stories, we get to Refine the Fires of heritage and self, to talk of the adversities we have transcended. In talking about these adversities, we often diffuse the eruptions brewing beneath the surfaces of our minds and hearts; these eruptions transformed can move toward love. These eruptions left chained and unaddressed become volatile, resulting in death of character, of spirit, and of self. Refining the Fires of gratitude for life itself and for the uniqueness of our own stories is one initial point of departure in creating a proactive context of faithful justice towards self and others. Appreciating our own autobiographies gives an entrée for practicing mutuality in other relationships with other living autobiographies. Our autobiographies emerge out of a particular cultural environment with particular values, vocabularies, and visions.

Culture and Human Behavior

The world is a cosmos comprised of many cultures and subcultures. Culture is the dynamic, integrated, complex patterned system of human behavior, symbols, ideas, traditions, habits, meanings, morals, beliefs, knowledge, art, and artifacts that respond to basic human needs and depends upon our capacity for learning and transmitting knowledge through generations. Within this matrix, we are not all the same, nor do we all deal with experiences in the same manner.[26] Our way of being or doing occurs within the borders and the limits of culture. We Refine the Fires of self, community, and desire, individually, and collectively. Consequently, as individuals and community we must Refine the Fires of justice, of creative nonviolence to stay and halt the trend of negative aggression, manipulation, and evil. Such behavior is blasphemous; it is an assault upon holiness, upon creation. If every human being is created *imago dei,* then what those same beings are divinely inspired to create have in themselves holiness. That holiness, like the great works of J. S. Bach, Ludwig von Beethoven, Wolfgang Amadeus Mozart, Giuseppe Verdi, Giacomo Puccini, Peter Ilich Tchaikovsky, Duke Ellington, Stevie Wonder, and Quincy Jones, is resplendent in color, light, sound, fury, and love. Such holiness is beautiful and aesthetic.

Aesthetics is a body of knowledge that comes from experiencing imagination, sensation, and the feeling or the idea of the beautiful. Beauty, along with truth and goodness, is a transcendental, a property that must accompany being and exists within every being. Beauty, therefore, is a path for the desire and longing that goes back and forth between God and us. From an anthropological view, human beings are designed to know and to welcome God's revelation through their senses. We can ascend to God, through sacred or secular art, with God as the catalyst that allows us to value beauty. The human imagination is an authentic form of rationality and a vital means of understanding God.[27] In seeing that which is holy in humanity, we Refine the Fires of noble grace. We see that which is beautiful, and true, and good; we can see God, if we but look. Beauty is available to us in powerful ways in nature itself, which presses us to explore the realms of the ecological.

The term *ecology* comes from the Latin word *eco* and the Greek word *oikos,* which mean the family household, and concerns the study of the relationship between organisms and their environment. This relationship includes an organism's physical and biological living conditions and its relatedness and interactions with other species and members of its own species. The study of ecology began with Aristotle's colleague, Theophrastus, who primarily wrote about plant bio-geography.[28] To Refine the Fires of justice and responsible ecological stewardship demands that we be concerned with world populations and ecosystems. We can no longer think in terms of having an infinitesimal number of children, of constructing an infinitesimal number of buildings, of mining the earth, or of creating toxic waste, without first calculating the destruction and the break in the relationship with God because we have taken advantage of nature. To have dominion over something is to be held accountable for something. That excessive occurrences of depression, leukemia, lupus, and ovarian and prostate cancers occur in economically poor communities is no coincidence. Communities that are poor in dollars, not in spirit or zeal, have more toxic waste areas and more petrochemical plants per capita. Further, we cannot localize the wastes. The mercury and other poisons seep through to the groundwater and evaporate into the atmosphere, in both instances only to resettle elsewhere. To wreck the earth and despoil creation is to Refine the Fires of filth and to initiate slow homicide for all of us who breathe the air and drink the water. Consequently, we must be diligent citizens and conscientious consumers to ensure that we are not complicit in the desecration of our planet. To stem the tide of creating more unusable land requires the commitment of individuals and communities.

Ekklesia: A Group of Friends

A community can involve people with common interests living in a particular area, or those living together in a certain area out of common interests. Other kinds of community pertain to those linked by a common policy, or a body of people or nations that have a common history or common socio-economic and political interests. Communities can inspire common ownership or participation. Healthy communities involve individuals who can get many of their own needs satisfied, yet they are willing to transcend small egotistical needs to fulfill larger goals. One such form of community is an *ekklesia*.

An *ekklesia* is a group of friends who seek the place that opposes oppression, makes room for spiritual and theological spaces and communion, and seeks the renewal of divine/human and human/community in covenantal relationships. In so doing, an ekklesia creates a sphere of justice, antithetical to the traditional patriarchal church. These experiences of grace allow for Refining the Fires of justice, imagination, and dialogue. As such, a community can listen well, have horizontal patterns of interaction, and create new visions for modes of being ekklesia, for doing theology. Building on the many stories and the community of faith(s), one can engage in theology as a praxis of emancipatory God-talk and ministry. Such a ministry, which educates for freedom and in so doing Refines the Fires of risk-taking, consciously seeks to transform oppression, recreate symbols, images, and dogma, Refined, rewoven, reshaped as lived practices that empower, nurture, and revive. Rooted in emancipatory dialogue,[29] such community-based, generated activity can truly liberate all people. Such possibility engenders hope; its antithesis Refines the Fires of death.

Hope and Hopelessness

Hopelessness is pathological and leads to a sense of loss, distortion, fatalism, and pessimism. Hope, as an ontological need, must be practiced and concretized. Hope and struggle, as dialectical companions, rise above tragic despair toward Refining new Fires of possibility. When hope and struggle, an offspring of rage and love, meet, they can produce tolerance.[30] The daughters of Zelophehad lived out of hopeful action. A Womanist, emancipatory theology and ethics of violence create strategies rooted in Refining the Fires of hope and possibility, respecting the *imago dei* in all persons. This mode of analysis is theoretical, ontological, experiential, and existential. With analytical, critical listening from all possible places, and a commitment to the wholeness and survival of all people, this liberative practice then Refines the Fires of radical, revolutionary, realistic relationships. Negative, destructive violence makes us insensitive, wounded, despondent, hateful, mean-spirited; we look for a way out, for escapism, but have nowhere to go—that which haunts our reality, sleeps, eats, and exists within us, sometimes like a Consuming Fire, rather than a Refining Fire. When we destroy nature and that which makes us human, we betray God and all of humanity. If we can commit to a radical, revolutionary, realistic relationality, God can then trouble the waters that quench our Fires or give us more fuel to Refine the Fires of life: a symphonic dance of peace, joy, and love unspeakable.

Womanist Theory Embodies God's Powerful Grace

Womanist theory embodies a Refiner's Fire: God's powerful grace lived out in humanity toward transformation. In the crucible of life, this Refiner's Fire can assist us in addressing issues related to women, humanity, religion, and violence. Womanist theory Refines our seeing, thinking, hearing, and living so that our discernment allows us to see the oppression and the possibilities, the gifts and graces, the complexities and ambiguities, the stereotypes and healthy balanced lifestyles in daily life. By definition, Womanist theology and ethics requires that we both celebrate and honor the holiness and sacrality of all humanity and of creation itself and that we see, name, and help transform the numerous personal and systemic injustices. Womanist thought serves as a corrective for the oppression in religious and secular institutions.

Womanist theory seeks to Refine dysfunctional systems by firing up healthy relationships and opportunities for renewal and reconciliation, for admitting the androcentric and patriarchal nature of many of our religious traditions and dogma. The theology and ethics that emerge from a Womanist ethos seek to save the whole person and are diametrically opposed to divisive and fractured ways of being. In seeing and then helping to redeem the violence of our religious traditions and systems, Womanist theory can affect violence in larger society. The separation of church and state, notwithstanding religious practices, faith, and spirituality, has a tremendous influence on our daily lives, even when the religious rhetoric is couched in secular terms. In mapping out strategies for wholeness, Womanist thought and praxis can serve as a powerful catalyst to help us to embark on Refining the Fire of life in our hearts, which resurrects love, hope, and faith—as a blessing to God and humanity and ourselves.

The multifaceted voices and structures that bring together the divine and human, exemplified in Jesus Christ, remind us that though change seems impossible, the indefatigable God—all that is holy and just and good and beautiful—empowers us to Refine the Fire of life. A transformed theology and ethics of violence Refines the grace-endowed creative Fires that call us to live in an exemplary manner, cognizant of who we are, why we are here, and to see and respect our lives and our universe as gift. The theological Refines the Fire of openness to see and embrace a healthy plan of action, which becomes lived in the realm of ethics. Womanist theology and Womanist ethics provide the lens for constructing and reading stories and analysis of violence in living and written texts, as we Refine the Fire of oppression to weld visions of hope and possibility from the radical to the risky and the resilient.

A Womanist theology and a Womanist ethics or religious engagement of violence are radical: we must own up to our own complicity, perhaps even our desire for violence. We must be willing to be suspended in the moment toward complicity, to experience loving grace that will stay our own demise into the practice of evil. The radical calls us to rebel against dominant cultural theologies that contain oppressive categories and are parasites that feed on the violence of otherness. As revolutionary engagement, this religiosity is revolutionary and sees that the place to begin is that God created us and that creative act makes every human being sacred and holy, nothing more and nothing less. Those persons who do bad things either have congenital pathologies or they are so tortured in some way that they have a compulsion to torture others. The righteousness of a Womanist notion of violence refutes naysayers and reiterates the health, honor, faithfulness, and grace-filled sacredness of each individual.

God's revelation of love frames the process and not only allows us to discover our own complicity, but also gives us the freedom to disclose our plight to our community or spiritual director, towards fully hearing the prophetic voices in our midst. Womanist love and care for all people is the signal for the engagement of rhetoric. As we value the stories and orality of others and as we celebrate our own sensuousness and our own ability to express, we can take delight in the eloquent amid poverty, getting by, and wealth. The loving power that this transformative process generates is one of the many kinds of realizations that take place when we educate and live for freedom, thereby knowing a heightened sense of awareness, understanding, and actualization.

Despite the risky nature of this kind of deep tissue work, a Womanist theological ethic of violence is offensive to some and is dangerous complex work. To do this work involves offending the egocentric, bitter sensibilities of another. A Womanist religious engagement of violence is representational as it has a purpose or function, is artistic in the best sense of the word, and is organic, girded by a visceral sense of "what is so." The more intimate we are with ourselves in loving ways, the more we are able to Refine the Fire of relational life happenings through conversations and relationship building. There are things to which we must say yes. There are other situations that this paradigm demands we respond with "No!" And there are other situations where we must say "maybe" or "not just yet." Making such choices in relationship building has a rising impetus, an intense movement across the strata of socioeconomic class, gender, race, and age. The intensity comes at the moment of choice. The possibility for choice in and of itself gives the impetus for the restorative.

Like the daughters of Zelophehad, we must ask for restoration, for new models that exact healing and visibility of the others toward justice. A Womanist paradigm for engaging the intersection between violence and the spiritual Refines the Fires of resilience: an adventure that is buoyant, flexible, and expansive. This is an invitation to dance, to live, to sing, to be, and to Refine the Fires of justice, peace, and anticipatory love—naming the lies and deceit before giving utterance via word or deed, as we fully comprehend that God loves us, God loves us just the way we are, and there is nothing we can do to change that love of God for us. God made us sacred and holy, and God did not make a mistake in speaking all people into existence and qualifying humanity as good.

> And hope beckons me
> To come into sanctuary
> Where unconditional love
> Forever shrouds violence into nothingness.

9. Death as Worship: Celebrating Dying as Part of Life

Death: just a breath away
Life and death,
Point and counterpoint
Face off each moment:
between inhale and exhale.
Between each breath we take,
People live, People die.
Life comes;
Death takes no holiday,
Death visits:
Noisily, quietly, repulsively, peacefully, enigmatically—
Where did all that hot air go?
Butterflies fly,
Death comes.
Praise, Adore, Embody God: Live life.
Die, dead, expire.
Death for me, death for you
When we let oppression
Snuff out our life force: our ideas, our actions,
Our very being:
Gloria in Excelsis Deo!
Our essence
Exits stage left.
We allow
Things and people
To break our sweet communion
with God,
Unadulterated theft.

I held her hand as she died. Fifty years before God had breathed life into her and she became a living being. I sang a few songs, read Scripture, and prayed. I told her to breathe down. She inhaled the Holy Spirit, exhaled all pain and suffering, and died. I saw breath and life leave and death enter in. The nurse confirmed that she was dead.

We called family members from the hall into the room to say good-bye. A nurse phoned members of our prayer band. Together, as a true body of Christ, we experienced death as worship. The Refining Fire of God had molded a cooling board for our friend.

Death: A Turnstile to the Unknown

Death, a turnstile to the unknown, is a rich, powerful, and painful cultural and theological experience that Refines the Fires of ultimate joyous encounter. Death is the way station of life that follows incarnated life,[1] when living and breathing consciousness has ceased. For the living dead, those who still breathe, physical death may or may not be the same type of experience; they are alive, but the depths of their woundedness, oppression, and resulting self-hatred deadens their spirits and vitality, their humanness. Death, the ultimate measure of life, is a door to active eternal life. Christians believe that God created them *imago dei*. That belief permits us to choose to experience Christian life and Christian death as liturgical celebrations, as worship.

Liturgy is thinking about and embodying God, creation, salvation, and other doctrines or beliefs into the context of worship and prayer. The worship experience is the adoration, praise, and thanksgiving to God for God's grace and glory by the corporate, gathered community. Using the liturgical experience as a metaphor illumines the relationship between death, life, and God as worship.

This chapter, in order to explore death as worship, uses liturgical expressions and seasons with their liturgical colors and the experience of certain moments during the worship service as moments of Refining divine Fires of praise and inspiration. That is, we explore the celebration of transition to eternal life by the African American Christian community from a Womanist perspective. In traditional African culture and in the Christian experience, death is transition and may be transforming. The mood of this chapter reflects a liturgical hermeneutic that integrates the writing and reading of this work into an act of praise. This hermeneutical or interpretative methodological dialogue of praise becomes a litany. The antiphonal moments engage my text with excerpts of Womanist poetry as response.

> . . . and only those who stay dead
> shall remember death.
> —Audre Lorde[2]

Death: A Transition of Time-Ordered Life

Death is a transition or translation of time-ordered life, but is not the absence of life. When we come together as children of God and stand next to the body of our beloved friend, we are multiracial, ecumenical, female and male, and diverse socio-economic classes. We gather in an act of praise, a profound liturgical moment of shifting realities. Amid joy and sorrow, we lay hands on her once again. Many times before, we had sung, read Scripture, and prayed together, had brought her food and drink, and took her to treatment centers. We had lived and Refined the Fires of compassion, generosity, and love. She had fought her disease and daily claimed her healing triumph in the Lord. Her courage allowed her to do the unbelievable. She led a normal life in the agony of terminal suffering. She gave her last recital, despite a medical death sentence, and her regal demeanor endured midst suffering and cloaked her in death. We celebrate her life and death as the process of living and ultimate healing. We cry and rejoice. She died. We are all in transition. Death is an ultimate transition, a mysterious journey Refining the Fires of immortality and difference.

Is Death the Enemy or a Pilgrimage of Joy?

This mysterious rite of passage becomes an experience of terror when death is the enemy. Death is a pilgrimage of joy when one knows that both life and death are gifts. Death brings humanity more fully into God's presence; thus, death is liberating. Death is inevitable, and it affects every area of our lives. Yet, we distance ourselves from death by worshipping youthfulness, immortality, and materialism. Examples of such distancing include the increased number of deaths at hospitals and sterile care facilities in the presence of strangers, instead of at home, in the presence of family and friends. This is not to say that we cannot be surrounded by love, relatives, and friends when the monumental nature of illness and dying demands that one is hospitalized. Once life is no longer present, an entire industry strives to make the dead corpse lifelike with the appearance of sleep or rest, a denial that death has visited the human.

The implicit denial of death and human finitude, the social abhorrence of death as a topic of conversation, is the dis-ease of ageism: the marginalization, discrimination, and exclusive behavior by persons and institutions. By facing the reality of death, we confront and combat human frailty, loneliness, feelings of dispensability, and actual incapacitation of aging with love. We combat the feelings of fear and meaninglessness by celebrating the God-presence in every aging person. We Refine the Fires of wellness and contentment when we fully grasp that every person at each stage of her or his life is sacred, holy. The responsibility of all communities is to celebrate this holy life and help us remember who each person is. Then we can embrace the dying person as necessary, wanted, and vital even when facing the awesomeness and often agony of the dying process. Death itself is a quiet release. To refuse to engage and minister to aging and dying persons is to violate one's own personhood and to forget that life itself is a gift. Life continuously evolves and embraces the fact that all who are born die.

A few years ago, I gave last rites to a beautiful 106-year-old spirit: what a privilege and a gift to stand at the bedside of one who had lived a thousand, thousand days. Those moments felt as if time was suspended. Nothing else mattered but sharing all the love, gentleness, and nobility that I could with an ancient, sweet soul. In that moment she and I were between the now and not yet, an eschatological moment of grace.

Life and Death Are Eschatological

Awareness about the essence of who we are and whose we are in life and death is eschatological. An eschatological life is one in which the experiences, visions, and ethics as praxis define how one deals with aging, the immediacy of death, and finitude. Seeing how we live in the now illumines and reflects what we expect to happen in our last days and in eternity. The goals of our life signal our sense of realized eschatology: that which we experience now shapes and manifests now and in the future. An eschatological sense of death has far reaching implications for all to expand beyond the experience of last things to daily goals, visions, and ethical imperatives. An eschatological view places life next to, around, and beside death. The collision of that confrontation can be either overwhelming or liberating when made pertinent to God's presence in individual and corporate life. Death is real, and it laughs in the face of mortality. Being mortal and spirit, we are "ecclesiastic" people—people fueled by the Holy Spirit and shaped by natural cycles and experiences of time. The life encounter expressed liturgically Refines the Fires of death as a moment for empowerment, tranquility, and reflection.[3]

Liturgical Seasons: Life Processes

A Womanist experience of the liturgical seasons embraces African American folk culture, the socio-political and religious ramifications of Black life, within the historical context of life and death. These encounters embrace the experiences and issues of Black women in life and literature as rituals of empowerment and liberation. Such rituals embrace celebration and social protest. Womanist thought gives voice to those silenced by the oppression of race/sex/class differences and gives voice with the tools and ideologies informed by history, economics, theology, and biblical witness. Womanist theory requires a universalist temperament. That universalism Refines the Fires of human self-expression as one who can love all people, as one who is outrageous and creatively embraces life that hinges on the survival and wholeness of all people.[4]

> . . . in memory of the bitter hours when we discovered we
> were black and poor and small and different and nobody
> cared and nobody wondered and nobody understood;
> For the boys and girls who grew in spite of these things
> to be man and woman, to laugh and dance and sing and
> play and drink their wine and religion and success, to
> marry their playmates and bear children and then die of
> consumption and anemia and lynching. . . .
> —Margaret Walker[5]

Such a view of death requires that people remember the liberation traditions of Black folk culture and community. We remember the personhood of women and men in our communities as we acknowledge all age groups and persons. We engage their voices and celebrate their thoughts and faith experiences that have enabled humanity to survive as the oppressions of racism, sexism, classism, and ageism have made most of us face off death moments on a daily basis. A Womanist study of death as worship is a rhythmic dance of Advent, Christmastide, Epiphany, Lent, Eastertide, and Pentecost. These seasons, moments of complex Refining Fires, mirror the Christian life process.[6]

The Advent Season
Advent begins with the fourth Sunday before Christmas. During this season, Christians rehearse the first coming of Christ, of the Incarnation, of God become human and await the coming of Christ in final judgment. Many observe this joyous, redemptive season as a time for prayer and fasting. We experience the Advent of persons and events: of Christ, of new babies, of transitional periods, of growth. Some get caught in the consumerism that can drown out the honest, simple beauty of this season. During antebellum slavery, the birth of each new babe was followed by the question, "Is this child the one, the one who will lead us out of bondage?" In contemporary African American communities, the Advents of new life experiences and death are constant. Death can and has visited us at the moment of birth, when the child leaves the womb and enters the world. Womanists anticipate and embrace this life and death dialectic. Womanists envision new life as a healthy community that welcomes the birth of equality and the death of racism/sexism/classism.

The royal color purple symbolizes both the Womanist experience and the solemn anticipation of Advent. Purple depicts majesty and heralds Christ's coming. This anticipatory sense invites us to note the majesty in all humanity, in life, and in death. For God loves "a mess of stuff [we] don't. . . . [God wants us] to share a good thing. . . . It pisses god [*sic*] off if you walk by the color purple in a field somewhere and don't notice it."[7] What kinds of rituals can we create to help people experience the color purple as they cross over life's joyful or painful hurdles and over the chilly and liberating Jordan? Suffering persons with deep spirituality and a strong God presence anticipate their imminent encounter with death. What about the living dead, alive to addictions and hopelessness, but dead to life itself? How do we help them Refine the Fires illumined by the color purple and thus anticipate transformation and renewal?

> . . . she's been dead so long
> closed in silence so long
> she doesn't know the sound
> of her own voice . . .
> let her be born
> & handled warmly.
> "dark phrases," lady in brown
> —Ntozake Shange[8]

Christmastide

Christmastide, the liturgical feast that celebrates the birth of Jesus, is the day that honors the gift of life, renewal, and God's incarnated love and mercy. This embodied light and hope of the world glows brightly. God's radiance eclipses the glare caused by the commercialization of Christmas. The true sense of the Christ-mass is the celebration of God's love in concert with human good will and the praxis of building relationships and family. Birth is the gateway to family.

Families—biological, extended, and/or created—are the context of lives conjoined: patterns of behavior, symphonies of voices, complexities and myths that juxtapose the real with the ideal. Physical, spiritual, emotional, and socio-psychological births or rebirths offer opportunities for transforming anger, violence, denial, domination, subordination, and patriarchal kinships into intimacy, egalitarianism, *agape,* mutuality, and respect. Birth evokes memory, and memory recreates the family—ancestors, contemporaries, the yet unborn. A concept of family that births an empowering attitude about the recontextualization of the African American family within an oppressive society can move us toward wholeness. In our society, children are not born with hate, but institutions and sick families quickly imbue infants with notions of otherness and inferiority. A Womanist view of the family sees and celebrates difference and similarity. Fear, ignorance, and the need to control thrive on subjugation of "those people," of others, and make difference pathological. That pathology issues a death warrant to mutuality and love of the neighbor.

Christmas offers an alternative prognosis. Christmas does not deny reality but Refines the Fires of possibility for attitude adjustments and transformation. The color white, the color for Christmas and Epiphany, the color of innocence and virginity, symbolizes the potential for magnificence that is in Christmas and Epiphany. Christmas and Epiphany refract the light of God that shines in every human being. Christmas awakens the opportunity; Epiphany makes the pronouncement.[9]

Epiphany

Epiphany is the church festival that observes the coming of the Magi as the first recognition of Christ by the Gentiles, or in the Eastern church, the baptism of Christ. This manifestation or pronounced reality echoes the power of the spoken word. The Magi, like God, spoke and that which was stated—the Logos— came into being. The spoken word brings forth and begets reality. The power of speech creates but can also destroy. Words become living entities, bringing life, death, or both. Words are bits of language. Language makes up conversation. Conversations for action are the crux of reality and can change the world.[10] The words of Epiphany live via signifying. In the Black vernacular, signifying is a rhetorical strategy or language game of double voicing. Double voicing embraces repetition, revision, and intertextuality, to express simultaneously meanings of an original utterance and multiple other meanings. This process draws upon the sounds of words as opposed to their meanings.

The signification of Epiphany is the adult naming and encoding ritual, the meta-discourse, that affords a Black rhetorical process of difference and independence. Signifying, a figure of speech, is a trope that details the life and death processes integral to being and existence. Health care practitioners signify the actuality, time, place, and date of birth and death. Birth and death certificates codify these significations. Epiphany invites us to signify or pronounce life and accept death in faith, Refining the Fires of existence as gift. Christian faith signifies death as confession, not explanation. Such faith teaches that physical death limits humanity but is not inherently evil. Physical death lets us know life and God in a different way. Spiritual death and human anxiety about physical death separate us from God. The confession of Epiphany is the mystery of life and death embodied within the incarnated Christ Jesus.

> Evil is no black thing: black
> may be the undertaker's hearse
> and so many of the civil trappings

of death, but not its essence:
. . . the grave shines
darkly; but these are the rituals
of the living.
                              —Sarah Webster Fabio[11]

Lent

The Lenten season is forty days long, forty days[12] that echo Jesus' time in the wilderness during his fasting and meditation, from Ash Wednesday to Easter Sunday. Lent evolved from a time of preparation for the Easter baptism, when the catechumens received instruction, fasted, and prayed, to a time when many Christians today observe penitence, fasting, thanksgiving, and reflections concerning God's promises. This reflection time allows one to contemplate personal and corporate sin, or living death, and move toward penitence and forgiveness. The juxtaposition of life and death at the cross on Good Friday creates a paradox, a dialectic of the now and the not yet. Each year, many give up or deny themselves a particular habit, pleasure, or experience as a means of distancing themselves from worldly pleasures, Refining the Fires of discipline and asceticism. This period of active fasting and waiting is an effort to prepare their hearts, to abstain from self, and to move toward a higher spiritual plane. Lent is a time to die to the secular and draw toward the sacrality of life. From a Womanist perspective, Lent is a time to test personal wholeness: a time to acknowledge betrayals, losses, alienation; a time to pray for the willingness to experience and offer God's forgiving grace and sustaining love.

During these reflective moments, an individual contemplates the previous instances of sin or living death as she or he repents, seeks divine forgiveness, and moves toward transformation. Lent is a corporate and an individual wilderness experience. The forty days embrace an Exodus motif in which one moves from Egypt to the promised land. The eminence of Good Friday sets a tone for one who wants new life. The cross stands ominously within a dialectic of despair and hope.

Many recognize the cross but question the whole nature of atonement, of being renewed to God. Some concede that the life-giving blood sacrifice, required for atonement, resulted in Jesus' death. Many ask how could a loving God require the death of any child, particularly the Child of the Divine? Some thus argue for focusing more on the revolutionary, life-giving ministry of Jesus as opposed to focusing on his death and then allowing oneself to be abused because one is allegedly carrying a cross. Some recognize the cross not as a sanctioning of violence and suffering but as testimony to such evil and as transformation.

Wherever one stands on atonement, every moment that we live brings us closer to our physical death. Every moment that we live is also an opportunity for our spiritual life. Amid the purple that symbolizes Lent, we all wait at the foot of all crosses, self-imposed and otherwise, and look and listen to receive Easter Sunday's good news. Lent opens us to a process of releasing Womanist melodies that embrace God's spirit as we struggle with trying to live harmoniously and to engage our critical voices within fragile personhood and a social order rife with double consciousness. Our purple lens enables us to set aside the mundane and awakens a hopeful imagination toward experiencing the glory of God amid the newness and the Resurrection, toward healing.

> . . . arched feet
> of deadly exuberant children . . .
> some singing some waving . . .
> their fathers knew tomorrow
> they will be dead.
> How can I mourn these children . . .
> Young do not dream of dying . . .
> the only dependable warmth
> is the burn of the blood.
> —Audre Lorde[13]

Eastertide

Resurrection is the activity of Eastertide. Eastertide begins with Easter Sunday and concludes on Pentecost. Easter celebrates life restored to a world previously devastated by sin. Easter implies the opportunity for recovery and Refines the Fires of life as gift, in which one celebrates this gift of choosing to live. Easter shares the reality that God is in charge and that life is God's gift to us. A true experience of Easter makes one uncomfortable and unwilling to remain in unhealthy relationships with self, God, and others, and a true experience of Easter reminds us that we cannot deny what we need to do to take care of ourselves. Easter is the manifestation of *agape*, love in action. The redemptive spirit of Easter pushes us toward gratitude and beyond the need to punish the other. Punitive otherness is a result of separation and ignorance. Easter strikes the death knell to the evils of separation, ignorance, idolatry, and sin. *"Mortis formidine, vitae percepit humanos odioum lucisque videndae"* (for fear of death human beings are seized by hatred of life and of seeing the light).[14] Having any person, place, or thing as ultimate concern other than God is idolatry. To have victimhood or egoism as the generating life source also intones idolatry. Easter confronts this idolatry, Refining the Fires of paradox—the tension between sin and grace.

This confrontation between sin and grace reorders individual and communal life experiences toward championing the sacrality of life. Life, as a sacramental confession, relies on rituals of penance and mercy. Easter worship involves rituals and symbols that focus on the ecclesial and christological reality of human life. Placing the church, the body of Christ, and the eternal Jesus Christ at the center of Christian life is an invitation for a life of service. A life that embraces altruistic behavior and Christian service is a most promising ethos and praxis for Christian leadership and discipleship. This resurrection lifestyle reconstructs reality and leads to socio-cultural, religious, and political solidarity. The color white,[15] a symbol of innocence, symbolizes the risen Christ's radiance, the living light and hope for all those who thirst for living water along with the solidarity of the Easter triumph over sin, suffering, and death.

The liberating force of Christian Womanist theology recognizes that Easter grants us the permission and in fact demands that we preach, teach, and practice a theology that posits a holistic, integrated reality of African American womanhood, the wholeness of Black women and ultimately of all women and men. Easter says "No!" to all forms of subjugation and destruction, including socio-economic oppression. Easter says "Yes!" to the concerns of the "least of these" for "all of us!" The Easter commemoration Refines the Fires of resurrection love, making us fishers (evangelists) of people. Our theology and ethics demand that now is the time to "fish or cut bait" through the empowerment of the Holy Spirit.

> . . . the pain
>   stopped
> I took a breath of
> life
> birth was completed
> growth was begun
> I was sister
> I had . . . Black
> Proud   IDENTITY.
>   —Johari Amini (Jewel C. Larimore)[16]

Pentecost

Christians move from Eastertide to celebrate the outpouring of the Holy Spirit during Pentecost, a word derived from the Greek term *pentekostos* applied to the fiftieth day after Passover, the Christian anniversary of the coming of the Holy Spirit. The Pentecost feast represents the manifestation of divine power and the beginning of the church. Passover marked the beginning of the harvest season; Pentecost, the Feast of Weeks, marked the end of the harvest season, the end of the Easter Refining Fire. At Pentecost, the Holy Spirit descended upon a group of 120 praying disciples, for Jesus told them to remain in Jerusalem until they received divine power. As the Holy Spirit descended upon them, via the sound of great winds and tongues of fire, the disciples began to speak in many other languages, so all could listen in their own languages, and these 120 disciples began to preach boldly in the name of Jesus the Christ.

The Holy Spirit Refines the Fires of empowerment, advocacy, and revitalization. Red, the liturgical symbol for Pentecost, depicts these flames and the outpouring of the power on the disciples. The color red represents the gifts of the outpouring: empowerment, expansion, and rebirth. Pentecost, from eleven to sixteen Sundays beginning with Pentecost Sunday, symbolizes the new life that combats living death. The red flames of expansion inspire humanity to desire healing and move actively toward transformation. The rebirth experience is the manifestation of people receiving the anointing. An anointed life is a life of awareness—the awareness of powers and principalities. An anointed life Refines the Fires of opportunity to know peace while living midst the dialectic of flesh and spirit. (Kingdom-tide is often symbolized by the color green, which depicts the prosperity of harvesttime, and is often subsumed under the Pentecost season, which continues until Advent.) Pentecost is a time of embracing newness that does not fear death. Pentecost anticipates possibility and welcomes the intimacy of a spirit-filled life in Christ. A Womanist vision of Pentecost Refines the Fires of healing old wounds and celebrates life as an unfolding journey and death as a consequence of life.

> Rest. In peace
> in me
> the meaning
> of our lives
> is still
> unfolding.
> —Alice Walker[17]

Liturgical Moments: Death as Process

The liturgical seasons reflect a life and death experience of mystery, miracle, and empowerment. We can describe what happens at birth and death, but we do not really know what happens. We see the wonderment of the miraculous realities and possibilities in a spiritual life in relationship. Relationships are paramount to life. Without relationships one can only know death. We also see the result of Refining the Fires of authority: changed attitudes, changed visions, and changed lives. The embodiment of mystery, miracle, and empowerment within human life undergirds liturgical moments of the worship service. In viewing selected liturgical moments common to many Protestant, Orthodox, and Roman Catholic worship services, we see that these liturgical moments parallel the human life/death experience as a procession toward the praise and adoration of God, which ends with a sending forth to live life.

The Processional

The introit or processional of the worship service is the moving toward God through Christ Jesus and the movement in life toward death. The candle-lighting represents the illumination that opens us to see God and opens us to let the light of God shine through us. This illumination gives us the courage to face the injustices of life and the reality of death. Death moves us toward eternal life. The greeting and call to worship invite the congregation to focus on the adoration of God. The adoration and praise of God always encourages us to be at one with God as a community of faith. Such praise assures us that we are never alone. Even in death, God never forsakes us. The hymn of praise, along with other musical selections, liturgical drama, and dance, follows the dictates of the Psalmist, who invites us to praise God with every breath and every fiber and act of our being: Refining the Fires of holy embodiment.

All such creative liturgical expressions reflect the beauty of creation and provide the opportunity for fulfillment not afforded us with the onset of physical death or the separation indicative of spiritual demise. Prayers, responsive readings, affirmations of faith, and covenant statements or creeds are reactions and supplications to God. These reactions denote what we believe, what we desire, and how we are called to live. The thanksgiving and pleas common to prayer and response are the inspiring encounters that help us face daily life and death experiences. The affirming nature of worship is concretized in the giving of gifts.

Tithes, Offerings, Sermon, and Benediction

Tithes and offerings are one way we concretely give back to God and to the community of believers. Tithing of time and other gifts is critical to a full experience of life, a full experience that negates any need to deny our own mortality, aging, and death.

Scripture readings feed us spiritually and provide the context for the sermon. The sermon or homily flushes out the theological and ethical implications for Christian life and discipleship. The eucharist, also known as the Lord's Supper or Holy Communion, offers us atonement, forgiveness, freedom, and intimate relationship with God, Refining the Fires of renewal, rebirth, and reclamation of *imago dei*. The life that we live reflects our sacramental hermeneutic and preaches a sermon more striking than the words we speak. Our living sermon also says a great deal about our perspective on death.

The benediction blesses us and admonishes us to go forth and proclaim the gospel. The last breath that we breathe is a benediction that opens the door of transition toward eternal life.

A Womanist Experience of Ritual

A Womanist experience of liturgical moments acknowledges the power and mystery of ritual. Womanist experience knows the mystery and power of Blackness, the symbol and embodiment of African American life. Blackness embraces all liturgical colors: the royalty and magnificence of purple, the illumination of white, the harvest and prosperity of green, and the Refining Fire power of red. Blackness does not stand in opposition to but is inclusive of life and death. Interestingly, from the view of physics, white light is the reflection of all colors; black is the absorption of all colors. Today in the West, black and white are usually deemed the colors of death.

> Death be not proud, though some have called thee
> Mighty and dreadful, for thou art not so,
> For those whom thou think'st thou dost overthrow,
> Die not, poor Death. . . .
> One short sleep past, we wake eternally,
> And death shall be no more; Death, thou shalt die.
> —John Donne[18]

Life and death are two experiences on the continuum of living. Neither life nor death is necessarily fair, convenient, or predictable. There are no fixed ways to live, although ethical and moral imperatives do exist. The realities of life offer many options for our use of time, meaning, and memory. But death confronts those realities and causes problems ranging from the familial to the financial. There are no set patterns for how those left to mourn will deal with death.

Even the stages posited by Elisabeth Kübler-Ross[19] (denial and isolation, anger, bargaining, depression, acceptance), which Kübler-Ross recently recanted when faced with her own impending demise, are not everyone's experience of death and dying. Scholars hold opposing views as to how we should cope with death, the pattern of grief, and the place of friends, the support of fellow sufferers. Much needs to be said about ways to deal with the funeral in a manner that allows the church to proclaim a significant resurrection doctrine. We need more analysis and reflection as well as preparation of the faith community family, so that the funeral event can become a time of affirmation that invites humanity to stand before the ultimate of existence and face it with fortitude and faith, not anxiety and fear.

Womanist Liturgics: Hurting, Pain, and Grief

Womanist liturgics invite us to embrace and legitimize all hurting and pain, especially the grief process as ministry to the body of Christ. Womanist liturgics also celebrate and teach us the values of balance. Thus, just as we cannot preach the entire Bible in one sermon, we cannot fully explore all the ramifications of life and death here. We can conclude that the mysterious, miraculous, powerful experiences of life and death not only mirror each other, but also are often separated only by the giving and ceasing of breath. Womanist liturgics invite each of us to Refine the Fires of celebration and praise as we breathe, dance, adore, and pray. In so doing, we build friendships and nurture each other's souls, to live and die in the faith and love of a God who never sleeps and a God who breathes life into us.

> The spirit within
> Loses touch with reality,
> Oh what Pain
> for the Creator who never sleeps!
> Yes, Jesus wept and still weeps.
> The tears flow, knowing the grief
> when *imago dei*
> Separates from the Almighty Beloved,
> And from the Almighty in humanity:
> The self, the neighbor,
> The addict, the thief, the liar,
> all who mirror you and me.
> Forget bout MTV!
> Are the children home?
> Seasons of purple,
> Red, green, white
> Be present, doing praise
> All are sacred in God's sight.
> We are invited, without fright
> To see God is here.
> And what of our children?
> Are they part
> Of a heart too filled with
> The gods of Death?
> They, so close to the divine,
> Still trust,

Until we deaden their souls.
But Jesus also laughs.
We laugh, and we live, and we sneeze, even as we die:
"Say Amen, Somebody!"

Notes

1. Eyes on the Prize: Womanist Reflections

1. Alice Walker, *In Search of Our Mothers' Gardens: Womanist Prose* (New York: Harcourt Brace Jovanovich, 1967, 1983) xi; Jacquelyn Grant, *White Woman's Christ and Black Woman's Jesus: Feminist Christology and Womanist Response* (Atlanta: Scholars, 1989) 200–202.

2. Grant, *White Woman's Christ, Black Woman's Jesus,* 205.

3. Guy Carawan and Candie Carawan, *Sing for Freedom: The Story of the Civil Rights Movement through Its Songs* (Bethlehem, Pa.: Sing Out, 1990) 111. Alice Wine, one of the first "graduates" of the voter education schools of Johns Island, South Carolina, created this redacted version of the Spiritual "Keep your hand on the plow," in which she changed the words to "keep your eyes on the prize." This song is the theme song for the ten-part video documentary series, "Eyes on the Prize," covering the Civil Rights Movement from 1954 to 1978, edited by the late Henry Hampton, Blackside, Inc.

4. Walker, *Our Mothers' Gardens,* ix.

5. Kelly Brown Douglas, "To Reflect the Image of God," in Cheryl J. Sanders, ed., *Living the Intersection: Womanism and Afrocentrism in Theology* (Minneapolis: Fortress, 1995) 76–77.

6. Sheldon Solomon, taped lecture on "The Thought of Ernest Becker," presented by the Ernest Becker Foundation, University of Washington, Seattle (April 28, 1994). See also Ernest Becker, *Escape from Evil* (New York: Free, 1975).

7. James H. Cone, *For My People: Black Theology and the Black Church* (Maryknoll, N.Y.: Orbis, 1984) 125, 128–29.

8. Ibid., 129. Deborah Gray White, *Ar'n't I A Woman: Female Slaves in the Plantation South* (New York: W. W. Norton, 1985) 14, 23.

9. Kelly Delaine Brown, "God Is as Christ Does: Toward a Womanist Theology," *The Journal of Religious Thought* 46 (summer–fall, 1989) 11.

10. See Deane William Ferm, *Contemporary American Theologies* (San Francisco: Harper & Row, 1981, 1990) 58.

11. See Joan Wilen and Ludia Wilen, *The Perfect Name for the Perfect Baby* (New York: Fawcette/Columbine, 1993).

12. Cheryl Townsend Gilkes, "Mother to the Motherless, Father to the Fatherless: Power, Gender, and Community in an Afrocentric Biblical Tradition," *Semeia: An Experimental Journal for Biblical Criticism* 47 (1989) 57–85.

13. M. Shawn Copeland, "Wading through Many Sorrows": Toward a Theology of Suffering in Womanist Perspective," in Emilie Townes, ed., *A Troubling in My Soul: Womanist Perspectives on Evil and Suffering* (Maryknoll, N.Y.: Orbis, 1993) 109–29.

14. Katie G. Cannon, "The Wounds of Jesus: Justification of Goodness in the Face of Manifold Evil," in Townes, 222–31.

15. Grant, *White Women's Christ, Black Woman's Jesus,* 212–22; Jacquelyn Grant, "The Sin of Servanthood and the Deliverance of Discipleship," in Townes, 199–210.

16. Grant, "The Sin of Servanthood," in Townes, 210–16.

17. Delores S. Williams, *Sisters of the Wilderness: The Challenge of Womanist God-Talk* (Maryknoll, N.Y.: Orbis, 1993) 2–6, 15–33, 60–62. See Genesis, chapters 16 and 21. The experience of motherhood also involves institutionalization of mammy; the reinstitutionalization of denominational "mothers" of the church; the shift of authority from Black women to a Black male patriarchal authority; the literary concretization of that shift in blues songs and postbellum Black male protest thought; the patriarchal, androcentric African American denominational liturgy and the male religious leaders who exploit Black female constituency; the celebration of Black female spirituality by Black female postbellum writers; the role of Black women as catalysts for social change; and the impact of structures of domination on the lives of African American mothers and nurturers.

18. Delores S. Williams, "A Womanist Perspective on Sin," in Townes, 137–47.

19. Williams, *Sisters of the Wilderness,* 164–67.

20. Ibid., 108–9, 113, 117. The wilderness is the place where God meets Black women in times of trouble, impending death or destruction; where God cares and gives the believer personal direction, which helps her make a way out of no way, a religious wilderness experience of transformation. Wilderness had a different connotation for the dominant White American culture. Early pioneers envisioned the wilderness as a hostile place that required conquering not living in. The wilderness was a remote, strange place of solitude and freedom for European Romanticism.

21. Douglas, "To Reflect the Image of God," in Sanders, 67–77.

22. Kelly Brown Douglas, *The Black Christ* (Maryknoll, N.Y.: Orbis, 1994) 116–17.

23. Emilie Townes, "Living in the New Jerusalem: The Rhetoric and Movement of Liberation in the House of Evil," in Townes, 73–86.

24. Ibid., 86-91; Emilie Townes, *In A Blaze of Glory: Womanist Spirituality as Social Witness* (Nashville: Abingdon, 1995), 11, 48, 58, 60, 64–67, 71, 77, 81–84, 87, 109, 115, 117–19, 130–36, 143–44.

25. Delores S. Williams, "Womanist Theology: Black Women's Voices," in Judith Plaskow and Carol P. Christ, eds., *Weaving the Visions: New Patterns in Feminist Spirituality* (San Francisco: HarperCollins, 1989) 183–85.

26. See Abraham Maslow, *Motivation and Personality* (2d ed.; New York: Harper & Row, 1970).

27. *The Auburn Lecture: A Day with Alice Walker,* the second annual Auburn Lecture at Union Theological Seminary, April 25, 1995.

28. bell hooks, *Killing Rage: Ending Racism* (New York: Henry Holt, 1995) 12.

29. Ibid., 16, 19, 47.

30. Ibid. 4, 8, 11, 19, 47, 57, 61.

2. Take No Prisoners: Biblical Women Engaged in Violence

1. This phrase is a parody of the movie *What's Love Got to Do with It?* starring Tina Turner, a film rife with violence, transformation, and religious elements.

2. Leila L. Bronner, "Valorized or Vilified? The Women of Judges in Midrashic Sources," in Athalya Brenner, ed., *The Feminist Companion to the Bible,* vol. 4: Judges (Sheffield, Eng.: JSOT Press, 1993) 78–79, 81–86.

3. Carol Blessing, "Judge, Prophet, Mother: Learning from Deborah," *Daughters of Sarah* (winter 1995) 34–36.

4. Barnabas Lindars, "Deborah's Song: Women in the Old Testament," *Bulletin of the John Rylands University Library of Manchester* 2 (spring 1983) 160, 162, 165, 166–72. Daniel Block, "Deborah among the Judges: The Perspective of the Hebrew Historian," in A. R. Millard, James Hoffmeier, David W. Baker, eds., *Faith, Tradition, and History: Old Testament Historiography in Its Near Eastern Context* (Winona Lake, Ind.: Eisenbrauns, 1994) 249, 251–52; Danna Noland Fewell and David M. Gunn, *Gender, Power, and Promise: The Subject of the Bible's First Story* (Nashville: Abingdon, 1993) 124–26.

5. Richard Patterson, "The Song of Deborah," in John Feinberg and Paul Feinberg, eds., *Tradition and Testament: Essays in Honor of Charles Lee Feinberg* (Chicago: Moody, 1981) 148–49.

6. Phyllis Trible, "The Odd Couple: Elijah and Jezebel," in Christina Büchmann and Celina Spiegel, eds., *Out of the Garden: Women Writers on the Bible* (New York: Fawcett Columbine, 1994) 166–79. Elijah vanishes into a whirlwind; Jezebel is reduced to dung.

7. Judith Todd, "The Pre-Deuteronomistic Elijah Cycle," in Robert Coote, ed., *Elijah and Elisha in Socioliterary Perspective* (Atlanta: Scholars, 1992) 1–2.

8. Ibid., 3–10. Deuteronomistic history sees the revolution as the cause for the loss of the land.

9. Trible, "The Odd Couple," in Büchmann and Spiegel, 167–169, 173–75.

10. Tina Pippin, "Jezebel Re-Vamped," in Athalya Brenner, ed., *The Feminist Companion to the Bible,* vol. 5: Samuel and Kings (Sheffield, Eng.: Sheffield Academic, 1995) 20, 21, 196–97, and Athalya Brenner, "Introduction," in Brenner, vol. 5, 13–25.

11. Pippin, "Jezebel Re-Vamped," in Brenner, vol. 5, 197. On doubles in mother-daughter relationships, see Jane Gallop, "The Monster in the Mirror: The Feminist Critic's Psychoanalysis," in Richard Feldstein and Judith Roof, eds., *Feminism and Psychoanalysis* (Ithaca, N.Y.: Cornell University Press, 1989) 13–24.

12. Jacob Katzenstein, "Who Were the Parents of Athaliah?" *Israel Exploration Journal* 5 (1955) 194–97. Katzenstein argues that based on the dates of Athaliah's birth and of Omri becoming sole ruler, Ahab could be the father, but Jezebel would not be the mother. Based on 2 Kings 8:26 and 2 Chron. 22:2, one could posit that Athaliah was the daughter of Omri but grew up as an orphan in Ahab's court under the supervision of Jezebel.

13. Sidnie Ann White, "In the Steps of Jael and Deborah: Judith as Heroine," in James C. VanderKam, ed., *"No One Spoke Ill of Her": Essays on Judith* (Atlanta: Society of Biblical Literature, 1992) 5–6.

14. Ibid., 7, 12–13. Women-directed salvation occurs often in the Hebrew Bible.

15. André LaCocque, *The Feminine Unconventional* (Minneapolis: Fortress, 1990) 35, 46.

16. Toni Craven, *Artistry and Faith in the Book of Judith* (Chico, Calif.: Scholars, 1983) 95. See Judith 8 and 9.

17. Craven, *Artistry and Faith*, 96.

18. John Craghan, "Judith Revisited," *Biblical Theology Bulletin* 12 (April 1982) 51–53.

19. Patricia Montley, "Judith in the Fine Arts: The Appeal of the Archetypal Androgyne," *Anima* 4 (spring 1978) 38.

20. Ibid.

21. Brian McNeil, "Reflections on the Book of Judith," *The Downside Review* 96 (July 1978) 202–4.

22. Aristobulus, like her grandmother Marianne I, was assassinated by order of her grandfather. Josephus does record Herodias as married to a Philip in Rome and later to Herod Antipas. Antipas's first wife's father, Aretas IV, the Nabatean King of Arabia, attacked and invaded Antipas's territory in revenge with such a force that Antipas had to get help from Roman soldiers.

23. Salome's name does not appear in the biblical text. Joan Conway and Ronald Brownrigg, eds., *Who's Who in the Bible: Two Volumes in One* (New York: Bonanza, 1980) 143, 393.

24. Several sources support a historical reconstruction of John the Baptist. The Baptist sources or disciples that formed a community after his death might provide the commentary about John's death as found in Mark 6:14-29 (Matt. 14:1-12, Luke 9:7-9): John dies as a result of offending Herodias and her entrapment of Herod through Salome's dance. Some suggest that this legend developed in the Gospel tradition because many of John's and Jesus' disciples did not want people to know that their teachers had been executed and because the authorities saw them as a threat to socio-political order and as possible insurrection leaders. See W. R. Farmer, "John the Baptist," in George A. Buttrick, ed., *The Interpreter's Bible Dictionary,* vol. 2 (Nashville: Abingdon, 1962) 955, 957.

25. Ibid., 955, 957. Josephus' account, in *Antiquities* 18, describes John as a pious, influential person. Herod feared John's power and sent John away as a prisoner to Macherus so he could not start a revolt.

26. Frederick Greenspahn, "A Typology of Biblical Women," *Judaism* 32 (winter 1983) 43, 46, 49.

27. Hoda Mahmoudi, "The Role of Men in Establishing the Equality of Women," *World Order* 26 (1995) 32.

28. Lillian R. Klein, "A Spectrum of Female Characters in the Book of Judges," in Brenner, vol. 4, 25.

29. Yairah Amit, "Judges 4: Its Contents and Form," *Journal for the Study of the Old Testament* 39 (1987) 100–101.

30. Peter C. Craigie, "Deborah and Anat: A Study of Poetic Imagery (Judges 5)," *Zeitschrift für die alttestamentliche Wissenschaft* 90 (1978) 375–81. The ancient northern Hebrews in the text probably knew of Anat's warlike reputation.

31. Adrien Janis Bledstein, "Is Judges a Woman's Satire of Men Who Play God?" in Brenner, vol. 4, 34–35, 38–42, 52.

32. Priscilla Denam, "It's Hard to Sing the Song of Deborah," in *Spinning a Sacred Yarn: Women Speak from the Pulpit* (New York: Pilgrim, 1982) 62–64.

33. Lillian Sigal, "Models of Love and Hate," *Daughters of Sarah* (March/April 1990) 8, 10.

34. Susan Niditch, "Eroticism and Death in the Tale of Jael," in Peggy Day, ed., *Gender and Difference in Ancient Israel* (Minneapolis: Fortress, 1989) 43, 45–47, 48, 50, 51–53.

35. Raymund Schwager, *Must There Be Scapegoats? Violence and Redemption in the Bible* (San Francisco: Harper and Row, 1987) 27.

36. Tamis H. Rentería, "The Elijah/Elisha Stories: A Socio-Cultural Analysis of Prophets and People in Ninth-Century BCE Israel," in Coote, 91, 124, and Calum Carmichael, "Biblical Laws of Talion" in Ahroni Reuben, ed., *Biblical and Other Studies in Memory of S. D. Goitlein, Hebrew Annual Review* 9 (1985) 110, 123.

37. Omri and later Ahab had an open border policy with Tyre, which appeared to assure cultural and economic development. Jezebel was a Tyrean princess.

38. Hannelis Schulte, "The End of the Omride Dynasty," *Die Entstehung der Geschichtsschreibung im Alten Israel, Zeitschrift für die alttestamentliche Wissenschaft* 128 (1972) 135–39, 144–46. Jehu had power in Samaria, Athaliah's former alliance, and she was cut off from her mother's homeland of Phoenicia.

39. Craven, *Artistry and Faith,* 75, 81, 89, 95–96. The three-fold chiastic pattern includes: Part I (a) campaign against disobedient nations; (b) Israel is terrified and prepares for war; (c) Holofernes talks with Achior and the latter put out of the Assyrian camp; (c') Achior received at Bethulia and talks with Israelites; (b') Holofernes calls for war preparations; Israel greatly terrified; (a') campaign against Bethulia and Israelites ready to surrender; Part II (a) Judith introduced; (b) Judith plans to save Israel; (c) Judith and her maid leave Bethulia; (d) Judith overwhelms Holofernes; (c') Judith and her unnamed maid return to Bethulia; (b') Judith plans to destroy Israel's enemy; (a') conclusion about Judith.

40. Jan Willem van Henten, "Judith as Alternative Leader: A Rereading of Judith 7–13" in Brenner, ed., *The Feminist Companion to the Bible,* vol. 7: Esther, Judith, and Susanna (Sheffield, Eng.: Sheffield Academic, 1995) 245–51.

41. John Craghan, "Esther, Judith, and Ruth: Paradigms for Human Liberation," *Biblical Theology Bulletin* 12 (January 1982) 11–15.

42. Ibid., 16–17.

43. Van Henten, "Judith as Alternative Leader," in Brenner, vol. 7, 228.

44. Patricia Montley, "Judith in the Fine Arts: The Appeal of the Archetypal Androgyne," *Anima* 4 (spring 1978) 39–40.

45. Amy-Jill Levine, "Sacrifice and Salvation: Otherness and Domestication in the Book of Judith," in Brenner, vol. 7, 211, 212. Manasseh, Judith's husband, dies ingloriously; Holofernes is unsuitable; Bagoas, who assists Holofernes, is a eunuch; and Achior passes out when he sees Holofernes's head.

46. Betsy Merideth, "Desire and Danger: The Drama of Betrayal in Judges and Judith," in Mieke Bal, ed., *Anti-Covenant: Counter-Reading Women's Lives in the Hebrew Bible* (Decatur, Ga.: Almond, 1989) 75.

47. Ibid., 75–76.

48. Craven, *Artistry and Faith,* 84, 85, 94.

49. M. Shawn Copeland, "Editorial Reflections," in Elisabeth Schüssler Fiorenza and M. Shawn Copeland, eds., *Violence against Women* (Concilium series; Maryknoll, N.Y.: Orbis, 1994) 119.

50. Ibid., vii–x.

51. Hoda Mahmoudi, "The Role of Men in Establishing the Equality of Women" *World Order* 26 (1995) 27–29.

52. Mark O. Hatfield, "No Limits to Love: The Bible and Violence," *Sojourners* 5 (April 1976) 22–23, and "Introduction," in Schüssler Fiorenza and Copeland, xvi, xciii.

53. Joanne Carlson Brown, "Because of the Angels: Sexual Violence and Abuse," in Schüssler Fiorenza and Copeland, 10.

54. In this section I apply to the biblical narratives some of the ideas of René Girard and Raymund Schwager. See Raymund Schwager, *Must There Be Scapegoats?* 21, 29, 30–31.

55. James Williams, "The Innocent Victim: René Girard on Violence, Sacrifice, and the Sacred," *Religious Studies Review* 14 (October 1988) 320.

56. Gale Yee, "By the Hand of a Woman: The Metaphor of the Woman Warrior in Judges 4," *Semeia* 61 (1993) 102–3, 104–5, 107–9, 114–16.

57. Thus perhaps before the reception of Judges 4 and 5, Deborah's story as a warrior and major character throughout was part of a women's oral tradition. Notably, whenever there are female deities, the females in a particular society tend to have more power and make greater contributions to that particular society.

58. Rachel C. Rasmussen, "Deborah the Woman Warrior in Judges and Judith," in Bal, 79–81, 85–87, 91–93.

59. Alice Ogden Bellis, *Helpmates,, Harlots, Heroes: Women's Stories in the Hebrew Bible* (Louisville, Ky.: Westminster John Knox, 1994) 117, 122.

60. Rasmussen, "Deborah the Woman Warrior," in Bal, 91.

61. Else K. Holt, "Urged On by His Wife Jezebel: A Literary Reading of 1 Kings 18 in Context," *Scandinavian Journal of the Old Testament* 9 (1994): 83–96.

62. Duane Christensen, "Huldah and the Men of Anathoth: Women in Leadership in the Deuteronomic History," in Kent H. Richards, ed., *Society of Biblical Literature 1984 Seminar Papers* (Atlanta: Scholars, 1984) 399–402.

63. Calum Carmichael, "Biblical Laws of Talion" *Hebrew Annual Review* 9 (1985) 108, 110, 111, 113.

64. Fewell and Gunn, *Gender, Power, and Promise,* 167.

65. Schulte, "The End of the Omride Dynasty," 145.

66. Craven, *Artistry and Faith,* 79.

67. Elizabeth Philpot, "Judith and Holofernes: Changing Images in the History of Art," in David Jasper, ed., *Translating Religious Texts: Translation, Transgression and Interpretation* (New York: St. Martin's, 1993) 83–84, 85–88.

68. Montley, "Judith in the Fine Arts," 41.

69. Schüssler Fiorenza and Copeland, *Violence against Women,* xv–xvi.

70. Cain H. Felder, "The Bible, Black Women, and Ministry," *The Journal of Religious Thought* 41 (fall-winter, 1985) 48–49.

71. Mahmoudi, "The Role of Men," 33–39.

72. Freema Gottlieb, "Three Mothers," *Judaism* 30 (spring 1981) 194–200.

73. Schulte, "The End of the Omride Dynasty," 142–44.

74. Todd, "Pre-Deuteronomistic," in Coote, 34, 35.

75. Craghan, "Judith Revisited," 53, 60; Toni Craven, "Tradition and Convention in the Book of Judith," *Semeia* 20 (1981) 49–52.

3. Lay My Burden Down: Spirituality Transcends Antebellum Violence

1. See James Weldon and J. Rosamond Johnson, *The Books of American Negro Spirituals* (New York: Harper & Row, 1926) Book 2, 142–43.

2. See Cheryl A. Kirk-Duggan, *Exorcizing Evil: A Womanist Approach to the Spirituals* (Maryknoll, N.Y.: Orbis, 1997).

3. Arthur C. Jones, *Wade in the Water: The Wisdom of the Spirituals* (Maryknoll, N.Y.: Orbis, 1993) 21.

4. Molefi Kete Asante, *The Afrocentric Idea* (Philadelphia: Temple University Press, 1987) 4–6.

5. Paul Jacobs and Saul Landau, *Natives and Slaves,* vol. 1 of *To Serve the Devil* (New York: Random House, 1971) 89. See William Z. Foster, *The Negro People in American History* (New York: International, 1954) 37.

6. See the accounts of insurrections led by Nat Turner, Gabriel Prosser, Denmark Vesey in the colonies, and Toussaint L'Ouverture in Haiti and Jamaica. See Eugene Genovese, *Roll, Jordan, Roll: The World the Slaves Made* (New York: Vintage, 1972, 1974).

7. John Fletcher, *Studies on Slavery in Easy Lessons: Compiled into Eight Studies, and Subdivided into Short Lessons for the Convenience of Readers* (Miami, Fla.: Mnemosyne, 1852, reprint 1969) 53, 62, 178, 507.

8. Slaves and women counted toward representation in Congress, but only White men could vote. "Representatives and direct Taxes shall be apportioned among the several States which may be included within this Union, according to the respective Numbers, which shall be determined by adding to the whole Number of free Persons [white males], including those bound to Service for a Term of Years, and excluding Indians not taxed, three fifths of all other Persons" (U.S. Constitution, Art. I, sec. 2). This compromise assured the slave-holding states that the slave-holding states would be over represented in the House of Representatives, and thus abolishing slavery would be beyond the power of the new nation. Constitutional Amendments must be approved by both the Senate and the House of Representatives before being submitted to the States. Chief Justice Taney's convoluted logic and erroneous historical analysis of the Dred Scott Case changed Blacks from humans to property. "Scott v. Sandford, 19 How. (60 U.S.) 393 (1857), argued 11-14 Feb. 1856 and 15-18 Dec. 1856, decided 6-7 Mar. 1857 by vote of 7 to 2; Taney for the Court, Curtis and McLean in dissent." See Kermit Hall, ed., *The Oxford Companion to the Supreme Court of the United States* (New York: Oxford University Press,

1992) 759. This avoidable, erroneous case denied the humanity of the Black population. See Jethro K. Lieberman, *Milestones! 200 Years of American Law* (St. Paul, Minn.:
West, 1976) 135.

9.   George Frederickson, *The Arrogance of Race: Historical Perspectives on Slavery,
Racism, and Social Equality* (Middletown, Conn.: Wesleyan University Press, 1988)
209–14. See for example, Thomas Dixon's pseudo-historic romances, which influenced his confidant, President Woodrow Wilson to impose segregation upon an integrated federal civil service, as well as the translation of Dixon's novel *The Klansman,*
into Griffith's film, "Birth of a Nation."

10.   Eugene Genovese, *Rebellion to Revolution: Afro-American; Slave Revolts in the
Making of the Modern World* (Baton Rouge: Louisiana State University Press, 1979)
46.

11.   John Blassingame, *The Slave Community: Plantation Life in the Ante-bellum South*
(New York: Oxford University Press, 1979) 6, 47, 297; John Earl Taylor, "The Sociological and Psychological Implications of the Texts of the Ante-bellum Negro Spirituals" (Ed.D. diss., University of Northern Colorado, 1971) 189, 192. Albert Beckham, "The Psychology of Negro Spirituals," *The Southern Workman* 60 (1931) 393.

12.   Ida Mukenge, *The Black Church in Urban America: A Case Study in Political
Economy* (Lanham, Md.: University Press of America, 1983) 1, 6. The leadership and
membership of the Black church is now and has always been Black.

13.   Charles T. Davis and Henry Louis Gates Jr., *The Slave's Narrative* (New York:
Oxford University Press, 1985) 306, 308.

14.   Juan Williams, et al., *Eyes on the Prize: America's Civil Rights Years, 1954–1965*
(New York: Penguin, 1987) vi.

15.   For reflections on the philosophies and roles of Black intellectuals, Booker
T. Washington and DuBois, pan-Africanist Marcus Garvey, and social protest orga-
nizer, A. Philip Randolph, see the following works: Louis R. Harlan, *Booker T. Wash-
ington: The Making of a Black Leader, 1856–1901* (New York: Oxford University
Press, 1972); Louis R. Harlan, *Booker T. Washington: The Wizard of Tuskegee,
1901–1915* (New York: Oxford University Press, 1983); Elliot Rudwick, *W. E. B.
DuBois: A Study in Minority Group Leadership* (Philadelphia: University of Pennsylva-
nia Press, 1960); Edmund D. Cronon, *Black Moses: The Story of Marcus Garvey and the
Universal Association* (Madison: University of Wisconsin Press, 1955); William H.
Harris, *Keeping the Faith: A. Philip Randolph, Milton P. Webster, and the Brotherhood of
Sleeping Car Porters, 1925–1937* (Urbana: University of Illinois Press, 1977);
Theodore Cross, *The Black Power Imperative: Racial Inequality and the Politics of Nonviolence* (New York: Faulkner, 1987). "For example, President Roosevelt issued Executive Order 8802, which forbade discrimination by those holding government war
contracts when Randolph, president of the Brotherhood of Sleeping Car Porters,
threatened a march on Washington by African Americans to obtain better job possibilities" (Leonard Broom and Norval Glenn, *Transformation of The Negro American*
[New York: Harper & Row, 1965] 60).

16.   George D. Kelsey, *Racism and the Christian Understanding of Man* (New York:
Charles Scribner's Sons, 1965) 9.

17. Ibid., 19–35, 98, 156–61.

18. C. T. Vivian, "Racial Violence In the '80s," *Sojourners* (November 1987) 24.

19. Anne Wortham, *The Other Side of Racism: A Philosophical Study of Black Race Consciousness* (Columbus: Ohio State University Press, 1981) ix.

20. Jean-Jacques Rousseau coined the phrase "civil religion" in Enlightenment France. *Civil religion* means religious nationalism: a religious system existing alongside churches, with a creed (theology or mythology), a code (ethic), and a culture (set of symbols and rituals), related to the political state or nation. Catherine L. Albanese, *America: Religions and Religion* (Belmont, Calif.: Wadsworth, 1981) 284–85.

21. C. Eric Lincoln, *Race, Religion, and the Continuing American Dilemma* (New York: Hill and Wang, 1984) xiv–xviii.

22. Kenneth Clark, *Pathos of Power* (New York: Harper & Row, 1974) 32–33. The use of the term "god" here is apropos, using a Tillichian idea, that the object of one's ultimate concern is that person's god.

23. Paul Dumochel, ed., *Violence and Truth: On the Work of René Girard* (London: Athlone Press, 1988) 54–55; see also Burton Mack, "Introduction: Religion and Ritual," in Robert Hammerton-Kelly, ed., *Violent Origins: Walter Burkert, René Girard, and Jonathan Z. Smith on Ritual Killing and Cultural Transformation* (Stanford, Calif.: Stanford University Press, 1987) 4, 6.

24. René Girard, *The Scapegoat,* trans. Yvonne Freccero (Baltimore, Md.: Johns Hopkins University Press, 1986) 17, 19.

25. René Girard, *Things Hidden Since the Foundation of the World,* trans. by Stephen Bann and Michael Metteer (Stanford, Calif.: Stanford University Press, 1987) 283–90, 338. Mimetic rivalry includes anything from eroticism to all types of ambition.

26. Michael Paul Rogin, "The Sword Became a Flashing Vision: D. W. Griffith's *The Birth of a Nation,*" chap. in *Ronald Reagan, the Movie and Other Episodes in Political Demonology* (Berkeley: University of California Press, 1987) 197–98.

27. Theophus H. Smith, "King and the Nonviolent Religion of Black America," in Mark I. Wallace and Theophus H. Smith, eds., *Curing Violence: Religion and the Thought of René Girard* (Sonoma, Calif.: Polebridge, 1994) 250–51.

28. Ibid.

29. Raimu Panikkar, *Myth, Faith And Hermeneutics: Cross-Cultural Studies* (New York: Paulist, 1979) 4–5.

30. Ibid., 98–99; See also 30–33.

31. Lee Gibbs and W. Taylor Stevenson, eds., *Myth and the Crisis of Historical Consciousness* (Missoula, Mont.: Scholars Press/American Academy of Religion, 1974) 3–5.

32. Louis N. Williams, *Black Psychology: Compelling Issues and Views* (3d ed.; Washington, D.C.: University Press of America, 1981) 49–57.

33. Frederickson, *The Arrogance of Race,* 131–32, 193–205.

34. Ibid., 133. Slavery ceased because it became incompatible with the push toward a unified nation-state shaped by a liberal, republican base.

35. Kelsey, *Racism,* 9–11, 19–33.

36. The Compromise of 1877, or The Redemption, dates the overthrow of the carpetbagger system. Redeemers were the Southern leaders who executed the overthrow. Though used by writers in the 1890s, the origin of the term "Jim Crow" as applied to African Americans is unknown. Thomas D. Rice wrote a dance and song named "Jim Crow" in 1832. The term was in use as an adjective by 1838. Jim Crow sensibilities led to laws that paralleled the massive papering of the South with "Colored" or "White Only" signs (C. Vann Woodward, *The Strange Career of Jim Crow* (rev. ed.; New York: Oxford University Press, 1957) vii, 3–4, 7, 26–52, 77–87.

37. Clark, *Pathos of Power,* 166.

38. Asante, *The Afrocentric Idea,* 125.

39. Taylor, "Implications," 189, 192; Albert Beckham, "The Psychology of Negro Spirituals," *The Southern Workman* 60 (1931) 393. Beckham claims that singers languishing in pity relayed their dire plight. Many knew pity, but they did something about it. Some of the Spirituals were palliative, that is, they mentally reduced the intense pain of slavery. Some were sorrow songs. Depending upon the text and performer, these categories are not mutually exclusive. Sometimes the emotional context overlapped.

40. Henry Hampton and Steve Fayer, *Voices of Freedom: An Oral History of the Civil Rights Movement from the 1950s through the 1980s* (New York: Bantam, 1990) 94–96; see also 38, 108.

41. Williams, *Black Psychology,* 74.

42. See Manfred Clynes, "The Communication of Emotion: Theory of Sentics," in R. Plutchhik and H. Kellerman, eds., *Emotion, Theory, Research, and Experience* (New York: Academic, 1989) 271–300; Manfred Clynes, "The Living Quality of Music," in Manfred Clynes, ed., *Music, Mind, and Brain* (New York: Plenum, 1982) 47–82.

43. Norman Harris, *Connecting Times: The Sixties in Afro-American Fiction* (Jackson: University Press of Mississippi, 1988) 5, 10–12. The folk and the formal, the competing forces in African American life, are the African and American phases of double consciousness. Engaging the formal literary aspects of the text circumvents the critique of 1960s Black aesthetics as being too proscriptive when attentive to making political assessments about Blackness.

44. Ibid., 3. According to Arnold Rampersand, DuBois relied on the work of nineteenth-century psychologist, Oswald Kulpe, and the thought of William James. The divided self is characterized "by the existence of a more or less complete separation of two aggregates of conscious process . . . often times of entirely opposite character." See Gates, "Introduction," in W. E. B. DuBois, *The Souls of Black Folk* (reprint 1989; New York: Bantam, 1903) xix; see also Arnold Rampersand, *The Art and Imagination* (Cambridge, Mass.: Harvard University Press, 1976).

45. Olly Wilson, "Black Music as an Art Form," *Black Music Research Journal* (1983) 21; see also 7, 9.

46. John Lovell Jr., *Black Song: The Forge and the Flame: The Story of How the Afro-American Spiritual Was Hammered Out* (New York: Macmillan, 1972) 637.

47. James Standifer, "Musical Behaviors of Black People in American Society," *Black Music Research Journal* (1980) 57.

48. Houston Baker Jr., *Blues, Ideology, and Afro-American Literature: A Vernacular Theory* (Chicago: University of Chicago Press, 1984) 110–11.

49. See Michel Foucault, *The Archaeology of Knowledge* (New York: Harper & Row, 1972) 56, 131. Discourse occurs in modes (e.g., economics, history, music).

50. Ibid., 79–87; Baker, *Blues,* 17–19.

51. Vincent Harding, *Hope and History: Why We Must Share the Story of the Movement* (Maryknoll, N.Y.: Orbis, 1990) 1–10; 77–78, 80–95.

52. Henry Louis Gates Jr., *Figures in Black: Words, Signs, and the "Racial" Self* (New York: Oxford University Press, 1987) xxxi.

53. Baker, *Blues,* 60; Henry Louis Gates Jr., *The Signifying Monkey: A Theory of Afro-American Literary Criticism* (New York: Oxford University Press, 1988) xxiii, 45, 50–51.

54. Gates, *Signifying,* xi, xix. One example of difference is the way in which a person talks about life under oppression versus experiencing freedom, justice, and the distribution of power, coded in the Spirituals: "I'm On My Way to Freedom Land," and "I'm Gonna Sit at the Welcome Table" (Guy and Candie Carawan, *Sing for Freedom: The Story of the Civil Rights Movement through Its Songs* [Bethlehem, Pa.: Sing Out, 1990] 18, 45, 70–71).

55. Gates, *Signifying,* 30.

56. Traditional Spiritual.

57. Gates, *Signifying,* xix, 44, 54. Gates explores the relationship of Black vernacular traditions to African American literary traditions, symbolized by the Signifying Monkey in Signifying. In the signifying monkey tales and poems, the Signifying Monkey always repeats to his friend, the Lion, some insult purportedly generated by their mutual friend, the Elephant.

58. Ibid., xxv, 46. Gates distinguishes between the Black and white terms of signification visually: Signification (Black) with the capital 'S' and signification (White); signifyin(g) has the bracketed 'g' (Black) and signifying (White).

59. Gates, *Signifying,* 50–52.

60. Ibid., 80, 86, 88.

61. Harding, *Hope and History,* 127.

62. Ibid., 135.

63. Ibid., 136.

64. For example, by identifying distinctive musical patterns in a system of oral traditions, the music intimates a human social response. The use of call-and-response without boundaries between leaders and audience suggests a pattern of community where people value unity as they work to experience solidarity and justice.

65. Jon Michael Spencer, ed., "Preface," *The Theology of American Popular Music; Black Sacred Music: A Journal of Theomusicology* 3 (fall 1989) v.

66. Andrew Greeley, *God in Popular Culture* (Chicago: Thomas More, 1988) 13–14, 16, 87.

67. Ernst Bloch, *Essays on the Philosophy of Music,* trans. Peter Palmer (Cambridge, Eng.: Cambridge University Press, 1985) 227, in Spencer, "Preface," vi. Note that prior to the 1960s, both church and society accepted the "hidden cracks" of racism, sexism, and classism as the status quo. Further, both church and society usually

ignored the ramifications of these "cracks;" e.g., denial of their humanity, and legal violence against minorities.

68. Jon Michael Spencer, *Theological Music: Introduction to Theomusicology* (New York: Greenwood, 1991) xi.

69. Ibid., 116.

70. Ibid., 162. See James W. Button, *Blacks and Social Change: Impact of the Civil Rights Movement in Southern Communities* (Princeton: Princeton University Press, 1989) 77. Button analyzes and documents changes caused by the impact of the Civil Rights Movement within southern communities from the 1950s to the mid-1980s. Theomusicology, not limited but conducive to the study of Christian, African American cultures, must account for "the actual lack of liberation at levels and in areas that elude national attention," and must explain those nuances in music that scholars have difficulty articulating.

71. Marcia Herndon and Norma McLeod, *Music as Culture* (Darby, Penn.: Norwood Editions, 1982) 12–23; Steven Feld, "Sound Structure as Social Structure," in Kay Kaufman Shelemay, ed., *Ethnomusicological Theory and Method* (New York: Garland, 1990) 299.

72. C. Marcel-DuBois, "L'ethnomusicologie, as vocation et as situation," *Revue de l'enseignement supérieur* 3 (1965) 38; Barbara Krader, "Ethnomusicology," in Stanley Sadie, ed., *The New Grove Dictionary of Music and Musicians* 6 (New York: St. Martin's, 1980) s.v. There remains ambiguity about the meaning and intent of this discipline. Timothy Rice, "Toward the Remodeling of Ethnomusicology," in Shelemay, 329, 331; Bonnie Wade, "Prolegomenon to the study of Song Texts," in Shelemay, 207. The term *ethnomusicology* first occurs in the sixth edition of the Grove dictionary. Some non-Western scholars find "ethnomusicology" offensive because they sense certain biased analytical techniques; other scholars find the shape and focus of the questions addressed problematic.

73. Krader, "Ethnomusicology," in Sadie; Alan Lomax, "Folk Song Style," in Kay Kaufman Shelemay, ed., *Music as Culture* (New York: Garland, 1990) 59, 61.

74. Jones, *Wade in the Water,* xi, xiii, xv.

75. Standifer, "Musical Behaviors of Black People," 61; See also 54–55.

76. Since the nineteenth century includes the time from the DuBois and Washington era, the World War years, the 1954 Brown decision, through the 1960s readiness of grassroots socio-political groups to protest.

77. Music is a way of perceiving the world. See Alan Durant, "Improvisation in the Political Economy of Music," in Christopher Norris, ed., *Music and Politics of Culture* (New York: St. Martin's, 1989) 255. Silence means the moments of rest or pause. Metaphorically, silence refers to (1) instances where African Americans were voiceless, disenfranchised, and powerless; and (2) the diminished use (silence) of music because Black power activists do not use singing as a tool.

78. Jon Michael Spencer, *Protest and Praise: Sacred Music of Black Religion* (Minneapolis: Fortress, 1990) 93, 97.

79. Samuel Floyd, "Black American Music and Aesthetic Communication," *Black Music Research Journal* 1 (1980) 4. The idioms include patterns, cadences, timbres, nuances, inflections, and devices.

80. Asante, *The Afrocentric Idea*, 160; Robert Schmidt, *Hearing, Calling and Naming: Aspects of Nommo in Toni Morrison's Beloved* (Bowling Green, Ohio: Bowling Green University, n.d.), photocopied.

81. Catherine Albanese, *America: Religions and Religion* (Belmont, Calif.: Wadsworth, 1981) 120–21.

82. Samuel Floyd, "Black American Music And Aesthetic Communication" *Black Music Research Journal* 1 (1980) 7, 10, 11; Hall Johnson, "Notes on the Negro Spiritual," in Eileen Southern, ed., *Readings in Black American Music* (New York: W. W. Norton, 1971) 269.

83. Richard Rorty, *Contingency, Irony, and Solidarity* (Cambridge, Eng.: Cambridge University Press, 1989) xiii–xvi.

84. Cornel West, "The Historicist Turn in Philosophy of Religion," in Leroy S. Rouner, *Knowing Religiously* (Notre Dame, Ind.: University of Notre Dame Press, 1985) 44–49.

85. See Dominique Zahan, *The Religion, Spirituality, and Thought of Traditional Africa* (Chicago: University of Chicago Press, 1979) 4–5, 9, 14–17, 125, 156–57; John S. Mbiti, *African Religions and Philosophy* (New York: Praeger, 1969) 1–3, 15–16.

86. DuBois, *Souls,* xxxi, xxxii, 43–48, 56–65.

87. Bernice Johnson Reagon, "Songs of the Civil Rights Movement 1955–1965: A Study in Culture History" (Ph.D. diss. Howard University, 1975) 7–9.

88. Karen Labacqz, *Six Theories of Justice: Perspectives from Philosophical and Theological Ethics* (Minneapolis: Augsburg, 1986) 9.

89. Ibid., 9-10.

90. Spencer, *Protest and Praise,* 32.

91. Martin Buber, *I And Thou,* trans. Walter Kaufman (New York: Charles Scribner's Sons, 1970) 56, 62–63, 68, 75; Stephen Panko and Martin Buber, *Makers of the Modern Theological Mind* (Waco, Tex.: Word, 1976) 24, 47–48, 150.

92. Walter Wink, *Naming the Powers: The Language of Power in the New Testament* (Philadelphia: Fortress, 1984) 5.

93. Nicholas Cooper-Lewter and Henry H. Mitchell, *Soul Theology: The Heart of American Black Culture* (San Francisco: Harper & Row, 1986) viii–11; 29–42, 95–111.

94. James H. Cone, "Black Spirituals: A Theological Interpretation," in Mary Collins, David Power, and Mellonee Burnim, eds., *Music and the Experience of God, Concilium: Religion in the Eighties* (Edinburgh, Scotland: T. and T. Clark, 1989) 48–49.

95. Jones, *Wade in the Water,* 146.

96. Ibid., 8, 11, 24.

97. Hall Johnson, "Notes," in Southern, 271.

98. Jones, *Wade in the Water,* 90.

99. Peter Kivy, *Sound and Semblance: Reflections on Musical Representation* (Princeton, N.J.: Princeton University Press, 1984) 12, 17; Carl E. Seashore, *Psychology of Music* (New York: Dover, 1967) 14.

100. Gordon C. Bruner, II, "Music, Mood, and Marketing," *Journal of Marketing* 54 (October 1990) 94.

101. Slave bards produced over six thousand still extant Spirituals, despite the prohibition of slave education (Lovell, *Black Song,* 637).

102. Peter Kivy, *Sound Sentiment: An Essay on Musical Emotions* (Philadelphia: Temple University Press, 1989) 256, 258.

4. Sojourner's Sisters: 1960s Women Freedom Fighters Right Civil Wrongs

1. Cornel West, "The Prophetic Tradition in Afro-America," *The Drew Gateway* 55 (spring 1985) 104–6.

2. Ibid., 106.

3. Katie Cannon, "Women in the African American Church Community," in Miriam Winter, Adair Lummis, Allison Stokes, eds., *Defecting in Place: Women Claiming Responsibility for Their Own Spiritual Lives* (New York: Crossroad, 1994) 215.

4. Clayborne Carson, *In Struggle: SNCC and the Black Awakening of the 1960s* (Cambridge, Mass.: Harvard University Press, 1981) 147–48. Lech Walesa, Polish leader of Solidarity, observed in the midst of the 1986 Polish free elections: "Women are to have fun with. In politics, I prefer not to see a woman. Instead of getting all worked up, they should stay as they are—like flowers." Interestingly, ten years later, in 1996, his Prime Minister—a woman named Hanna Suchova—was instrumental in revitalizing the Polish economy, whereas Walesa had been relegated to a titular figurehead status fulminating against limited abortion laws (Ross and Kathryn Petras, *The Stupidest Things Ever Said by Politicians* [New York: Pocket, 1999] 153).

5. James H. Cone, "Martin Luther King Jr.: Sixty-Fifth Anniversary Overview and Assessment," *The Journal of the Interdenominational Theological Center* 21 (spring 1994) 2–3.

6. Howard Zinn, *SNCC: The New Abolitionists* (Boston: Beacon, 1964) 32–33. See also James Forman, *The Making of Black Revolutionaries* (Washington, D.C.: Open Hand, 1985); Jessie Carney Smith, ed., *Notable Black American Women* (Detroit: Gale Research, 1992) 40.

7. Gerna Lerner, ed., *Black Women in White America* (New York: Pantheon, 1972) 345, 351.

8. Forman, *Black Revolutionaries,* 161, 215.

9. Ibid., 215–17, 293.

10. Zinn, *New Abolitionists,* 106, 186.

11. Carson, *In Struggle,* 31, 41–42.

12. Emilie Townes, "Keeping a Clean House Will Not Keep a Man at Home: An Unctuous Womanist Rhetoric of Justice," in David Batstone, ed., *New Visions for the Americas: Religious Engagement and Social Transformation* (Minneapolis: Fortress, 1993) 128, 134.

13. Carol Mueller, "Ella Baker and the Origins of Participatory Democracy," in Vicki L. Crawford, Jacqueline Rouse, Barbara Woods, eds., *Women in the Civil Rights Movement: Trailblazers and Torchbearers, 1941–1965* (Bloomington: Indiana University Press, 1990, 1993) 51–67.

14. Smith, *Notable Black American Women,* 41–42.

15. Grace McFadden, "Septima Clark and the Struggle for Human Rights," in Crawford et al., 85–87.

16. Septima Poinsette Clark with LeGette Blythe, *Echo* (New York: E. P. Dutton, 1962) 117.

17. Darlene Clark Hine, ed., *Black Women in America: An Historical Encyclopedia* (Brooklyn, N.Y.: Carlson, 1993) 191.

18. Ibid.; Clark with Blythe, *Echo,* 186, 206–17.

19. Grace Jordan McFadden, *Oral Recollections of Septima Poinsette Clark* (Columbia, S.C.: USC Instructional Services Center, 1980) cited in McFadden, "Septima Clark," in Crawford et al., 93.

20. McFadden, "Septima Clark," in Crawford et al., 95, 96.

21. Fannie Lou Hamer, "Sick and Tired of Being Sick and Tired," *Katallagete* 1 (fall 1968) 19; Danny Collum, "Fannie Lou Hamer: Prophet of Hope for the Sick and Tired," *Sojourners* 11 (December 1982) 4.

22. Zinn, *New Abolitionists,* 93, 95, 113, 121.

23. Mamie E. Locke, "Is This America? Fannie Lou Hamer and the Mississippi Freedom Democratic Party," in Crawford et al., 27–29; Collum, "Fannie Lou Hamer," 11–13.

24. Collum, "Fannie Lou Hamer," 13.

25. Juan Williams, *Eyes on the Prize: America's Civil Rights Years, 1954–1964* (New York: Viking-Penguin, 1987) 241.

26. Locke, "Is This America?" in Crawford et al., 32–33.

27. Cornel West, "The Prophetic Tradition in Afro-America," *The Drew Gateway* 55 (spring 1985) 104.

28. Fannie Lou Hamer, "It's in Your Hands," in Lerner, 613.

29. Collum, "Fannie Lou Hamer," 16.

30. Bernice Johnson Reagon and Sweet Honey in the Rock, *We Who Believe in Freedom: Sweet Honey in the Rock . . . Still On the Journey* (New York: Anchor, 1993) 134–36.

31. Ibid., 145–50.

32. Dick Cluster, ed., *They Should Have Served That Cup of Coffee: Seven Radicals Remember the '60s* (Boston: South End, 1979) 16–18.

33. Ibid., 19–20.

34. Ibid., 11–15, 28–30.

35. Reagon and Sweet Honey in the Rock, *We Who Believe,* 152–62.

36. Ibid., 163–67; Cluster, *They Should Have Served,* 20–22, 28–30; Smith, *Notable Black American Women,* 926–27.

37. Cluster, *They Should Have Served,* 22–24.

38. Smith, *Notable Black American Women,* 927–28.

39. Jo Ann Robinson, *The Montgomery Bus Boycott and the Women Who Started It: The Memoir of Jo Ann Gibson Robinson,* ed. David J. Garrow (Knoxville: University of Tennessee Press, 1987) xii, 23; Darlene Clark Hine, "Jo Ann Gibson Robinson," in Hine, 989.

40. Ibid., x–xi.

41. Ibid., 8, 10, 20, 36, 45; Mary Fair Burks, "Trailblazers: Women in the Montgomery Bus Boycott," in Crawford et al., 71–75.

42. Ibid., 28–36, 71, 74, 91–97, 168–71; Hine, "Jo Ann Gibson Robinson," in Hine, 989.

43. Lenwood Davis, *I Have A Dream . . . The Life and Times of Martin Luther King Jr.* (Westport, Conn.: Negro Universities Press, 1969) 31, 37, 60–63, 88–89, 212–13.

44. See Darlene Clark Hine, "Coretta Scott King," in Hine, 678–80; and Jessie Smith, "Coretta Scott King," in Smith, 631–34.

45. Coretta Scott King, "The Indivisible Cord," *Otherside* 21 (October 1985) 54.

46. Interview of James Breeden by author, Yale University, summer 1996.

5. Ballads, Not Bullets: The Nonviolent Protest Ministry of Martin Luther King Jr.

1. George Lipsitz, "The Drum Major Instinct: American Religion since 1945," *Telos* 16 (winter 1983–1984) 96–98, 100. Congress added "under God" to the pledge of allegiance in 1954, and "In God We Trust" became the nation's overarching creedal statement in 1956.

2. Ibid., 101.

3. Wilson J. Moses, "Civil Religion and the Crisis of Civil Rights," *The Drew Gateway* 57 (winter 1988) 25, 29, 30, 37.

4. Ibid., 29, 30, 37–40.

5. Riggins R. Earl Jr., "Two Consciences: An Afro-American Reflection on Barth, Barmen and the Confessing Church Today," *Katallagete* (fall 1987) 34–35. See also Martin Luther King Jr., *Strength to Love* (New York: Harper & Row, 1963) 40.

6. James Cone, "Black Theology in American Religion," in Ray L. Hart, ed., *Trajectories in the Study of Religion* (Atlanta: Scholars, 1987) 211–28.

7. King preached this sermon on February 4, 1968, from Mark 10:35f, at Ebenezer Baptist Church. See James M. Washington, ed., *A Testament of Hope: The Essential Writings and Speeches of Martin Luther King Jr.* (San Francisco: Harper & Row, 1986) 259–67.

8. Lipsitz, "Drum Major Instinct," 102–4.

9. Preston Williams, "Contextualizing the Faith: The African American Tradition and Martin Luther King, Jr.," in Ruy O. Costa, *One Faith, Many Cultures: Inculturation, Indignization, and Contextualization* (New York: Orbis and Boston Theological Institute, 1988) 130–33.

10. James Baldwin, "The Highroad to Destiny," in C. Eric Lincoln, ed., *Martin Luther King, Jr.: A Profile* (New York: Hill and Wang, 1984) 99–100.

11. Ibid., 100.

12. Ibid., 90, 93, 96, 97; Louis Lomax, "When 'Nonviolence' Meets 'Black Power,'" in Lincoln, 157.

13. Robert M. Franklin Jr., "Martin Luther King as Pastor," *The Iliff Review* 42 (spring 1985) 4. See Martin Luther King Jr., "Letter From Birmingham Jail," in his *Why We Can't Wait* (New York: Harper, 1963) 90–91. See also Richard Lischer, *The Preacher King: Martin Luther King, Jr. and the Word That Moved America* (New York: Oxford University Press, 1995) 3–4, 8, 10–11.

14. Lomax, "Nonviolence," in Lincoln, 165–73.

15. Ibid., 158–59.

16. James H. Cone, "Martin Luther King, Jr.: Sixty-Fifth Anniversary Overview and Assessment," *The Journal of the Interdenominational Theological Center* 21 (spring 1994) 8.

17. Lischer, *The Preacher King,* 171, 180, 181.

18. Paul R. Garber, "Black Theology: The Latter Day Legacy of Martin Luther King, Jr.," *The Journal of the Interdenominational Theological Center* 2 (spring 1975) 100, 103, 107, 113.

19. William Donnel Watley, "Against Principalities: An Examination of Martin Luther King, Jr.'s Ethic" (Ph.D. diss., Columbia University, 1980) 352, 356, 358, 361, 364, 368, 369.

20. James Cone, "Black Theology—Black Church," in Lincoln, 217, 243–50.

21. Andrew Young, "Martin Luther King as a Political Theologian," in Theodore Runyon, ed., *Theology, Politics, and Peace* (Maryknoll, N.Y.: Orbis, 1989) 79–81, 82, 84.

22. Ibid., 79–82; Baldwin, "Highroad," in Lincoln, 91–92.

23. Lewis V. Baldwin, "Martin Luther King, Jr., the Black Church, and the Black Messianic Vision," *The Journal of the Interdenominational Theological Center* 12 (1984–1985) 93–108. See Martin Luther King Jr., *Stride Toward Freedom: The Montgomery Story* (New York: Harper & Row, 1958) 223, and *Strength to Love,* 62–63.

24. Robert Harrison and Linda Harrison, "The Call from the Mountain Top: Call–Response and the Oratory of Martin Luther King, Jr.," in Carolyn Calloway-Thomas and John Louis Lucaites, eds., *Martin Luther King, Jr. and the Sermonic Power of Public Discourse* (Tuscaloosa: University of Alabama Press, 1993) 165–69, 177. On *nommo,* see Molefi Asante, *The Afrocentric Idea* (Philadelphia: Temple University Press, 1987) 160; Robert Schmidt, *Hearing, Calling and Naming: Aspects of Nommo in Toni Morrison's* Beloved (Bowling Green, Ohio: Bowling Green University, n.d.) photocopy. See Janheinz Jahn, *Muntu: The New African Culture* (New York: Grove, 1961) 121–57.

25. Chuck Fager, "Selma and the Spirit," *The Other Side* 21 (1985) 20–21.

26. Jon M. Temme, "Jesus as Trailblazer: The Christology of Martin Luther King, Jr.," *The Journal of Religious Thought* 42 (spring/summer 1985) 75, 77, 79. See also Martin Luther King Jr., *The Trumpet of Conscience* (New York: Harper & Row, 1963) 75, and *Stride Toward Freedom.*

27. Cone, "Black Theology in American Religion," in Hart, 218, 220–21, 223.

28. Ibid., 223; also see King, "Nonviolence: The Only Road to Freedom," *Ebony* (October 1966) 218.

29. John Cartwright, "The Black Church and the Call For Peace," *The Drew Gateway* 54 (1983) 54.

30. Franklin, "King as Pastor," 6, 8, 11–14; King, *Why We Can't Wait,* 151, and *Strength to Love,* 27–33.

31. James R. Ecklund, "The Church and the Civil Rights Movement 1955–1970: An Overview," *The Covenant Quarterly* 29 (May 1971) 33, 35. See also King, *Why We Can't Wait,* 63–64.

32. On the events of August, 1963, see Robert S. Lecky and H. Elliott Wright, eds., *Black Manifesto* (New York: Sheed & Ward, 1969) 83.

33. William R. Jones. "Liberation Strategies in Black Theology: Mao, Martin, or Malcolm?" *The Chicago Theological Seminary Register* 73 (winter 1983) 38–39, 42–43, 44–47.

34. Cone, "Martin Luther King, Jr.: Sixty-Fifth Anniversary," 2; James Cone, *Malcolm & Martin & America: A Dream or a Nightmare* (Maryknoll, N.Y.: Orbis, 1991) 280.

35. Harrison and Harrison, "The Call from the Mountain Top," in Calloway-Thomas and Lucaites, 165–69, 177. See Martin L. King Jr., *Where Do We Go From Here? Chaos or Community* (Boston: Beacon, 1967) 167.

36. Mary Sawyer, "Legacy of a Dream," in Lincoln, 260, 263.

37. John H. Patton, "'I Have A Dream': The Performance of Theology Fused with the Power of Orality," in Calloway-Thomas and Lucaites, 105, 118, 121. As a child, King resolved to hate all White people, because a White friend's father had said that he could no longer play with King. King did hate, until he went to college and worked with interracial organizations.

38. Warren E. Steinkraus, "The Dangerous Ideas of Martin Luther King," *The Scottish Journal of Religious Studies* 4 (1985) 16–23.

39. Franklin, "King as Pastor," 5–6, 8, 10. See Martin Luther King, Jr., *The Measure of a Man* (New York: Christian Education, 1959) 20–22.

40. Cone, "Black Theology—Black Church," in Lincoln, 243, 245–50.

41. James Cone, "Martin Luther King, Jr., Black Theology, and the Black Church," *The Drew Gateway* 56 (1985) 2–3, 5, 9–13.

42. Cone, "Black Theology in American Religion," in Hart, 217.

43. Calloway-Thomas and Lucaites, *Martin Luther King, Jr., and the Sermonic Power of Public Discourse,* 1–8.

44. Ibid., 9, 10.

45. Lomax, "Nonviolence," in Lincoln, 161–63.

46. James Forman, *The Making of Black Revolutionaries* (Washington, D.C.: Open Hand, 1985) 147, 148, 275, 313.

47. Lomax, "Nonviolence," in Lincoln, 173.

48. Sawyer, "Legacy of a Dream," in Lincoln, 254–57.

49. Cone, "Black Theology in American Religion," in Hart, 219. See Martin Luther King, Jr., "Christmas Sermon on Peace," Ebenezer Baptist Church, Atlanta, December 24, 1967.

50. Cone, "Black Theology in American Religion," in Hart, 220.

51. Craig Anderson, "Martin, Malcolm, and the NAACP," *The Covenant Quarterly* 41 (February 1983) 27–35.

52. Ibid., 36.

53. Archie Smith Jr., "Martin Luther King, Jr.: A Twentieth Century Pied Piper?" *The Journal of the Interdenominational Theological Center* 19 (spring 1992) 28–29.

54. Cone, "Black Theology—Black Church," in Lincoln, 257–58.

55. Vincent Harding, "Martin Luther King Jr. and the Twenty-First Century," *The Journal of the Interdenominational Theological Center* 16 (spring 1989) 290.

56. Martin Luther King Jr., "A View from the Mountain Top: Dr. King's Last Message," in *Renewal* 9 (1969) 4–5.

57. John Louis Lucaites and Celeste Michelle Condit, "Universalizing 'Equality': The Public Legacy of Martin Luther King, Jr.," in Calloway-Thomas and Lucaites, 85–86, 93, 100.

58. James H. Cone Jr., "Two Roads to Freedom: Martin Luther King, Jr., and Malcolm X," *Bangalore Theological Forum* 22 (June 1990) 46, 49.

59. See L. M. Friedel, *The Bible and the Negro Spirituals* (Bay St. Louis, Miss.: St. Augustine Seminary, 1947); John Lovell Jr., *Black Song: The Forge and the Flame: The Story of How the Afro-American Spiritual Was Hammered Out* (New York: Macmillan, 1972) 3–11.

60. Guy Carawan and Candie Carawan, eds., *Sing for Freedom: The Story of the Civil Rights Movement through Its Songs* (Bethlehem, Pa.: Sing Out, 1990) 11, 115. Also see the companion compact disc, along with Bernice Johnson Reagon, ed., *Voices of the Civil Rights Movement: Black American Freedom Songs 1960–1966* (Washington, D.C.: Smithsonian Institution Program in Black Culture, 1980) phonodisc R023.

61. Howard Zinn, *SNCC: The New Abolitionists* (Boston: Beacon, 1964) 128–29.

62. Bernice Johnson Reagon, "Songs of the Civil Rights Movement 1955–1965: A Study in Culture History" (Ph.D. diss. Howard University, 1975) 22–23.

63. Ibid., 95–96. See also Alfred Mound, "Around the U.S.A.," *The Nation* 3 (March 1956).

64. Reagon, "Songs of the Civil Rights Movement," 102–3.

65. Carawan and Carawan, *Sing for Freedom,* 11, 115.

66. Ibid., 32–36.

67. Ibid., 40–41, 48, 81, 136–37, 138–39, 188, 200.

68. Ibid., 30.

69. Ibid., 42, 46, 48.

70. Reagon, "Songs of the Civil Rights Movement," 106–8.

71. Ibid., 110–14.

72. Cone, *Martin & Malcolm & America,* 273–78.

73. Charles Payne, "Men Led, but Women Organized: Movement Participation of Women in the Mississippi Delta," in Vicki L. Crawford, Jacqueline Rouse, Barbara Woods, eds., *Women in the Civil Rights Movement: Trailblazers and Torchbearers, 1941–1965* (Bloomington: Indiana University Press, 1990, 1993) 1–12.

74. Franklin, "King as Pastor," 7, 9, 10.

75. Lischer, *The Preacher King,* 168–69.

76. Ibid., 140–41.

77. Stephen B. Oates, *Let the Trumpet Sound: The Life of Martin Luther King, Jr.* (New York: Harper & Row, 1982) 265, 280–84.

78. Frederick J. Antczak, "When Silence Is Betrayal: An Ethical Criticism of the Revolution of Values in the Speech at Riverside Church," in Calloway-Thomas and Lucaites, 130.

79. Rufus Burrow Jr., "Some African American Males' Perspectives on the Black Woman," *The Western Journal of Black Studies* 16 (1992) 64–65, 69.

80. "Editorial: The Theses of Martin Luther King, Jr.," *First Things: A Monthly Journal of Religion and Public Life* 10 (February 1991) 5–7.

6. Soul Sisters: Girls in Gangs and Sororities

1. "Research Review: Gang Violence and Prevention," Washington State University, 1996; on the Web: http://www.caho.wai.du/~cherfey/issue4.com.

2. Carl S. Taylor, *Girls, Gangs, Women, and Drugs* (East Lansing: Michigan State University Press, 1993) 201.

3. Anne Campbell, *The Girls in the Gang: A Report from New York City* (New York: Basil Blackwell, 1984) 176–80.

4. "Research Review: Gang Violence and Prevention."

5. Edward Humes, *No Matter How Loud I Shout: A Year in the Life of Juvenile Court* (New York: Simon & Schuster, 1996) 46–56, 120–23, 345–49.

6. Jim Wallis, *The Soul of Politics: Beyond "Religious Right" and "Secular Left"* (San Diego: Harcourt Brace, 1995) 4-5.

7. William Sanders, *Gangbangs and Drive-Bys: Grounded Culture and Juvenile Gang Violence* (New York: Aldine De Cruyter, 1994) 8, 12–20.

8. Ibid., 3–4.

9. Margaret Ann Rose, *R*U*S*H: A Girl's Guide to Sorority Success* (New York: Villard, 1985) 3, 82–83.

10. Barbara Forisha and Barbara Goldman, *Outsiders on the Inside: Women and Organizations* (Englewood Cliffs, N.J.: Prentice-Hall, 1981) xiii.

11. Arnold Goldstein and Barry Glick with Wilma Carthan and Douglas Blancero, *The Prosocial Gang: Implementing Aggression Replacement Training* (Thousand Oaks, Calif.: SAGE, 1994) 9.

12. George W. Knox, *An Introduction to Gangs* (Buchanan, Mich.: Vande Vere Publishing, 1993) 31, 39.

13. Joyce Carol Oates, *Foxfire: Confessions of a Girl Gang* (New York: Dutton, 1993) 44, 83.

14. Anne Campbell, "Self Definition by Rejection: The Case of Gang Girls," *Social Problems* 34 (December 1981) 452–53.

15. Ibid., 459; Knox, *Introduction to Gangs,* 1–5, 365; Campbell, *Girls in the Gang,* 2–3, 23–26; Goldstein et al., *Prosocial Gang,* 3.

16. Paula Giddings, *In Search of Sisterhood: Delta Sigma Theta and the Challenge of the Black Sorority Movement* (New York: William Morrow, 1988) 43–45.

17. Ibid., 54–57, 67.

18. Ibid., 90.

19. Ibid., 102, 278.

20. Campbell, "Self Definition," 11–12. Frederick Thrasher, an American criminologist who did extensive gang research on Chicago gangs, supports this argument.

21. James Diego Vigil, *Barrio Gangs: Street Life and Identity in Southern California* (Austin: University of Texas Press, 1988) 102–3.

22. Ibid., xiii–xv, 1, 4.

23 Taylor, *Girls, Gangs,* 8.

24 Sanders, *Gangbangs and Drive-Bys,* 139–49.

25 Vigil, *Barrio Gangs,* 102–3.

26 Ibid., 100–103.

27. Mary G. Harris, *Cholas: Latino Girls and Gangs* (New York: AMS, 1988) 4, 8, 80–81, 96–97, 116, 120.

28. Taylor, *Girls, Gangs,* 1–3.

29. Ibid., 4–7.

30. Campbell, "Self Definition," 436–38; George Knox, Thomas Currie, Edward Tromanhauser, "Findings on African-American Female Gang Members Using a Matched-Pair Design: A Research Note," *Journal of Gang Research* 2 (spring 1995) 65, 71.

31. Knox et al., "Findings," 71.

32. Goldstein et al., *Prosocial Gang,* 78–80.

33. Humes, *No Matter,* 123.

34. Knox et. al, "Findings," 65; Campbell, "Self Definition," 458; Maria Hinojosa, *Crews: Gang Members Talk to Maria Hinojosa* (San Diego: Harcourt Brace, 1995) 188–96.

35. Campbell, "Self Definition," 459–62.

36. William J. Swart, "Female Gang Delinquency: A Search for 'Acceptably Deviant Behavior,'" *Mid-American Review of Sociology* 15 (1991) 46–47.

37. Hinojosa, *Crews,* 6, 10, 11, 70–73.

38. Sanders, *Gangbangs and Drive-Bys,* 65–107.

39. Ibid., 16.

40. Hinojosa, *Crews,* 74, 76, 78, 80.

41. Ibid., 83.

42. Ibid., 90–97, 99, 100.

43. Humes, *No Matter How Loud I Shout,* 19.

44. Ibid., 16–18.

45. Ibid., 122.

46. Walter Wink, "The Myth of Redemptive Violence: Exposing the Roots of 'Might Makes Right,'" *Sojourners* 21 (April 1992) 18.

47. Vern Redekop, *Scapegoats, the Bible, and Criminal Justice: Interacting with René Girard* (Akron, Pa.: MCC [Mennonite Central Committee] and U.S. Office of Criminal Justice, 1993) 6–7.

48. Ibid., 7–11.

49. Theophus H. Smith, "King and the Nonviolent Religion of Black America," in Thee Smith and Mark I. Wallace, eds., *Curing Violence: Religion and the Thought of René Girard* (Sonoma, Calif.: Polebridge, 1994) 230–51.

50. James G. Williams, "Sacrifice, Mimesis, and the Genesis of Violence: A Response to Bruce Chilton," *Bulletin for Biblical Research* 3 (1993) 34–36.

51. See *NWO: A Directory of National Women's Organizations,* compiled by Paulette Tulloch (New York: National Council for Research on Women, 1992).

52. Richard Rorty, *Contingency, Irony, and Solidarity* (Cambridge, Eng.: Cambridge University Press, 1989) xiii–xvi.

53. Wink, "Myth of Redemptive Violence," 20, 21, 35.

54. Sanyika Shakur, aka Monster Kody Scott, *Monster: The Autobiography of an L.A. Gang Member* (New York: Penguin, 1993) 381.

55. Allison Anders, *Mi Vida Loca* (My Crazy Life), produced by Daniel Hassid and Carl-Jan Colpaert; directed by Allison Anders, 92 min., Cineville, 1994.

56. Taylor, *Girls, Gangs,* 196–200.

57. Wallis, *Soul of Politics,* xiii–xv. as recalled by Arun Gandhi from the teaching of Mohandas's grandfather.

58. Ibid., 18–20.

59. Ibid., 288.

60. Ibid., 291.

61. Ibid., 293–95.

62. Ibid., 139.

63. Ibid., 139–43.

64. Taylor, *Girls, Gangs,* 206.

65. Humes, *No Matter,* 354–71.

66. Children's Defense Fund, "Moments in America for Children," April 19, 2000 (http://www.childrensdefense.org/moments.html).

7. Build Up, Break Down: Language as Empowerment and Annihilation

1. See the work of Ernest Becker.

2. See the work of René Girard.

3. Sidney Sheldon, "The Thought of Ernest Becker" Ernest Becker Foundation cassette tape, 1994.

4. Ernest Becker, *The Denial of Death* (New York: Free, 1973) ix, 70, 96.

5. Ernest Becker, *Escape From Evil* (New York: Free, 1975) xvii, 3, 4, 5.

6. Becker, *Denial of Death,* 148–49.

7. Charles Bellinger, "Ernest Becker and Søren Kierkegaard on Political Violence" in *Church Divinity* (1987) 21; Becker, *Escape,* 95.

8. Becker, *Escape,* 141; Becker, *Denial,* 95. Bellinger, 25, 124, 135, 141.

9. Becker, *Escape,* 102, 113; Bellinger, 181.

10. Robert Hammerton-Kelly, *The Gospel and the Sacred: Poetics of Violence in Mark* (Minneapolis: Fortress, 1994) 3–6, 130–32, 137.

11. Ibid., x–xi, 129.

12. Robert North, "Violence and the Bible: The Girard Connection," *Catholic Biblical Quarterly* 47 (n.d.) 1, 3–7.

13. Ibid., 8-10, 18-20. See René Girard, *Things Hidden Since the Foundation of the World,* trans. by Stephen Bann and Michael Metteer (Stanford, Calif.: Stanford University Press, 1987), and Delores S. Williams, *Sisters in the Wilderness: Womanist God-Talk* (Maryknoll, N.Y.: Orbis, 1993).

14. James Gleick, *Chaos: Making a New Science* (New York: Viking, 1987) 3, 5. Gleick's discussion of chaos theory points us toward two factors related to studying racism: free will and critical thought.

15. See René Girard, *Violence and the Sacred* (Baltimore and London: Johns Hopkins University Press, 1977).

16. See James Allen, Hilton Als, John Lewis, and Leon F. Litwack, *Without Sanctuary: Lynching Photography in America* (Santa Fe, N.M.: Twin Palms, 2000): "*Without Sanctuary* brings to life one of the darkest and sickest periods in American history. . . . The photographs in this book make real the hideous crimes that were committed against humanity" (7).

17. Conversations with Diana Culbertson, Professor of Literature, Kent State University, summer 1995.

18. Allen et al., *Without Sanctuary,* 204–5.

19. Leon Litwack, "Hellhounds," in Allen et al., 8–9.

20. Ibid.

21. Paul Dumochel, ed., *Violence and Truth: On the Work of René Girard* (London: Athlone, 1988) 54–55; see also Burton Mack, "Introduction: Religion and Ritual," in Robert Hammerton-Kelly, ed., *Violent Origins: Walter Burkert, René Girard, and Jonathan Z. Smith on Ritual Killing and Cultural Transformation* (Stanford, Calif.: Stanford University Press, 1987) 4, 6.

22. Nancy Armstrong and Leonard Tennenhouse, eds., *The Violence of Representation: Literature and History of Violence* (London: Routledge, 1989) 25; Michael Kowalewski, *Deadly Musings: Violence and Verbal Form in American Fiction* (Princeton, N.J.: Princeton University Press, 1993) 7.

23. Jean-Jacques Lecerle, *The Violence of Language* (London: Routledge, 1990) 51.

24. Ibid., 49, 51, 69, 182, 229, 233, and David Bond, "Marie Cardinal's *Comme si de rien n'était:* Language and Violence," *The International Fiction Review* 21 (1994) 68.

25. Lecerle, *Violence of Language,* 2, 25, 48, and Irving Massey, *Find You the Virtue: Ethics, Image, and Desire in Literature* (Fairfax, Va.: George Mason University Press, 1987) 3.

26. See Ludwig Wittgenstein, *Philosophical Investigations* (Cambridge, Mass.: Blackwell, 1958).

27. See Paul Rabinow, ed., *The Foucault Reader* (New York: Pantheon, 1984); Michel Foucault, *The Archaeology of Knowledge and The Discourse on Language,* trans. A. M. Sheridan Smith (New York: Pantheon, 1982); Michel Foucault, *Power/Knowledge: Selected Interviews and Other Writings, 1972–1977,* ed. Colin Gordon (New York: Pantheon, 1980).

28. See Noam Chomsky, *The Logical Structure of Linguistic Theory* (New York: Plenum, 1975); Noam Chomsky, *Language and Mind* (New York: Harcourt Brace Jovanovitch, 1968), *Language and Responsibility* (New York: Pantheon, 1975), and *Language and Thought* (Wakefield, R.I.: Moyer Bell, 1994).

29. Françoise Lionnet, "Geographies of Pain: Captive Bodies and Violent Acts in the Fictions of Myriam Warner-Vieyra, Gayl Jones, and Bessie Head," *Callaloo* 16 (1993) 132–33.

30. Irving Massey, *Find You the Virtue: Ethics, Image, and Desire in Literature* (Fairfax, Va.: George Mason University Press, 1987) xiii.

31. Robert McAfee Brown, *Religion and Violence* (2d ed.; Philadelphia: Westminster, 1973, 1987) 1–14; Teresa de Lauretis, "The Violence of Rhetoric," in Armstrong and Tennenhouse, 240, 249–50.

32. Catharine MacKinnon, *Only Words* (Cambridge, Mass.: Harvard University Press, 1993) 3–20, 75.

33. Arno Gruen, *The Insanity of Normality—Realism As Sickness: Toward Understanding Human Destructiveness,* trans. Hildegarde and Hunter Hannum (New York: Grove Widenfeld, 1987, 1992) 91.

34. Brown, *Religion and Violence,* vii–xxii; Becker, *Denial,* 7; Lionnet, "Geographies of Pain," 137; MacKinnon, *Only Words,* 45–50, 59–60.

35. Armstrong and Tennenhouse, *Violence of Representation,* 24.

36. Bond, "Marie Cardinal," 70–71.

37. Gruen, *Insanity of Normality,* vii–viii, 87–90.

38. Lecerle, *Violence of Language,* 230–32, 241.

39. Sharon Quint, *Schooling Homeless Children: A Working Model for America's Public Schools* (New York: Teachers College Press, 1994).

8. Daughters of Zelophehad: A Constructive Analysis of Violence

1. Katharine Doob Sakenfeld, "Numbers" in Carol Newsome and Sharon Ringe, eds., *The Women's Bible Commentary* (Louisville, Ky.: Westminster John Knox, 1992) 45, 50–51.

2. Thomas B. Dozeman, "Numbers," *The New Interpreter's Bible: A Commentary in Twelve Volumes,* vol. 2 (Nashville: Abingdon, 1998) 212, 214.

3. Carol L. Myers, "Everyday Life: Women in the Period of the Hebrew Bible," in Newsome and Ringe, 244–50.

4. Ibid., 250

5. Myers, "Everyday Life," in Newsome and Ringe, 250–51.

6. Dozeman, "Numbers," 217, 218, 266–67.

7. Katherine Doob Sakenfeld, "Feminist Biblical Interpretation," *Theology Today* 46 (1989) 154–68, and Alice Ogden Bellis, *Helpmates, Harlots, and Heroes: Women's Stories in the Hebrew Bible* (Louisville, Ky.: Westminster John Knox, 1994) 106–8.

8. Tikva Frymer-Kensky, "Deuteronomy," in Newsome and Ringe, 58.

9. The term "Munchausen syndrome by proxy" (MSBP) was coined around twenty years ago, and hundreds of reports have appeared since then. In most cases, a mother either claims that her child is sick or goes even further to actually make the child sick. This "devoted" parent then continually presents the child for medical treatment, all the while denying any knowledge of the origin of the problem—namely, herself. As a result, MSBP victims may undergo extraordinary numbers of lab tests, medication trials, and even surgical procedures that aren't really needed. See http://www.shpm.com/articles/parenting/hsmun.html

10. *National Vital Statistics Reports,* vol. 47, no. 19 (June 30, 1999): http://www/cdc.gov/nchswww/data/nvs47_10.pdf.

11. Sergio Cotta, *Why Violence? A Philosophical Interpretation,* trans. Giovanni Gullace (Gainesville: University of Florida Press, 1985) viii, 2, 3, 9, 10, 12–16, 17.

12. Ibid., 17.

13. Ibid., 18.

14. Ibid., 18, 115–26.

15. Ibid., ix.

16. Ibid., 126, 128, 138–40.

17. See Delores S. Williams, *Sisters in the Wilderness: The Challenge of Womanist God-Talk* (Maryknoll, N.Y.: Orbis, 1993).

18. David Crystal, ed., *The Cambridge Encyclopedia of Language* (2d ed.; Cambridge, Eng.: Cambridge University Press, 1997) 40.

19. Robert Audi, "Personal Identity," in Robert Audi, ed., *The Cambridge Dictionary of Philosophy* (Cambridge, Eng.: Cambridge University Press, 1995) 574.

20. Aristotle, *Poetics,* trans. by Gerald F. Else (Ann Arbor: University of Michigan Press, 1967, 1970) 32–37, 43.

21. Shakespeare, *As You Like It,* Act II, scene vii, 139.

22. David N. Power, *Worship: Culture and Theology* (Washington, D.C.: Pastoral, 1990) 19.

23. bell hooks, *Killing Rage: Ending Racism* (New York : Henry Holt, 1995).

24. Ibid., 16, 19, 47.

25. Ibid., 4, 8, 11, 19, 47, 57, 61.

26. Jill Kerper Mora, "Understanding Multiculturalism: Culture and Values," San Diego State, 1998 (http://coe.sdsu.edu/people/jmora/CulturalValues/Default.htm).

27. See Richard Viladesau, *Theological Aesthetics: God in Imagination, Beauty, and Art* (New York: Oxford University Press, 1999), and Alejandro Garcia-Rivera, *The Community of the Beautiful: A Theological Aesthetics* (Collegeville, Minn.: Liturgical, 1999). Garcia-Rivera, exploring U. S. Hispanic popular Catholicism as a model, reminds us that too often we forget that the transcendental involves truth, goodness, beauty, and God.

28. Jim Merickel, "What is Ecology," from http://ecology.miningco.com/education/ecology/library/weekly/aa012400.htm.

29. Rebecca Chopp, *Saving Work: Feminist Practices of Theological Education* (Louisville, Ky.: Westminster John Knox, 1995) 15–18, 21, 34–41, 45, 54, 56, 62, 70, 94.

30. Paulo Freire, *Pedagogy of Hope: Reliving Pedagogy of the Oppressed* (New York: Continuum, 1994) 8.

9. Death as Worship: Celebrating Dying as Part of Life

1. Cf. Maya Angelou, "Is Love," in *I Shall Not Be Moved* (New York: Bantam, 1990) 8.

2. Audre Lorde, "Memorial I," in *Chosen Poems Old and New* (New York: W. W. Norton, 1982) 3.

3. Cf. Gwendolyn Brooks, "The Children of the Poor," in Abraham Chapman, ed., *Black Voices: An Anthology of Afro-American Literature* (New York: New American Library, 1968) 464.

4. Alice Walker, *In Search of Our Mothers' Gardens: Womanist Prose* (New York: Harcourt Brace Jovanovich, 1983) xi.

5. Margaret Walker, "For My People," in Stephen Henderson, ed., *Understanding the New Black Poetry: Black Speech and Black Music as Poetic References* (New York: William Morrow, 1975) 163–65.

6. Cf. Angelou, "Preacher Don't Send Me," in *I Shall Not Be Moved,* 38.

7. Alice Walker, *The Color Purple* (New York: Pocket, 1982) 203.

8. Ntozake Shange, *For colored girls who have considered suicide/when the rainbow is enuf: a choreopoem* (New York: Macmillan, 1977) 2.

9. Cf. Gwendolyn Brooks, "The Chicago Defender Sends a Man to Little Rock," in Chapman, 467.

10. Rayona Sharpnack, "Women Leading Change," workshop at the Institute for Women's Leadership, Santa Clara, California, January 2000.

11. Sarah Webster Fabio, "Evil Is No Black Thing," in Henderson, 241–42.

12. It also echoes the forty years that the Israelites wandered in the wilderness before entering the promised land.

13. Audre Lorde, "Holographs," in *Our Dead Behind Us: Poems* (New York: W. W. Norton, 1994) 59–60.

14. Lucretius Carus, *De Rerum Naturam,* III, 79 in *Anchor Book of Latin Quotations,* compiled by Norbert Guterman (New York: Anchor, 1990, 1996) 92.

15. White is also the color of mourning in Eastern cultures.

16. Johari Amini, "Identity," in Henderson, 352–54.

17. Alice Walker, "Rest in Peace," in *Horses Make a Landscape Look More Beautiful*: *Selected Writings, 1973–1987* (New York: Harcourt Brace Jovanovich, 1988) 88–89.

18. See *The Oxford Dictionary of Quotations* (2d ed; London: Oxford University Press, 1955) 185; *Merriam-Webster's Encyclopedia of Literature* (Springfield, Mass.: Merriam Webster, 1995) 338.

19. See Elisabeth Kübler-Ross, *On Death and Dying* (New York: Macmillan, 1969) and *On Life After Death* (New York: Celestial Arts, 1991); Elisabeth Kübler-Ross and Mal Warshaw, *To Live Until We Say Good-bye* (Englewood Cliffs, N.J.: Prentice Hall, 1982).

Index